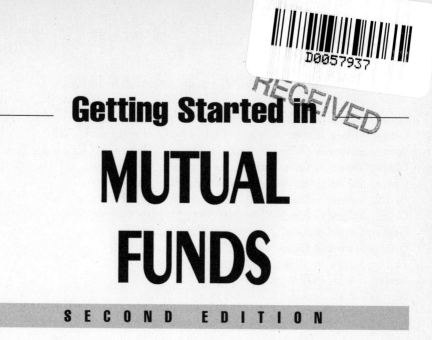

Getting Started in

MUTUAL FUNDS

SECOND EDITION

Books in the *Getting Started In* Series

Getting Started in Online Day Trading by Kassandra Bentley

Getting Started in Asset Allocation by Bill Bresnan and Eric P. Gelb

Getting Started in Online Investing by David L. Brown and Kassandra Bentley

Getting Started in Investment Clubs by Marsha Bertrand

Getting Started in Internet Auctions by Alan Elliott

Getting Started in Stocks, Third Edition by Alvin D. Hall

Getting Started in Mutual Funds by Alvin D. Hall

Getting Started in Estate Planning by Kerry Hannon

Getting Started in Online Personal Finance by Brad Hill

Getting Started in 401(k) Investing by Paul Katzeff

Getting Started in Internet Investing by Paul Katzeff

Getting Started in Security Analysis by Peter J. Klein

Getting Started in Global Investing by Robert P. Kreitler

Getting Started in Futures, Fifth Edition by Todd Lofton

Getting Started in Financial Information by Daniel Moreau and Tracey Longo

Getting Started in Emerging Markets by Christopher Poillon

Getting Started in Technical Analysis by Jack D. Schwager

Getting Started in Real Estate Investing by Michael C. Thomsett and Jean Freestone

Getting Started in Tax-Savvy Investing by Andrew Westham and Don Korn

Getting Started in Annuities by Gordon M. Williamson

Getting Started in Bonds, Second Edition by Sharon Saltzgiver Wright

Getting Started in Retirement Planning by Ronald M. Yolles and Murray Yolles

Getting Started in Online Brokers by Kristine DeForge

Getting Started in Project Management by Paula Martin and Karen Tate

Getting Started in Six Sigma by Michael C. Thomsett

Getting Started in Rental Income by Michael C. Thomsett

Getting Started in REITs by Richard Imperiale

Getting Started in Property Flipping by Michael C. Thomsett

Getting Started in Fundamental Analysis by Michael C. Thomsett

Getting Started in Chart Patterns by Thomas N. Bulkowski

Getting Started in ETFs by Todd K. Lofton

Getting Started in Swing Trading by Michael C. Thomsett

Getting Started in Options, Seventh Edition by Michael C. Thomsett

Getting Started in A Financially Secure Retirement by Henry Hebeler

Getting Started in Candlestick Charting by Tina Logan

Getting Started in Forex Trading Strategies by Michael D. Archer

Getting Started in Value Investing by Charles Mizrahi

Getting Started in Currency Trading, Second Edition by Michael D. Archer

Getting Started in Options, Eighth Edition by Michael C. Thomsett

Getting Started in Rebuilding Your 401(k), Second Edition by Paul Katzeff

Getting Started in Mutual Funds, Second Edition by Alvin D. Hall

Getting Started in Hedge Funds, Third Edition by Daniel A. Strachman

Getting Started in

MUTUAL FUNDS

SECOND EDITION

Alvin D. Hall

WILEY

John Wiley & Sons, Inc.

Published by John Wiley & Sons, Inc., Hoboken, New Jersey.
Published simultaneously in Canada.

For general information on our other products and services or for technical support, please
contact our Customer Care Department within the United States at (800) 762-2974, outside
the United States at (317) 572-3993 or fax (317) 572-4002.

Wiley also publishes its books in a variety of electronic formats. Some content that appears in
print may not be available in electronic books. For more information about Wiley products, visit
our web site at www.wiley.com.

Library of Congress Cataloging-in-Publication Data:
Hall, Alvin D.
  Getting started in mutual funds / Alvin D. Hall. – 2nd ed.
     p. cm. – (Getting started in..... ; 84)
  Includes index.
  ISBN 978-0-470-52114-4 (pbk.)
  1. Mutual funds.   2. Investments.   3. Mutual funds – United States.   4. Investments – United
States. I. Title.
  HG4530.H335 2010
  332.63'27–dc22

                                                                        2010023266
Printed in the United States of America

10 9 8 7 6 5 4 3 2 1

To
John Keefe (Chicago, Illinois),
who shares my belief that mutual funds
are one of the best ways for individuals to learn
about the benefits of long-term investing and wealth building

Contents

Acknowledgments   ix

Introduction   1

Chapter 1
Definition and Structure of a Mutual Fund   15

Chapter 2
Investment Objectives and Risks of Stock and Bond Funds   35

Chapter 3
Fees and Expenses: Load, No-Load, and Pure
No-Load Funds   79

Chapter 4
Buying, Redeeming, and Exchanging Mutual Fund Shares   107

Chapter 5
Analyzing Mutual Fund Performance   121

Chapter 6
Shareholder Services   151

Chapter 7
Seven Wisdoms of Mutual Fund Investing   161

Glossary   171

Index   217

Acknowledgments

Thanks to Van Morrow of Type-Right, Inc., for diligently and expertly turning my drawings into the illustrations and tables in this book, and for helping me to prepare the manuscript during the time when I was simultaneously traveling (literally around the world) for business and writing this edition. Thanks to my long-time friend, Edward Fleur, for helping me to decipher some of the new mutual fund regulations and practices so that I could explain them clearly in this book. John Keefe's commitment to reading and commenting on the final manuscript and page proofs was invaluable. His questions and insights helped me to make the book more informative and appropriate to the needs of a wide range of mutual fund investors.

My thanks also go to Bill Falloon, Tiffany Charbonier, and Michael Lisk at John Wiley & Sons. They were forthright, patient, and honest throughout the process of this revision. I truly appreciated their understanding of and dedication to my (and any author's) desire to produce the best book possible. Their work throughout was supportive and encouraging in all the right and honorable ways.

And finally, my thanks to all of the inquisitive people who have attended my lectures and classes over my more than 25 years of conducting training programs in the financial services industry. All of the questions they have asked, especially those that were complex or difficult to answer, have enabled me to improve continually the way I present the information in my classes and in the books I write. I know that the readers of my books are the true beneficiaries of all the wisdom and practical insights I've learned from teaching financial information in front of real people in classes all over the world.

Introduction

I am writing this second edition of *Getting Started in Mutual Funds* during a worldwide recession and one of the worst bear markets in recent U.S. history. Many of the funds in which we—you and I—invested the money we earned or inherited, set aside for our retirement or our children's education, or saved hoping to fulfill some lifelong dream, are down in value 25, 35, even 50 percent. Trillions of dollars have disappeared from our collective personal net worth. Many investors have decided they cannot stand to see their life savings being slowly wiped out, so they have sold their mutual funds and other investments, putting the proceeds in money market funds. Others are holding on, feeling it's too late to sell and take their losses. Instead they hold on to the traditional long-term investment philosophy that the market and the value of their mutual funds will eventually recover—or so they hope and pray.

Regardless of which camp you fall in, we all must admit that this current crisis in the economy and investment markets has made us aware of three important facts. First, each of us must be more knowledgeable about the products in which we invest our money. Second, we must be more conscientious and proactive in reviewing and adjusting to our asset allocations in light of changing market conditions and the need to preserve the money we've made. And third, each of us must be much more aware of our real individual tolerance for risk, and not let it be overly influenced, or even blinded, by the optimism of a prolonged bull market.

This second edition of *Getting Started in Mutual Funds* is revised and expanded with these three facts in mind. My goal is to help you understand what you invest in when you purchase mutual funds and the risks associated with those investments. I want to enable you to have a clearer understanding of your choices when you invest in mutual funds, whether it's via a 401(k) plan, a 403(b) plan, a 529 college savings plan, an IRA, a SEP (Simplified Employee Pension plan), a personal cash account, or any other type of account. Too often when deciding what to do with our money, we are left essentially on our own—without any guidance, explanation, or reasonable understanding of what we should do and why. This book will be your educational tool, your useful reference guide, and your secret helper, enabling you to make better investment choices for yourself, whether you are a beginning investor or an experienced one wondering what to do in the future.

Despite what has happened in the markets, you most likely know that some of the money you have set aside for retirement, a child's education, or some future purchase should be invested in the stock market. However, you are apprehensive and gun-shy because of the recent losses you've experienced or read about, or you don't feel you have enough knowledge of investments in general—of mutual funds, specifically. Not only do you want a clearer and more useful understanding of the terminology of mutual funds, you want, per-haps most importantly, to know how to evaluate and select those most appro-priate for you from among the group of funds presented to you by your broker, financial advisor, the administrator of the retirement plan at your job, or that you see on web sites, in newsletters and in newspapers you use for research as you make your own investments.

There could be other reasons you need the information in this book. Maybe you are a person who has invested in a fund because "a friend said it was a good one" or because "it was one of the choices in my company's 401(k) plan." When asked what fund you own, you say offhandedly, "Oh, Fidelity or Vanguard something-or-other." Your choice had done well, but now it has dropped in value by a greater percentage than the decline in the major market indices. You now want to be both more knowledgeable and proactive. You want to know about asset allocation, about sector-specific funds, target-date funds, green funds, and about bond funds. In short, you want to be more involved in shaping your financial future, with a renewed understanding of the need to preserve your capital along the way.

Or you have some investment experience but are seeking to understand a particular aspect of mutual funds in more detail—such as the risk associated with a fund, the experience and investment approach of the fund manager, the different classes of mutual fund shares, expense ratios, or turnover ratios. You want to learn about these specific areas quickly and efficiently.

Getting Started in Mutual Funds, Second Edition, is written, like the first edition, to make you smarter and more confident about choosing and monitor-ing your mutual fund investments. I make two assumptions in this book. First, you are motivated to invest in mutual funds and want to learn more about them. And second, you are looking for a book that will give you a sound under-standing of the basic concepts and terms, as well as explain the complexities of evaluating mutual funds in clear, easy-to-follow, and easily readable language. Among the important topics covered in this book are:

- The structure and workings of a typical mutual fund.
- The roles of the various entities involved in operating a fund (i.e., port-folio manager, board of directors, custodian bank, underwriter).

- How to understand the risk evaluations of a particular fund during bull and bear markets.

- Investment minimums.

- Fees and expenses.

- Measurements (e.g., past performance, expense ratios) to be examined and compared before investing.

- Common shareholder services.

- Sources of information about and evaluations of mutual funds.

This book will help you (1) understand what a fund's return or yield actually means, (2) comprehend the impact of the fund manager's investment style on your return, and (3) evaluate the ongoing expenses associated with mutual fund investing. The ultimate goal of *Getting Started in Mutual Funds, Second Edition* is to enable you to choose a mutual fund that will, given your investment objective, risk tolerance, and time horizon, be one of the top performers in its group or sector.

Benefits of Investing in Mutual Funds

Mutual funds are the primary means by which most individuals in the United States invest in the stock and bond markets. Funds offer an opportunity for a group of people with the same investment objective to pool their resources and gain greater buying power. Investors, whether beginning, small, or experienced, are attracted to mutual funds for four widely touted benefits.

Diversification

A mutual fund's investment portfolio consists of stocks and/or bonds from different companies, usually in many different industries or business sectors. As a result, an investor's money is somewhat shielded against a decline in any one company, or depending on the fund, any one business sector. Diversification does *not* mean, as I have heard a beginning investor say, "The value of my money is safe and can only go down a little in value." If the overall stock market declines sharply, as all of us saw in 2008–2009, then the value of a mutual fund, no matter how well diversified, will also decline. And depending on the types of securities and the business sectors they represent, the mutual fund may decline in value more than the overall market, as measured by indices such as the Standard & Poor's 500 Index or the Dow Jones Industrial Average. Diversification does not and cannot protect shareholders against adverse moves in the broad investment market. (This is known as market risk.) It protects only against the risk of "putting too many eggs in one basket" (i.e., putting too much money in one stock).

Professional Management

The specific stocks and/or bonds in which the fund invests shareholders' money are carefully selected by a professional portfolio manager or investment advisor. This may be a single person, or, as is more common today, a team of people. Most have an advanced degree from a business school and have taken additional courses to achieve the Certified Financial Analyst (CFA) designation. Recent business school graduates often work under the guidance of a more experienced or senior portfolio manager before being given primary responsibility for a particular fund. Also, the fund (or its management company) employs or contracts researchers as well as investment analysts and strategists to provide the manager with detailed information, insights, and interpretations about specific companies, sectors, and the overall market that are important considerations when choosing individual stocks and bonds. These data and opinions enable the manager to fulfill the fund's objective and select those securities that will, hopefully, produce a substantial positive return.

Lower Transaction Costs

Compared with buying individual stocks and bonds to build a diversified portfolio on your own, the costs associated with investing in a mutual fund which contains these financial instruments are lower. A fund's administrative, operations, and trading expenses are spread over all of the shareholders in the fund. This might be thousands of people. Therefore, the transaction costs per person for every dollar invested are less—some would say minuscule.

This benefit is, however, being challenged by the low-cost order execution services available through deep-discount and on-line brokerage firms. Some services will execute trades for up to 5,000 shares in any stock for a commission as low as $7.00. For the person who buys and holds individual securities over the long term, the trading costs of building his or her own diversified portfolio using these services may be less than the ongoing expenses (explained in Chapter 3) of holding a group of mutual funds. This would most likely be true for a person who buys substantial amounts of securities. However, for the majority of people who invest modest amounts of money, the low cost of mutual fund transactions remains an advantage.

Convenience

Large mutual fund companies and supermarkets offer investors numerous funds, often by different providers, that have different objectives and that concentrate on different industries, markets (e.g., international) or types of securities (stocks, bonds, mortgage-backed securities). They also provide an increasing array of customer services. Investment "help" in screening funds for potential investment, automatic investment plans, online purchases and redemptions, automatic dividend and capital gains reinvestment, and asset allocation models are just a few of the services. (More are discussed in detail in Chapter 6.) The increasing breadth of mutual fund objectives and services afford you, the individual investor, a great deal of flexibility. Competition for your investment dollars has given funds the incentive to make it easy for you to implement your investment decisions, track their performance, and keep accurate records for tax-reporting purposes. In many ways, financial institutions have succeeded in their efforts to make mutual fund investing as convenient as one-stop shopping.

Since the early 1980s, the public has come to understand and believe in the benefits of investing through mutual funds. The result is that, despite the recent distressing downturn, funds remain the investment vehicle of choice for all levels of investors—for the person with as little as $25 per month to invest to the person with hundreds of thousands of dollars. The amount of money Americans poured into mutual funds over the years illustrates this point. In 1990, the public invested $12.8 billion in stock funds *for the entire year.* In 1996, the public invested $28.9 billion dollars in stock funds in just *the first month of the year!* In 2000, the amount of money in mutual funds had soared to nearly $4 trillion, and was still growing—up 600 percent during the decade leading up to the millennium. As the long bull market was approaching its peak, at least one new mutual fund was being created every business day. By the end of 2009, mutual funds managed over $11 trillion of assets for nearly 90 million U.S. investors representing 21 percent of all households, according to the Investment Company Institute (ICI). Of these households, the average number of mutual funds owned per household is four.

Today there are around 8,600 mutual funds available from approximately 600 sponsors (mutual fund companies, brokerage firms, banks and other financial institutions). Many industry experts expect the numbers will decrease the longer the bear market lasts. Some mutual funds will merge and some will liquidate, but fewer new funds will be created. Unlike their older brethren, the newer funds created today often have more focused investment objectives and investment strategies. The result: target marketing has become a permanent feature of the mutual fund industry.

Mutual funds are one of the more established products through which small investors have pooled their funds to gain access to the stock and bond markets and to professional management. And as the following brief history and time line reveal, mutual funds have had, like the stock market itself, their ups and downs with the public.

A Brief History of Mutual Funds

1924-1970

In 1924, the Massachusetts Investors Trust and the State Street Investment Trust created the first mutual funds in the United States. Like today's mutual funds, these trusts enabled investors to purchase shares of a professionally managed portfolio that consisted of a diverse selection of stocks. This product was not immediately popular with individual investors. At that time, people were more interested in owning individual stocks.

Following the Market Crash of 1929 and the Great Depression, individual investors avoided all types of securities, including mutual funds. The entire industry was dubbed "the plague" and stockbrokers "the carriers of the plague." Beginning in 1933, Congress and the newly created Securities and Exchange Commission (SEC) developed and implemented a series of Acts designed to reform the securities industry. These new laws also sought to protect investors from the fraudulent and manipulative practices that pervaded the market during the Roaring Twenties. One Act, the Investment Company Act of 1940, classified and regulated the various types of pooled investment vehicles. The Act defined three types of investment companies (see Figure I.2) and detailed rules governing the creation, marketing, and operation of these entities and

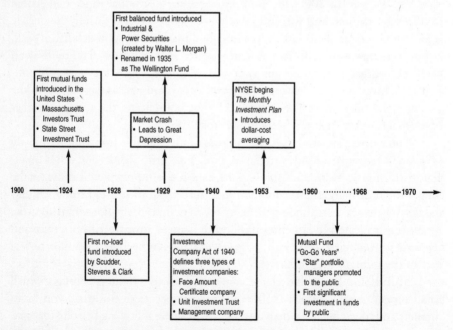

FIGURE I.1 Mutual fund timeline: 1924–1970.

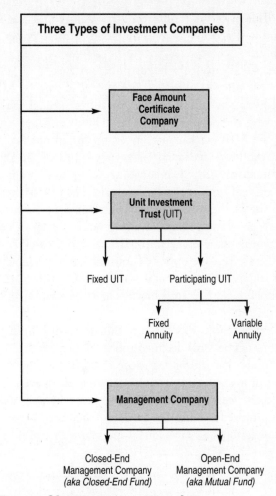

FIGURE I.2   Types of investment companies.

their products. As Figure I.2 shows, a mutual fund is a type of a management company. It is, by its legal name, an open-end management company. At the time the Act was passed, there were only 68 mutual funds in the United States.

From the 1929 crash through World War II, Americans did not invest in the stock markets. The U.S. securities markets were virtually moribund. Recognizing that bringing people back to the markets was essential for their survival, the New York Stock Exchange (NYSE) and its member firms started the *Monthly Investment Plan (MIP)* in January 1954. Using the tag-line, "Own Your Share of American Business," this campaign had two purposes: (1) to educate prospective investors about the basic benefits of buying stocks and bonds, and (2) to offer them an opportunity to invest in NYSE-listed stocks with as little as $40 a month. A participant could buy small numbers of shares, including fractional shares computed to three places to the right of the decimal point.

MIP gave small investors hands-on experience with three important investment-related concepts. The first was *payroll deduction.* MIP participants could elect to invest the quarterly amount either through payroll deduction plans or by making the deposit themselves. The second was *dividend reinvestment.* Virtually all MIP participants signed up for automatic reinvestment of dividends. And the third, *dollar-cost averaging,* is one of the keystones to successful mutual fund investing. It involves investing modest amounts of money into a stock or mutual fund at regular intervals. The ease of this strategy, combined with the rise in the stock market, contributed to the success of MIP. It introduced a new generation to the advantages of investing in stocks.

The increase in share ownership MIP created, however, did not extend to mutual funds. There were only 161 mutual funds available to investors in 1960. Even as late as 1970, the total was only 361. (Forty-six of these were bond and income funds.) Few stockbrokers had ever written an order ticket for a mutual fund.

The severe bear market of 1973–1974 made mutual funds even less attractive (see Figure I.3). The Dow declined nearly 50 percent during that two-year period. Many funds shares dropped more than 40 percent in value and the resulting deluge of investor redemptions contributed to even further declines. Among stockbrokers and the few mutual fund investors, the cynical view about mutual funds is captured in what was then an oft-repeated statement: "I can lose my money just as easily as a professional fund manager can."

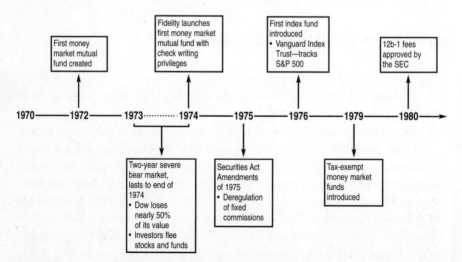

FIGURE I.3   Mutual fund timeline: 1970–1980.

1970–1980: The Disenfranchisement of the Small Investor

During the mid-1970s, two events made investing directly in stock and bonds more difficult for people with small amounts of money and consequently spurred the growth of mutual funds. First, the Federal Reserve Board (FRB) increased the minimum investment for Treasury bills. Interest rates on six-month Treasury bills had risen to more than 16 percent. This increase, combined with the prolonged bear market, caused investors to flee the stock market and begin purchasing large amounts of U.S. Treasury bills.

To stem the demand, the FRB raised the minimum purchase amount for Treasury bills from $1,000 to $10,000. (The minimum purchase has been reduced over the past decade and is currently $100.) This increase effectively placed T-bills out of the reach of small investors. The high interest rates associated with T-Bills could only be accessed through investment in the then-newly-created product called the "money market mutual fund." One of the first of these, The Fidelity Daily Income Trust, was offered to the public in 1974. Like today's money market mutual funds, it sought to maintain its net asset value at $1.00 and offered check-writing privileges. The yields on money funds closely tracked that of the six-month T-bill rate.

The second blow to the smaller investor came on May 1, 1975, when commissions on securities transactions became negotiable. This resulted in small investors becoming less attractive to full-service brokerage firms. The reason was simple: the commissions to be earned from their small trades were relatively insignificant. Most brokerage firms therefore chose to focus their efforts and attention on the institutional clients, who bought and sold large quantities of shares.

1980–Today: Mutual Funds Attract More Investors—Small and Large

The elimination of fixed commissions was good news for mutual funds and a newly created type of investment firm: the discount brokerage firm. These companies saw opportunity—and profit—in the small investors' periodic purchases of modest quantities of stocks and bonds and set out to attract those who would regularly invest in the securities market, either indirectly (i.e., through investment in mutual funds) or directly (i.e., by purchasing stocks and bonds). In doing so, they would capture an ongoing stream of fees and commissions. If the number of investors was large enough, these fees could provide substantial income for the company.

As a customer retention strategy, mutual fund companies began offering small investors a variety of products and services. Many of the services and benefits were tied to the amount of money invested. The more money you invested,

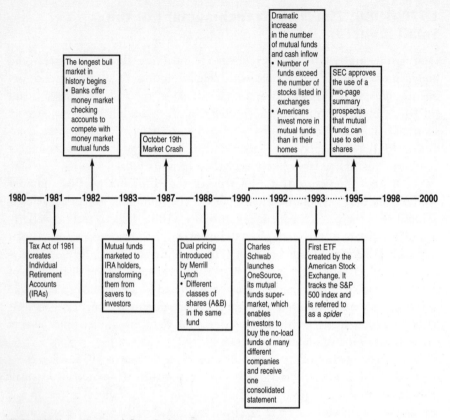

FIGURE I.4   Mutual fund timeline: 1980–2000.

the more benefits (usually discounts) you received—thereby lowering the over-all cost of your holdings. This strategy helped mutual fund companies capture a larger percentage of each person's investment dollars.

During the bull market of the 1980s (see Figure I.4), the number of mutual fund investors and the amount of money flowing into mutual funds increased rapidly. This growth was spurred by the creation of Individual Retirement Accounts (IRAs) under the Tax Act of 1981 and, as mentioned at the beginning of this introduction, the public's increasing awareness of the ben-efits of mutual fund investing. The movement of companies away from defined benefit plans, replacing them with defined contribution plans, also helped the growth of mutual funds. Most defined contribution plans—of which a 401(k) plan is one example—offer employees a group of mutual funds in which they can invest money for their retirement. Mutual fund companies began aggressive campaigns to attract new investors. The aim was—and remains—to convert people who "saved" for retirement into people who "invest" for retirement.

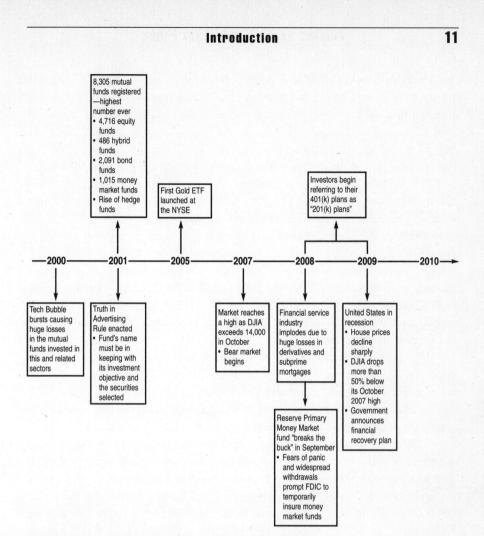

FIGURE I.5   Mutual fund timeline: 2000–today.

The Market Break of 1987 made many people aware of a feature about mutual funds that they had never fully focused on or understand. Although people talked about "trading" mutual funds, in reality these securities could not be bought and sold during the trading day like stocks. As the market plunged on October 19, many people wanted to sell their mutual funds before the market hit its lowest point. Instead they became aware that all orders to buy or redeem mutual fund shares are executed only at the end of the business day when the closing prices of the securities in the fund's portfolio are calculated. This prompted people to begin asking, "Why can't mutual funds be tradable?"

Some mutual fund companies experimented with executing orders for mutual fund shares based on stock and bond prices at specific times during the trading day. These intraday executions were not widely embraced by the industry and gradually stopped. The investment products group at the American Stock Exchange (AMEX), however, began to see if a "tradable mutual fund" could be created based on the increasing public interest in index mutual funds. What they discovered was that the legal structure of a mutual fund (discussed in Chapter 1) was not the best. So using another structure defined under the Investment Company of 1940, the AMEX launched the first tradable index fund shares based on the Standard & Poor's 500 index in 1993. Widely referred to as "spiders" (an acronym based on the first letters in Standard and Poor's Depositary Receipts, the proper name for this product), this security became the first exchange-traded fund (ETF) to be introduced in the United States, and it eventually became a direct challenge to traditional index funds, which are redeemable, not tradable. ETFs have become one of the most successful products introduced into the investment markets in recent years. There are broad-market ETFs, sector-specific ETFs, and country-specific ETFs. And many of the largest, traditional mutual fund companies such as Vanguard are creating ETF-versions of its most popular and successful index funds.

Today, the primary inflows to (and outflows from) traditional mutual funds are monies invested through company retirement plans—e.g., 401(k), profit-sharing, Simplified Employee Pension (SEP), defined benefit plans—and some private sector plans. Small investors and personal IRAs still represent a significant percentage of the monies invested.

Like any industry that's growing quickly—much more quickly than regulators envisioned—the mutual fund industry has encountered some problems. One was *portfolio drift*. In trying to achieve higher returns, some investment managers would slowly begin buying securities for the fund's portfolio that were not totally in keeping with the fund's investment objective. To correct this problem, a rule was implemented in 2001, generally called the "Truth in Advertising" rule, which requires that a fund's name and the securities bought into its portfolio must be in keeping with the fund's stated investment objectives. This was designed to reduce confusion among investors.

During 2001, the number of mutual funds in the United States reached 8,305. This record number included 4,716 equity funds, 486 hybrid funds, 2,091 bond funds, and 1,015 money market mutual funds. Staggering amounts of money were flowing into funds. As the Dow Jones Industrial Average went above 14,000 in October 2007, few investors would have imagined that this represented a market top and that 2008 would be one of the worst bear markets in history. Mutual fund investors, along with investors in other securities, have seen trillions of dollars of value wiped away. Undoubtedly one of the most disturbing events of 2008 was when the Reserved Primary Money Market fund "broke the buck." This means the market value of the assets in the money market account fell below $1 per share. Investors who had put money into this fund would get back less, but they did not know how much less. Because money market accounts were considered a totally safe place in which to hold cash while earning a low amount of interest, this incident caused a run on money market accounts. The U.S. government stepped in and temporarily insured all money market accounts in order to restore investor confidence.

As the losses deepened throughout 2008, mutual fund holders all across the United States debated whether to sell or continue to hold their funds. For those who continued to hold, the big question became—and remains—"Have the markets reach the bottom?" Many pundits and mutual fund portfolio managers saw this severe drop in the stock market in 2008 as one of the best buying opportunities to come along in decades. They reason that buying at these low levels could yield substantial gains when the markets recover. Certainly the market gains in 2009–2010 would support that point of view. Today, however, the markets remain quite volatile, with no clear direction in sight. Clearly such times require diligence and patience. Among all these investors, both individual and professional, an old adage still rings true: "Money always seeks the best return." *Getting Started in Mutual Funds, Second Edition*, will, I hope, make your search for, analysis of, and decisions about which funds to invest your money in better informed and more successful—through all market conditions.

Definition and Structure of a Mutual Fund

The concept underlying a *mutual fund* has probably existed since securities were created. In its simplest form, it works as follows. A group of individuals, with a similar *investment objective* or goal, place their investment monies into a common pool. These funds are then used to buy and sell securities. By pooling their money, the participants reap two primary benefits. The first benefit is diversification. The collective buying power of the group's pooled resources enable it to purchase shares or bonds in a broader range of industries or business sectors than any individual in the pool could do on his or her own. The second benefit is lower transaction costs per participant. Because the commissions and other trading fees are spread over more shares and more investors, the cost per person is usually much lower than it would be if each individual had bought the same shares directly through a brokerage firm.

Originally, one person, usually a contributor to the pool, was designated by power of attorney or other legal means to select which securities to buy and sell. Each

mutual fund commonly used name for an open-end management company that establishes a portfolio of securities and then continually issues new shares and redeems already outstanding shares representing ownership in the portfolio.

investment objective
the strategy by which an investor wishes to increase the value of his or her assets.

bull market
a period during which the overall prices of securities are rising.

investment company
generic name for one of the many companies, like a mutual fund, whose primary business is investing and reinvesting in securities.

person in the pool shared in the gains and losses on the investments. Their percentage of gains and losses was equal to their percentage of the participation in the pool.

These loosely run and unregulated pools were especially popular in the United States during the *bull market* of the 1920s. In March 1924, Massachusetts Financial Services created the first true mutual fund in the United States. It was called the Massachusetts Investors Trust. Following the market crash of 1929, Congress passed legislation designed to give clearer structure to and better regulate the various type of investment pools (also called *investment companies*). The *Investment Company Act of 1940* was the first U.S. law to define the different types of pools.

One of the types of investment companies defined in the Act is a management company. It is a corporation or trust whose primary business purpose is to invest and re-invest in securities in accordance with a stated investment objective. The securities that a management company's professional advisor buys and sells are held in an investment portfolio. When an individual buys shares of a management company, he or she is, in reality, buying an undivided interest in the portfolio of securities created by the company.

When a management company is formed, it will have either a closed-end structure or an open-end structure. (See Figure 1.1.) The basic difference between the two forms is how frequently new shares are issued to the investing public. A closed-end management company creates an investment portfolio and then issues shares backed by that portfolio to the public *only one time*. Therefore, the number of shares outstanding, called the company's capitalization, remains relatively fixed. (This is discussed in more detail at the end of this chapter.)

An *open-end management company* also creates an investment portfolio and then issues shares to the public backed by that portfolio. In contrast, however, this company, continually issues new shares and buys back already outstanding shares each business day in direct response to investors' orders to put more of their money into or pull money out of the underlying portfolio. The number of shares outstanding—its capitalization—changes continually. An open-end management company is the legal name for what is widely called a mutual fund.

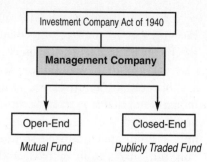

FIGURE 1.1   Types of management companies.

Open-End Management Company (aka, Mutual Fund)

Each mutual fund is legally registered as a separate management company or trust with the Securities and Exchange Commission (SEC). The financial services company that creates a fund is called the *sponsor*. It invests its own money to start the fund's portfolio. (The minimum dollar amount that the sponsor is required to invest is specified in the provisions of the Investment Company Act of 1940.) It also initially selects the fund's portfolio manager. The sponsor then seeks to bring additional money into the portfolio by marketing it to the public. The more shares it sells, the more money it has to invest in *stocks* and/or *bonds*.

A mutual fund is called an "open-end" management company because it stands ready to issue new shares and redeem outstanding shares every business day. As individuals buy (i.e., invest more money in) a fund, it issues more shares to the purchasers. The fund's portfolio manager then uses that money to purchase additional stocks and/or bonds into the portfolio. When investors sell (i.e., redeem or pull money out of) a fund, the total shares outstanding declines. If the number of redemptions is very high, then the fund's portfolio manager may have to sell some of the stock and/or bonds out of the portfolio in order to pay the investors who have sold (i.e., redeemed) their mutual fund shares. Thus, the number of a mutual fund's shares outstanding changes daily depending on the number of purchases or *redemptions*. Even when a mutual fund closes to new investors, those people who already have money invested in the fund can continue to buy and redeem that fund's shares.

Investment Company Act of 1940 the federal legislation that defines the types of organizations that qualify as investment companies and requires them to register with the SEC.

open-end management company legal name for a mutual fund under the Investment Company Act of 1940.

sponsor
the corporation or trust that creates a mutual fund or a family of mutual funds.

stock
a negotiable security representing ownership of a company and entitling its owner to the right to receive dividends.

bond
a long-term debt security or IOU issued by a corporation, municipality, or government that promises to pay interest periodically and to repay the bond's principal at maturity.

Mutual fund shares do not trade on stock exchanges or in the over-the-counter market. In fact, the Financial Industry Regulatory Authority (FINRA) expressly prohibits trading these shares in these *secondary markets*. It is, therefore, inaccurate to describe mutual fund shares as tradable securities. Investors cannot buy and sell shares among themselves. Instead, mutual funds are redeemable securities. An investor can only buy shares from or redeem them with the fund itself or one of the fund's authorized sales agents. Redeeming mutual fund shares is widely described as selling fund shares.

The emergence of *mutual fund supermarkets*, like those established by Charles Schwab & Co., OneSource, Fidelity Fund Network, E*Trade Mutual Funds Network. and others, has for some unknown reason caused some people to presume that they are actually trading mutual fund shares with other investors who have accounts at these companies. This belief is wrong. The supermarkets are authorized sales agents for many different mutual fund companies, in addition to selling their own. What many investors misconstrue as "trading" in the supermarket is nothing more than a purchase and a redemption, with the firm that runs the supermarket acting as an *agent*, directing the order to the specific mutual fund company. Again, there is no secondary market trading of mutual funds.

Structure of a Mutual Fund

Understanding the organization of a mutual fund and the responsibilities of each of its components makes clear two important features (See Figure 1.2):

1. The safeguards and separation of responsibilities designed to empower certain entities and individuals to act as watch dogs for the shareholders and thus protect their interests.
2. The various costs associated with its day-to-day operation, which are passed along to investors as fees and expenses.

The first feature does not imply that investors' shares are protected from market price fluctuations. Instead, it means that the fund's assets are protected from potentially inappropriate and fraudulent activities by the sponsor or portfolio manager. The diagram below illustrates the various participants or entities involved in a mutual fund. Their specific responsibilities and duties are detailed afterward.

redemption
the sale of mutual fund shares back to the fund or its selling agents at the fund's NAV.

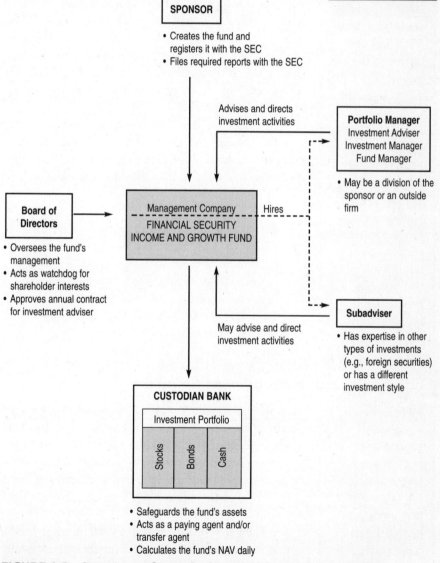

FIGURE 1.2 Structure of a typical mutual fund and the basic responsibilities of the various parties.

secondary market
also called the aftermarket market, a collective term for the markets—exchange and OTC—in which securities trade after they are issued to the public.

mutual fund supermarket
a select group of mutual funds from many different sponsors that can be bought and sold through one brokerage at nominal transaction fees.

agent
a registered person or business organization that acts as the intermediary in the purchase or sale of a security.

Sponsor

A sponsor is a company—typically a financial services organization such as a brokerage firm, bank, insurance company, or mutual fund company—that creates and makes the first investment in a particular mutual fund or series of mutual funds. For each new fund, the sponsor must file a registration statement with the Securities and Exchange Commission (SEC) and with the appropriate authority in any state in which it plans to offer or sell the fund to the public. This registration document, which becomes the *prospectus* for the mutual fund, must contain full and fair disclosure about the fund's sponsor, Board of Directors, investment objectives, types of investments permitted, expenses, fees, and risks.

Registration does not mean or imply in any way that the SEC or a state authority has approved or endorsed the mutual fund. In fact, all mutual fund prospectuses must contain the following statement in:

> *Like all mutual fund shares, these securities have not been approved or disapproved by the Securities and Exchange Commission or any state securities commission, nor has the Securities and Exchange Commission or any state securities commission passed upon the accuracy or adequacy of this prospectus. Any representation to the contrary is a criminal offense.*

Management Company

Each mutual fund is a separate open-end management company that the sponsor must register with the SEC when it is created. Janus Balanced Fund is an open-end management company. Vanguard's Long Term Bond Index Fund is an open-end management company. And Fidelity Select Gold Fund is a management company.

When a sponsor creates several mutual funds, it may choose to place them all under one umbrella or under different brand names. Such a grouping is called a *family of funds*. A family of funds may consist only of as few as three mutual funds—a stock fund, a bond fund, and a money market fund. Other companies (Fidelity, for example) create large fund families that include mutual funds that have different brand names (e.g., Fidelity Advisors, Fidelity Selects, Fidelity Spartan); invest in specific industries, specific countries, and specific combinations of securities; or have different investment approaches and different risk-to-reward characteristics.

Usually the shareholder services and benefits provided by one fund are also provided by all funds in the same family. Mutual fund companies view this grouping of different management companies as a way of being able to capture a larger percentage of each customer's investment dollars as, over time, individuals seek to diversify their holdings, or as their investment objects or economic circumstances change.

Board of Directors

The Board of Directors of a mutual fund is responsible for overseeing the day-to-day management of that fund as well as the trading activities of its portfolio manager or managers. Some of its specific responsibilities are: (1) deciding whether or not to renew the investment advisor's annual contract, (2) voting on any changes in the fees the manager charges the fund, (3) monitoring the specific investments within the portfolio to avoid undue concentration in any one sector or company, (4) making sure the advisor's investments comply with (and do not stray from) the fund's stated investment objectives, and (5) monitoring the fees charged by the fund to ensure that they are fair and reasonable to the shareholders. The primary purpose of all of the Board's responsibilities is to protect the interests of the fund's shareholders.

The members of the Board are initially appointed by the fund's sponsor. Afterwards, they are elected by the fund's shareholders. *Proxies* are distributed annually and are used by shareholders to vote. To prevent the sponsor, who may have large amounts of money invested in the fund, from having undue influence

prospectus
a printed summary of the SEC-filed registration statement that discloses the details of a particular mutual fund's objective, historical performance, portfolio composition, and other information an investor can use to judge the merits of investing in the fund.

family of funds
a group of mutual funds created by the same sponsor with different investment objectives or with portfolios of different securities.

proxy
a form on
which an
investor votes.
Shareholders
can also
vote via the
Internet or
phone.

over the Board, the Investment Company Act of 1940 mandates that although 60 percent of the Board can come from the sponsor, at least 40 percent must be independent directors (also unaffiliated or disinterested persons) that receive no compensation for either working for the fund or rendering services to the fund. These independent directors must also be individuals with no affiliation with the sponsor. In reality, the current percentages still give the sponsor a strong sway over the management. In many cases, the chairman of the Board of Directors is typically the same person who is the Chief Executive Officer (CEO) of the sponsor. Other Board members typically include individuals from the fund's law firm, its accounting firm, and the trading firm that executes its buy and sell orders, and important business associates of the sponsor.

Board members are paid fees for their services. (Importantly, this is not considered to be compensation.) The amounts are disclosed in the prospectus. It has become a widespread practice for individuals to serve on the boards of several funds, especially if those funds are sponsored by the same company. For example, if you compare the prospectuses for some of the large mutual fund groups, you will discover that many names appear again and again on the Boards of different funds.

Due to this overlap of directors, some shareholder activists and industry regulators have sought to make some changes in the board's composition. They argue that the large percentage of non-independent directors results in their merely rubber stamping the portfolio manager's activities, offering little oversight or expertise, failing to monitor expenses, and devoting less time than their fee warrants. Also activists (and regulators) question whether the non-independent board members, who already earn compensation working for a mutual fund or mutual fund company should also "double dip" by earning additional fees to serve as board members. Two important changes to a fund's Board of Directors have been proposed. First, the required number of independent board members (currently set at 40 percent) should be increased. Since these members are appointed specifically to watch out for the interests of the fund's shareholders, then the more of them on the board the greater the possibility that the shareholder's point of view would have greater representation during any conflicts with the fund's manager or sponsor. And second, there should be a review of member's compensation to see if it is excessive, perhaps resulting in less careful oversight of the fees charged by the portfolio manager.

Many mutual funds already appoint a number of independent board members in excess of the percentage required under the Investment Company Act of 1940.

[Note: The government had proposed changing the composition of the Board of a mutual fund, increasing the number of disinterested members to 55 percent. This change was proposed in response to scandals that occurred in the late 1990s and early 2000s. However, one of the largest mutual fund companies in the United States was able to challenge the proposed rule change and effectively stop it from being enacted. Given the current climate for financial reform that's focused on banks and brokerage firms, it seems unlikely that this rule change will be adopted for mutual funds. There are more important issues given the state of the U.S. economy. Nonetheless, increasing the number of unaffiliated, disinterested, or independent persons on a fund's board is thought to be a reasonable way of providing greater oversight on behalf of the investing public.]

Investment Advisor/Investment Manager/ Portfolio Manager/Fund Manager

When most people hear the term *investment advisor* or *portfolio manager*, they think of an individual who works directly for the sponsor or the fund itself. In reality, an advisor is generally a corporation that is a wholly owned subsidiary of the sponsor. Fidelity Funds, for example, is managed by Fidelity Management and Research (FMRCo), a subsidiary of Fidelity. Other mutual funds contract an outside investment advisory company, called an *asset-management firm* or a *sub-investment advisor*, to be the portfolio manager. Vanguard's Windsor Fund, for example, outsources portfolio management responsibility to the U.S. Value Equities at AllianceBernstein and Wellington Management Company. The person or persons listed as the portfolio manager is therefore an employee of an investment advisory firm. In the case of the Dreyfus Appreciation Fund, the Houston-based Fayez Sarofim & Company (where Mr. Sarofim is president, chairman of the board, and a director), has been the fund's sub-investment advisor since 1990. Fayez Sarofim & Company also serves as an advisor to several other Dreyfus funds.

An investment advisor is responsible for implementing the mutual fund's investment strategy by researching and selecting the specific securities that will be bought into and sold out of the portfolio. This individual or team manages the fund in accordance with the investment objective stated in the fund's registration statement and prospectus. He or she must also abide by any restrictions regarding the types of investment products (stocks, bonds, options, and futures) that can and cannot be traded in the portfolio, as well as the percentage of the fund's assets that the manager can, at his or her discretion, hold as cash in a money market account. These restrictions are detailed in the fund's prospectus.

The organization of the people within the investment advisory firm varies. At some firms, a portfolio manager works autonomously handling only one fund. At others, an individual portfolio manager will be responsible for several funds within the same sector or related sectors (e.g., consumer staples and pharmaceuticals) or with complementary investment objectives. When a team of managers is responsible for a mutual fund, usually one or two are designated as *team leader* or *lead managers*. These leaders are usually senior persons who supervise the activities of junior managers (relatively recent business school graduates) and sometimes researchers or analysts. (Research is sometimes a separate department.) The manager and/or the analysts may visit many of the companies that they are evaluating for possible investment. Then, using computer technology and proprietary analytical approaches, they use their findings and other factors about the company or business entity to create models of the security's potential performance. This arrangement is common throughout the mutual fund industry. At companies with formal training and development programs, like Fidelity, recently graduated professionals work with experienced managers in order to learn the business. This arrangement also enables the company to assess the individual's potential skill as a portfolio manager before assigning a fund to him or her.

As noted in the previously sited example of the Dreyfus Appreciation Fund, sponsors also hire outside investment advisory companies called *subadvisors*. These asset management firms typically provide skills in areas where the sponsor lacks expertise, such as emerging markets, international bonds, or certain industry sectors (e.g., precious metals, biotechnology, etc.). They may also employ a different or complimentary investment style to the one already being implemented in the fund. Asset management firms also provide research and information, which the managers can use in their other investment decisions. Outside asset management firms may have sub-advisory agreement with many different mutual funds or mutual fund companies. When a sub-advisor is used, each portfolio manager is usually an employee of the sub-advisor.

Each investment manager's professional experience must be disclosed in the prospectus in a section describing the fund's management. Here, an investor is told how long the sole manager or each member of the investment team has been in charge of that fund, any funds each manager has previously run, each manager's education, and other professional licenses that person has attained. This is important information to read, particularly if you are investing in an *actively managed mutual fund*. First, it gives you the ability to determine what period of the

actively managed mutual fund a fund that has a portfolio manager who decides which securities should be bought into and sold out of the fund's portfolio.

fund's performance has been under the direction of that specific individual or team. Second, if the advisor has managed another mutual fund previously, it enables you to research the performance of that fund under that manager's tenure. Finally, and perhaps most important, it enables you to determine the manager's depth of experience in the investment markets. Has he or she experienced both bull and *bear markets*? What returns did he or she produce during these periods relative to the overall stock or bond market? All of this information will help you to judge the expertise and talent of the manager or management team before you invest.

The longer a manager or investment team has been in charge of a mutual fund, the better. When a new or young manager takes charge of a fund, or there are management changes due to a merger or acquisition between mutual fund companies, future performance becomes even more uncertain. You should look for an experienced advisor with a proven track record of producing consistent results in good times and bad. The value of experience, tenure, and consistency should not be underestimated.

Mutual fund companies have become aware of the trust that these attributes can garner for the specific fund and the sponsor. In reaction, funds sometimes publicize successful portfolio managers in their promotional materials, advertisements, and *annual reports*. This "star system" is a double-edged sword. While it increases trust and cash inflows to the fund, it can backfire if the star portfolio manager leaves. Investors might redeem their shares and follow the manager to his or her new fund. While the old childhood rhyme, "hitch your wagon to a star and it will take you very far," might seem applicable, it is prudent for mutual fund investors to keep in mind that few portfolio managers make all investment decisions completely alone. There are analysts and researchers at the management company supporting these trading activities. For example, it is usually the analysts or even the fund's senior management who determine the fund's *asset allocation*—i.e., how much of it assets should be held in stocks, bonds, and cash. When a "star" leaves, it does not necessarily mean that the performance of a mutual fund will decline. There may be a great understudy trained and waiting to step into the role.

bear market
a period during which the overall prices of securities are declining.

annual report
a document containing audited financial statements as well as other information about the fund's performance that each fund must distribute to shareholders annually.

asset allocation
the systematic and thoughtful placement of investment dollars into stocks, bonds, and cash equivalents.

An investment advisor earns a management fee for its services. The specific individuals who manage the fund usually receive a base salary plus a bonus based on the return of the fund. The management fee is an annual fee based on the total amount of assets under management, and is deducted from the fund a little each day. It is therefore in the investment advisor's interest to make the fund's assets grow as well as attract new money to the fund because the amount of money they earn from fees increases. (Management fees are discussed in more detail in Chapter 3 on Fees and Expenses.)

Additionally, the advisory company or the individual portfolio manager may have its own money invested in the fund, and will profit if it makes the fund perform well. The amount of a manager's holdings in a specific fund is usually not disclosed to the public. Some analysts argue that this information is just as important as the manager's professional experience and education. If the manager doesn't invest his own money in the fund, the debate goes, then does he have a real incentive to make the fund grow? Will the manager "feel the shareholders' pain" during a period when the portfolio is significantly underperforming in the market, or will he be content to simply earn its fees, albeit lesser of them?

Many factors must be considered when evaluating the past and potential performance of an individual fund manager or team of managers. Unfortunately, there are no perfect models or formulas. Length of experience and consistency of returns are probably two of the best criteria for all investors to use.

Custodian Bank

The Investment Company Act of 1940 requires every mutual fund to appoint a qualified *custodian bank*. Its primary responsibility is to safeguard the fund's assets. It holds the securities and cash resulting from the portfolio manager's trading activities. This is one of the important protective features built into a mutual fund's structure. The portfolio manager does not and cannot have possession of the fund's assets. Therefore, he or she cannot abscond with the assets, as has happened in the past. Even if the management company were to be dissolved, the fund's assets would be at the bank where they could be distributed to the shareholders on a pro-rate basis or liquidated and the proceeds distributed to the shareholders. Further protection comes from the requirement that the bank must segregate the funds assets from other bank assets. This safeguards the mutual funds assets should the custodian go bankrupt.

custodian bank
the bank or trust company whose primary responsibility is safeguarding the fund's assets and calculating their value daily.

A key responsibility of the bank is to calculate the fund's net asset value (NAV) every business day and distribute this information to the public. The custodian bank may have other functions. It can be the fund's *transfer agent*, keeping track of how many shares each shareholder owns. It can also serve as *registrar*, maintaining a current and accurate list of the shareholders of the fund. This record is used for sending distributions (*dividends* and *capital gains*) as well as mailing reports, proxies, and other communications to shareholders. The custodian bank earns a custodial fee. The amount is disclosed in the prospectus.

The custodian bank may be an outside bank or trust company. However, it may also be a division of the mutual fund's sponsor. For example, either Merrill Lynch Bank USA or Merrill Lynch Bank and Trust acts as the custodian bank for Merrill Lynch funds.

Transfer Agent

While many mutual funds' custodian banks also act as transfer agent, other funds hire an outside organization to handle this function. A transfer agent is the primary record keeper and information distributor for a fund. It keeps detailed records of shareholders accounts, including calculating, distributing, and reinvesting dividends. The agent sends transaction *confirmations* to the customer and, at the end of each year, is responsible for mailing federal income tax information. A transfer agent prepares and mails shareholders monthly or quarterly account *statements*. It may also run the mutual funds customer service department, providing account information and answering shareholder questions.

Distributor/Underwriter

The *distributor* or *underwriter* is responsible for selling the mutual fund shares to the public. To accomplish this, the distributor prepares sales literature, brochures, advertising, and may even hold contests and promotions to give brokers an incentive to sell fund's shares. A mutual fund distributor can also act as a *retailer*, selling its shares directly to the public itself. Most of the major brokerage firms sponsor their own mutual funds. These are called *proprietary funds*. They are sold directly to the public by the brokerage firm. Merrill Lynch, Fidelity, and Charles Schwab,

transfer agent
usually a commercial bank or trust company appointed by a mutual fund to keep track of daily purchases and sales of fund shares.

registrar
usually a commercial bank or trust company responsible for maintaining an accurate list of the names and addresses of a mutual fund's shareholders.

dividend
that portion of the company's after-tax earnings that its board of directors decides to distribute to the shareholders.

capital gain
the profit that
results when
the proceeds
from the sale
of a security
are higher
than the price
at which the
security was
purchased.

confirmation
a notice sent
from the broker
to the customer
that discloses
the details of
the execution
of an order,
including the
execution
price, number
of shares, and
settlement date.

for example, all act as their own retailers (Figure 1.3). Merrill Lynch funds can only be bought through Merrill Lynch or Blackrock, a company that it partly owns. Today, some of these proprietary funds (especially those created by brokerage firms) are available through other sources, such mutual fund supermarkets. For example, Morgan Stanley Special Value Fund can be bought through Charles Schwab One Source. The reason for the change is the supermarkets' larger client base. The propriety funds can be marketed to a broader range of investors and their investment dollars. If successful, the result is an increase in assets under management and therefore more fee income for the investment advisor and sponsor.

The distributor can also act as a wholesaler (Figure 1.4). In this case, the fund signs up *selling groups* through which it sells its funds. Janus Funds and Dreyfus Funds are good examples of this. In addition to buying shares directly from Janus or Dreyfus, you can buy them through just about every bank, insurance company, brokerage firm, or mutual fund supermarket. These financial institutions act as a selling group. They receive a selling concession when their customers purchase one of the Janus or Dreyfus funds. In serving as its own retailer and wholesaler, a fund distributor is able to offer its shares to the broadest range of investors.

The members of the selling group are prohibited from "warehousing" mutual fund shares. This means the firm cannot hold an inventory of shares in anticipation of its customers placing orders. When you place an order to

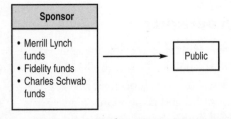

FIGURE 1.3 Retail distribution mechanism of mutual fund shares.
The sponsor acts as a retailer, selling its own mutual fund shares directly to the public. Until recently, proprietary funds created by brokerage firms could only be bought and redeemed directly with the sponsor. Today, some firms now sell their funds through other sales agents such as mutual fund supermarkets.

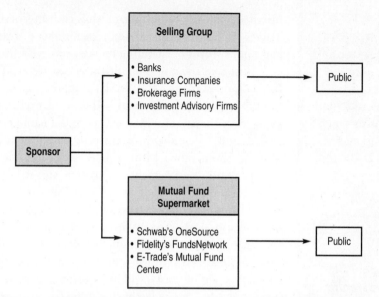

FIGURE 1.4 Wholesale distribution mechanism of mutual fund shares. Sponsor acts as a wholesaler, offering its funds' shares through individual selling groups or mutual fund supermarkets. This distribution method has become the most popular because the fund sponsor gains access to a broader customer base to which its funds can be sold. The same sponsor that sells its funds through selling groups can (and does) sell shares of the same fund directly to the public.

buy Janus fund shares through Charles Schwab OneSource or Fidelity FundsNetwork, for example, the supermarket forwards your order to Janus who executes the order to buy fund shares or redeem fund shares. Hence, a selling group member can only place an order to fill an existing customer order or for the firm's own proprietary investment account.

Closed-End Management Company (aka publicly traded fund)

Also called a publicly traded fund, a *closed-end fund* establishes a portfolio of securities, then issues shares to the public backed by the underlying portfolio. Like a mutual fund, each share represents an undivided interest in the portfolio of securities. However, a closed-end management company typically issues shares to the public only once. It does *not* continually issue new shares

statement
a summary of all transactions in an investor's account as well as the current value of all securities positions being held in the account.

distributor
the financial institution through which a mutual fund sells its shares to the public.

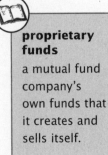

underwriter
the division of the sponsor responsible for creating the fund's prospectus and marketing the fund directly to the public or wholesalers.

proprietary funds
a mutual fund company's own funds that it creates and sells itself.

or redeem already outstanding shares each business day. Therefore, unlike a mutual fund, the number of a closed-end fund's shares outstanding remains relatively fixed.

Just like the common shares issued by a publicly held corporation (e.g., JNJ, MSFT, GOOG), closed-end fund shares can be bought and sold on stock exchanges or in the over-the-counter market; hence the name *publicly traded fund*. These shares are correctly described as being *tradable*. [Remember: Mutual fund shares (i.e., share of an open-end management company) are redeemable securities and cannot trade in the secondary markets.]

Historically, most closed-end funds have invested in the equity or debt securities of foreign countries or of specialized sectors (e.g., municipal securities, utilities). Today, closed-end funds invested in bonds make up the largest segment of this type of investment. The closed-end fund structure was originally chosen by the management company because the securities in the portfolio tended to lack the *liquidity* of those traded on major stock exchanges. If investors bought the securities directly in those local markets, they would have difficulty liquidating their holdings during market downturns. Because a closed-end fund shares trade on the highly liquid U.S. securities markets, it is easier for U.S. investors to buy and sell them.

The following example illustrates how a closed-end fund is established and how its shares trade. Suppose a brokerage firm determines that individuals are interested in investing in growth companies whose shares trade in India. It buys shares of companies traded on the local stock exchange or exchanges of India, creating a portfolio that it then registers with the SEC. Typically the portfolio or fund would be named after the country or region where the shares were purchased. Our theoretical fund will be called the India Growth Fund. Once the shares are issued, they then trade on the NYSE-Euronext. As with any publicly traded company, closed-end fund shares are issued at an initial public offering price. This initial price is based on the value of the equity or debt securities in the portfolio, plus any fees that the underwriter builds into the price. Once the shares are issued, their market value fluctuates daily based on expectations of the performance of the India-based companies whose stocks make up the underlying portfolio. The fund's shares on the NYSE-Euronext may trade at a price *equal to* the net asset value (NAV) of the shares in the portfolio, at a *discount* to the NAV, or at a *premium* to the NAV. Investors in the fund can place orders with their brokers to buy or sell their shares at their current market value or at specified prices during the trading day. A closed-end fund's shares are subject to the rules of the exchange where they are listed and traded. However, the companies' shares and/or bonds in the portfolio are regulated by the securities authorities of the markets in which those securities are listed and traded.

Closed-end funds allow the investment manager to maintain the portfolio, while at the same time giving investors a way to buy or sell in the secondary markets the shares backed by that portfolio. If there were a huge downturn in that particular country, market, or sector, the manager will not be forced to liquidate the portfolio during unfavorable conditions. As investors sell the fund's shares, their market value on the U.S-based stock exchange would be driven down, perhaps trading at a deep discount to the actual NAV of the stocks and/or bonds in the portfolio. In contrast, the manager of a mutual fund might be forced to liquidate positions in the portfolio if the number of redemptions resulting from the market's downturn was high. This forced sale could drive the market price for the securities in the portfolio even lower.

Today, closed-end funds are not limited to equity securities. Many of them are bond funds, particularly *municipal bonds*. Each Monday, *The Wall Street Journal* publishes a list of closed-end funds near the end of Section C. The excerpt from the online version of this column in Figure 1.5 shows that most of the funds trade at a discount to their NAV. This discount reflects, among other factors, the reality that many of closed-end fund portfolios consists of illiquid securities. If the fund had to sell them all at one time, it is virtually certain that such a large sale would cause the market value of the securities to decrease substantially. Hence the securities would be sold at low prices— well below their market value when the selling began.

The prevailing wisdom is that it is best to buy a closed-end fund when it is trading at a deep discount to the fund's NAV. The reasoning is that if you hold them over a long period of time, the price should eventually rise back to the fund's NAV. This price appreciation, combined with any dividends or interest, should provide the investor with a higher than

selling group
a group of registered brokers/ dealers responsible for offering and selling mutual funds created by other sponsors to the public.

closed-end fund
a type of management company that creates a portfolio of securities and then issues a fixed or limited number of shares to the public backed by the portfolio. The shares trade on exchanges or OTC markets.

CLOSED-END FUNDS: World Equity Funds
Friday, September 3, 2010

Weekly Statistics
(as of 9/03/2010)

Fund	NAV	Mkt Price	Prem/Disc %	52 Week Market Return %
Aberdeen Chile (CH)	22.25	20.84	-6.34	50.90
Aberdeen Em Mkt Telecomm (ETF)	19.68	17.37	-11.74	6.94
Aberdeen Indonesia (IF)	13.40	12.59	-6.04	59.05
Aberdeen Israel Fund (ISL)	16.58	15.02	-9.41	11.84
Aberdeen Latin America (LAQ)	45.93	42.87	-6.66	38.60
AGIC Gl Eq & Conv Income (NGZ)	15.23	14.66	-3.74	18.39
Alpine Glbl Dynamic Div (AGD)	6.17	6.21	+0.65	-18.03
Alpine Tot Dynamic Div (AOD)	5.54	5.31	-4.15	-22.09
Asia Pacific Fund (APB)	11.17	10.19	-8.77	9.22
Asia Tigers Fund (GRR)	20.56	19.34	-5.93	14.19
BlackRock S&P Qual Gl Eq (BQY)	13.45	12.10	-10.04	15.08
Calamos Glbl Dyn Inc (CHW)	8.51	7.59	-10.81	10.44
Calamos Glbl Tot Rtn (CGO)	14.01	13.93	-0.57	13.84
Central Europe & Russia (CEE)	38.91	35.36	-9.12	26.85
China Fund (CHN)	32.40	30.16	-6.91	30.83
Clough Glbl Allocation (GLV)	15.55	14.40	-7.40	11.68
Clough Glbl Equity (GLQ)	14.88	13.53	-9.07	13.39
Clough Glbl Opptys (GLO)	13.39	12.08	-9.78	10.38
Delaware Enh Gl Div & In (DEX)	12.05	12.02	-0.25	22.82
Eaton Vance Tx-Ad Gl Div (ETG)	14.16	13.35	-5.72	18.07
Eaton Vance Tx-Ad Gl Opp (ETO)	20.43	18.70	-8.47	16.64
First TrActive Div Inc (FAV)	9.47	10.20	+7.71	9.54
First Tr/Abrdn Emerg Op (FEO)	21.78	20.99	-3.63	42.38
Gabelli Global Deal (GDL)	15.35	13.85	-9.77	4.96
Global Income & Currency (GCF)	16.10	14.55	-9.63	8.35
Greater China Fund (GCH)	12.99	11.78	-9.31	-1.38
Herzfeld Caribbean Basin (CUBA)	6.75	6.18	-8.44	-1.75
India Fund (IFN)	35.53	33.88	-4.64	25.20
ING Infr Indus & Matr (IDE)	19.01	17.37	-8.63	NS
J Hancock Tx-Ad Gl Sh Yd (HTY)	12.53	12.62	+0.72	18.05
JF China Region Fund (JFC)	15.02	13.49	-10.19	5.78
Korea Equity Fund (KEF)	11.14	10.29	-7.63	26.88
Korea Fund (KF)	42.90	39.16	-8.72	23.65
Latin American Discovery (LDF)	18.52	17.36	-6.26	27.53
Lazard Gl Tot Ret & Inc (LGI)	15.63	14.20	-9.15	13.21
Lazard Wld Div & Inc (LOR)	12.82	11.67	-8.97	28.02
Malaysia Fund (MAY)	11.36	10.25	-9.77	52.48
Mexico Equity & Income (MXE)	10.57	9.25	-12.49	38.89
Mexico Fund (MXF)	26.42	23.51	-11.01	27.52
Morg Stan China A (CAF)	29.07	28.61	-1.58	1.33
Morg Stan East Europe (RNE)	17.99	16.09	-10.56	23.67
Morg Stan Emerg Mkts (MSF)	15.62	14.43	-7.62	18.66
Morg Stan Frontier Em Mk (FFD)	13.88	12.84	-7.49	18.90
Morg Stan India Inv (IIF)	26.85	25.04	-6.74	26.27
Nuveen Glbl Val Opps (JGV)	18.93	18.40	-2.80	21.67
Taiwan Fund (TWN)	16.81	15.16	-9.82	18.29

FIGURE 1.5 Closed-end fund listing from *The Wall Street Journal*. This separate listing of "Closed-End Funds" is published in *The Wall Street Journal* each Monday but the prices are updated daily online. During the rest of the week, a specific fund can be found in the listings of stock prices or at www.wsj.com. The listings above, labeled "World Equity Funds," are the type described in the example in the text. However, today's closed-end funds invest in a variety of securities: mortgage bonds, municipal bonds, high-yield bonds, government bonds, convertible securities, as well as domestic and international equities.

market rate of return. While this strategy seems simple, investing in closed-end funds requires considerable knowledge of the securities within the portfolio and the economic factors that affect them, as well as knowledge of the factors that influence the markets in which they trade. This information may not be readily available, especially for world equity funds. There are no simple, foolproof strategies.

>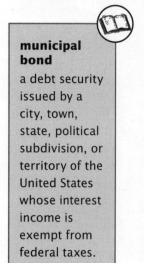
>
> **liquidity**
> the ease with which a security can be bought or sold.

Sometimes when a closed-end fund is selling at a deep discount to its net asset value (NAV), its Board of Directors and shareholders may vote to convert it to an open-end structure— i.e., a mutual fund. (It is rare for an open-end fund to covert to a closed-end fund.) At conversion, the fund's market price will be its net asset value. (Remember mutual funds are priced daily at their net asset value.) The difference between the discounted market price and the NAV will be a gain for holders of the once closed-end fund. Additionally, it also means that the fund can now begin to issue more shares, raising additional investment capital for the fund's portfolio.

Mutual Funds versus Closed-End Funds

Although mutual funds and closed-end funds are both management companies, they are quite different products. There is occasional mention in the financial media of a product called a *closed-end mutual fund.* The definitions of a closed-end fund and an open-end fund under the Investment Company Act of 1940 makes this term an oxymoron. When this term is used, it usually refers (1) to a mutual fund that is closed to new investors (this would be correctly called a closed mutual fund); or (2) to an actively managed closed-end fund. Many closed-end funds are not managed; therefore, the fund's investment portfolio of securities changes little. A closed-end fund that is actively managed might resemble a mutual fund to some people, but keep in mind that the number of outstanding shares remains relatively fixed, unlike a mutual fund. Given current legislation, however, a true closed-end mutual fund cannot exist.

> **municipal bond**
> a debt security issued by a city, town, state, political subdivision, or territory of the United States whose interest income is exempt from federal taxes.

Now that you understand the basic differences between the two types of funds, you probably wonder what caused mutual funds to become a more popular investment product than closed-end funds. There are four most-probable reasons for this development.

First, there are simply more mutual funds (over 8,600) than closed-end funds (around 630) available in the market. And they are more heavily marketed and advertised than closed-end funds. Hence, when people look at investment options, mutual funds show up and are recommended more often.

The second reason for their popularity is the certainty of pricing. At the end of each business day, a mutual fund (actually, its Custodian Bank) computes and publishes the value (minus applicable fees and expenses) of each share outstanding. In contrast, the "real" value of a closed-end fund is less certain. Market forces could drive the value of the fund's shares up, causing them to sell at a premium to their net asset value. Or the same forces could drive the price down, resulting in their selling at a discount. Price uncertainty is a concept that is emotionally (if not intellectually) anathema to most investors. They want to know exactly what their shares are worth.

The third reason is size. Mutual funds typically have more money to invest than do closed-end funds. Each time an investor buys a mutual fund share, the fund itself is getting new money that it can use to by more securities or can hold as cash in a money market account until it's ready to buy more shares into the portfolio. These additional dollars enables it to achieve greater diversity more easily than a closed end fund. It can purchase shares of more companies in different sectors. When a person buys a closed-end fund share on a stock exchange, the money goes to the person who sold the fund, not to the fund.

The final reason is for mutual funds' popularity is low initial investment cost. You can begin by investing as little as $25 a month in a fund. This makes the product available to a vast cross section of potential investors. These reasons, combined access to professional management, largely explain why mutual funds are the investment of choice of millions of people in the U.S. and abroad.

The remainder of this book focuses almost entirely on mutual funds. (Exchange-trade funds or ETFs will be occasionally mentioned.) Each chapter will examine particular features of a fund that you must evaluate to be able to select the mutual funds that are most suitable for your investment objectives, time horizon, and risk tolerance.

Chapter

2

Investment Objectives and Risks of Stock and Bond Funds

The first step in selecting a mutual fund is not looking at the fund's investment objective; instead, the first step is defining *your* investment goals. You must clearly determine why you want to invest *before* buying the shares of a mutual fund. By taking the time to think through and articulate the purpose for making the investment, you will be better able to choose a fund that is most appropriate. This, in turn, gives you a reasonable chance of achieving your stated goal in light of the risks you are willing to take.

Establishing Your Investment Objectives

Consider your response to the question: "What is your investment objective?" A surprising number of people would say, "My objective is to make money." This response, a statement of the blatantly obvious, is insufficient and far too general. Other people say, "I want to invest in mutual funds because they are safer than stocks." This answer understates the risk of certain types of funds (for example, sector funds) and fails to focus on the returns you wish to achieve over time. Still others answer, with some degree of sheepishness, "I want to invest in mutual funds because everyone is using them to get rich." This lemming-inspired

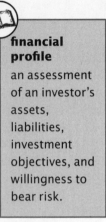

financial profile

an assessment of an investor's assets, liabilities, investment objectives, and willingness to bear risk.

answer fails to differentiate your risk-to-reward profile from those of other investors.

Individuals with virtually the same *financial profile* may want their money to work for them in very different ways. These are as varied as each person's ambition, lifestyle, and risk tolerance. For example, a person whose goal is to accumulate money for retirement or for a child's college education (e.g., a 529 plan) may want to invest in a mutual fund whose objective focuses on the rise in the stock prices (growth), instead of dividend payments (income), over the long term, but also wants the fund to become more conservative as the time approaches when the money will be needed. A recently retired person may wish to invest in a fund that provides supplementary income with little risk to principal. Perhaps a conservative, dividend-paying stock fund or interest-paying bond fund that distributes income monthly or quarterly may be suitable. Still another investor may wish to use mutual funds to enhance the return on his or her risk-free savings account at a bank. This person wants the money invested in funds to do at least as well as the overall stock market; hence, a mutual fund that tracks the overall performance of a benchmark market index might be appropriate.

Failure to clearly define your goals increases the possibility that you may choose a fund that is less than appropriate for achieving the returns you want. Each person must evaluate his or her own goals first. Three key questions must be answered when determining your investment objective.

What Is the Purpose of the Investment?

Why do you want to invest money in mutual funds? Are you using mutual funds as substitutes for a traditional bank savings account? Are you seeking to accumulate money for a child's college education, your retirement, or a down-payment on a house? Or are you trying to augment the return from a risk-free investment vehicle such as a bank certificate of deposit (CD)? Be specific when answering this question. During the inquiry, you may discover that you have more than one purpose for investing. If this is the case, you must think about the amount of money that you want to allocate to each purpose. This usually means investing in several different funds. There are few single mutual funds that can successfully satisfy multiple investment objectives.

What Is Your Time Horizon for Making the Investment?

Over what period of time do you plan to leave the money invested in a fund? Or, over what period of time do you plan to continue investing regularly in a mutual fund? Two years? Five years? Ten years? Again, it is important to have your target clearly in sight.

Your age must also be considered when establishing your investment's time horizon. Generally, the younger you are, the more growth-oriented your investments should be. Because your time horizon is long, you can withstand the inevitable downturns in the market. You should profit over the long term because historically the investment markets have always moved higher. As you age, you should periodically adjust the mix of funds in your portfolio to favor more conservative funds that focus on preservation of capital and perhaps provide a steady stream of income. Adjusting your investment for your age is a dynamic process. Regular periodic reviews—quarterly or annually—are essential so that the mix of funds remains appropriate.

A surprisingly large number of investors tend to make only the vaguest distinctions between money that is being invested for the long term (this money is sometimes called *investment dollars*) and that which they will need sooner. This tendency to meld the time horizons is probably due to two reasons. First, everyone likes to receive the highest possible return on the money invested regardless of the time horizon. Historically, long-term returns are usually more attractive and more predictable than short-term returns, so people tend to stretch (some would say exaggerate slightly) the time over which they plan to leave the money invested.

investment dollars
the money in excess of living expenses, savings, insurance, and other essentials that can be invested in securities and can be at risk.

The second reason is more complicated. Many individuals believe that a mutual fund is a relatively safe investment—that it will not fluctuate wildly in value over time. This belief arises because people equate the word *diversification* with the word *protection*. Thus, they lull themselves into thinking, erroneously, that the value of their mutual fund "cannot go down that much" over either the short term or the long term. Hence, the risks associated with both time horizons become similar in people's minds.

The shorter your time horizon, the less risk you should take with your investments. This money should probably be held as cash in a savings or money market account, or in a very liquid, low-risk investment. If this money were put in long-term securities, a sudden and long-lasting downturn in the stock market could mean that the value of your fund's shares would fall below (even far below) the price you paid for them—as many people experienced in 2008 to 2009. Until the market recovered, there would be no way for you to regain the value lost on the assets, especially in the short term. On the other hand, if you have a long time horizon, then you may want to choose a more growth-oriented fund as discussed earlier in this section. However, as a young person,

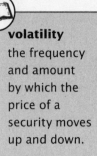

volatility
the frequency and amount by which the price of a security moves up and down.

you should choose this type of fund only if you can stand the *volatility*. Not all young investors are risk-tolerant.

Stock and bond mutual funds are considered to be long-term investment vehicles. However, the specific time period associated with the phrase "long-term" varies depending on the sectors or types of securities in which the fund invests. For a domestic stock fund, long-term may be five years, seven years, or longer. For some funds that focus on certain industries or countries, long-term may be only three to four years. These shorter time horizons mean that you can use some funds, especially bond funds, to achieve intermediate-term investment goals. Reading a fund's prospectus or talking with an investment professional should enable you to match your time horizon with that of an appropriate mutual fund.

What Is Your Risk Tolerance?

How much risk are you willing to accept in return for a potential gain? As noted earlier, many people assume that because mutual funds are diversified, they are not subject to price fluctuations as great as those of individual stocks. This may be generally true, but a specific mutual fund's volatility may leave investors feeling as if they are on the largest and fastest roller-coaster ride in the world. When the stock market plummeted during the recession of 2008 to 2009, some growth funds lost almost 50 percent of their value, while some conservative funds may have lost less than 20 percent. On the other hand, when the market began to rise from mid 2009 into 2010, several growth funds soared, regaining their position as top performers. Some conservative growth funds did quite decently, but not spectacularly. They were not top performers. Some investors would have found the growth funds' steep decline no more upsetting than accidentally losing $100. Others would have been up all night surfing the net and visiting chat rooms for information, talking to their friends for solace, or calling their brokers for advice.

No one likes to see the value of their investment assets decline. (Keep in mind, also, that not all of your assets should be invested in securities. Some should be allocated to risk-free savings products.) Still, some people can tolerate the market's drop better than others, and it is undoubtedly more distressing as you get older. If a 20 percent or 30 percent drop in the value of a particular mutual fund would upset you, then look for and choose a fund that has lower volatility. If you already own several funds, change the percentages of the money you have allocated among them so that your overall risk of loss is less. Or you can simply place your money in safer or risk-free instruments. Your goal (which is as much emotional as it is practical) in changing your allocation or mix is simple: to have fewer sleepless nights and fewer hours of worried Internet surfing.

Matching your investment objectives, time horizon, and risk tolerance to those of a mutual fund is not as simple as saying, "My objective is to achieve growth; ergo I will choose a growth fund." Gone are the days when a typical mutual fund company offered investors four options—a stock fund, a bond fund, a balance fund, and a guaranteed income fund—and only a few companies offered an *international fund* as well. Today, in order to select a suitable mutual fund, investors must: (1) be able to differentiate clearly among the numerous investment objectives that individual mutual funds have, and (2) understand the basic strategy or strategies by which the fund manager seeks to achieve the stated objective. (Chapter 5 contains a detailed discussion of the various investment styles a manager can use.)

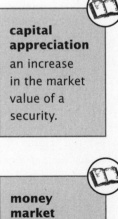

international fund
a mutual fund or closed-end fund that invests only in the securities of companies located outside the United States.

Mutual Fund Investment Objectives

A portfolio manager's selection of securities must be in keeping with the mutual fund's investment objective, which is stated in the fund's prospectus. A fund's objective denotes: (1) the primary method or approach (i.e., value investing, *capital appreciation*, dividend payments, interest payments) by which the manager seeks to make money for the shareholders, and (2) the class or classes of assets (e.g., stocks, bonds, *money market securities*—see Figure 2.2 later in this chapter) and types (as well as sizes) of securities (e.g., *growth stock, income stock,* large-cap, small-cap, municipal bonds, corporate bonds) within those classes that the portfolio manager can buy and sell. A mutual fund's investment objective is established when the fund is created. It can only be changed with a majority vote of the fund's shareholders.

capital appreciation
an increase in the market value of a security.

There has been a proliferation of new fund objectives in recent years. Currently, there are more than 40 different investment objectives for mutual funds. This increase has been spurred by several factors. The first is competition. Each mutual fund sponsor expands its choices of mutual fund objectives to imitate successful funds being offered by its competitors.

money market securities
short-term, highly liquid debt securities that mature in one year or less.

The second factor is shareholder retention. A mutual fund sponsor profits from being able to retain more of each shareholder's money in the funds it creates

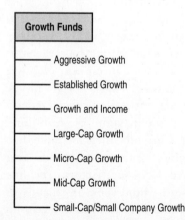

growth stock
stocks of
expanding
companies
whose market
values are
expected to
appreciate
rapidly.

income stock
equity
securities that
make regular
and substantial
dividend
payment to
shareholders.

and sells. The greater the variety of objectives offered, the greater the likelihood that customers will stay within the fund family even as their investment objectives and economic situations change. Shareholders would not have to transfer assets out of the mutual fund family.

The third factor is the refinement of traditional investment objectives as well as development of new objectives. In order to market a type of fund (for example, a growth fund) to groups of investors with different goals and varying risk tolerances, mutual fund sponsors are making the objectives more targeted—i.e., more specific or defined. Industry jargon for this further division is *splicing*. Figure 2.1 shows how a basic fund objective, in this case growth, can be spliced to create many more specifically targeted funds.

At the same time, mutual fund sponsors recognized that people want new kinds of funds that, given the analytical and mathematical modeling tools available today, can be more dynamically moved from one objective to another—such as growth to preservation of capital—following, for example, one's changing financial objectives and needs through life.

The increase in both the number of funds and the types of investment objectives gives mutual fund investors a broader arena for optimizing their

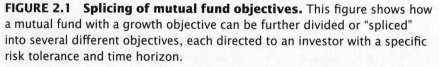

```
Growth Funds
    ├───── Aggressive Growth
    ├───── Established Growth
    ├───── Growth and Income
    ├───── Large-Cap Growth
    ├───── Micro-Cap Growth
    ├───── Mid-Cap Growth
    └───── Small-Cap/Small Company Growth
```

FIGURE 2.1   Splicing of mutual fund objectives. This figure shows how a mutual fund with a growth objective can be further divided or "spliced" into several different objectives, each directed to an investor with a specific risk tolerance and time horizon.

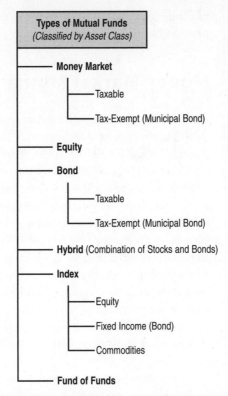

Types of Mutual Funds
(Classified by Asset Class)

— **Money Market**
   — Taxable
   — Tax-Exempt (Municipal Bond)

— **Equity**

— **Bond**
   — Taxable
   — Tax-Exempt (Municipal Bond)

— **Hybrid** (Combination of Stocks and Bonds)

— **Index**
   — Equity
   — Fixed Income (Bond)
   — Commodities

— **Fund of Funds**

FIGURE 2.2   Types of mutual funds classified by asset class.

returns. At the same time, it makes selecting a mutual fund that is suitable to your investment goal more complex and difficult. In order to help you understand the different investment objectives and, therefore, be better able to match your goal with that of a specific fund, this section takes a step-by-step approach.

Step 1. A figure in each section lists the mutual fund objectives associated with the asset class being discussed. The asset classes are shown in Figure 2.2.

Step 2. The objectives associated with each asset class are explained. The discussion follows the sequence shown in the figure, which will usually be in alphabetical order.

Step 3. The risks and rewards of each investment objective will be discussed under the objective itself. However, if they are the same for a particular asset class (e.g., *money market mutual funds*) or a group

money market mutual fund
a fund that invests in short-term, low-risk debt securities and thus seeks to maintain a net asset value per share of $1.

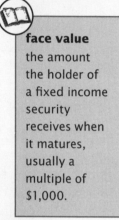

sector fund
a mutual fund
that invests in
one industry
or segment of
an industry.

face value
the amount
the holder of
a fixed income
security
receives when
it matures,
usually a
multiple of
$1,000.

**investment
grade**
the highest
quality of
fixed income
security with
the least
likelihood of
default.

of funds (e.g., *sector funds*), the risks and rewards will be discussed at the beginning of the appropriate section.

Money Market Mutual Funds

A money market mutual fund invests in high-quality, low-risk, short-term debt securities such as commercial paper, Treasury bills (T-bills), banker's acceptances, and negotiable certificates of deposit. Money funds attempt to maintain the net asset value of the fund at $1.00 per share. The money manager seeks to achieve this objective by purchasing these debt securities, which trade at a discount to their *face value,* when they have anywhere from one day to 60 days left to maturity. The discount is usually quite small because of the short time remaining to maturity. The difference between the security's discounted purchase price and its face value at maturity is the return or interest that you earn on your money market account. This interest accrues daily in your account.

The short-term maturity of money market securities provides investors with two advantages: low risk of default and high liquidity. Because the securities mature within a short period of time after purchase, the likelihood that one would default is extremely low to virtually nonexistent. Additionally, money managers are usually limited to buying only those short-term securities rated *investment grade* by both Moody's Investors Service and Standard & Poor's. This criterion further limits the risk of default. Short-term high-quality securities are also always in demand. If necessary, the money manager can quickly and easily sell the securities.

These advantages indicate that money market funds are an appropriate place for short-term investments that need to remain liquid—readily available—and perhaps earn a higher rate of interest than would be available through a traditional savings account. But, the safety of a money market mutual fund should not be interpreted to mean totally risk free. The failure of Lehman Brother in September 2008 caused the Reserve Primary Money Market Fund, which held Lehman's then worthless commercial paper, to "break the buck"—i.e., the value of the fund's shares fell below $1.00. This unexpected and surprising event demonstrated that money markets are indeed investments subject to the risk of loss. On the front of the prospectus of all money market funds you will find the following SEC-required disclosure statement:

> Investment in the fund is neither insured or guaranteed by the U.S. Government. Each Fund attempts to maintain a stable net asset value of $1.00 per share; however, there can be no assurance that the fund manager will be able to do so. The fund . . . is not insured by the Federal Deposit Insurance Corporation or any other agency, and involves risk, including possible loss of principal amount invested.

Because a money market mutual fund is a security, all deposited monies are usually insured by the *Securities Investor Protection Corporation (SIPC)*. Your deposits are not insured against the fluctuation in their market value or the manager's failure to maintain a net asset value of $1. Rather, SIPC insures your money only if the brokerage firm which is holding your money market shares goes bankrupt. The maximum SIPC coverage for cash is $250,000; however, most firms have excess SIPC coverage (referred to as *ex-SIPC insurance*) significantly above this amount. (Check with your brokerage company for the specific details and limitations to its coverage.)

There are five basic types of money market mutual funds, which are grouped into two categories: taxable money market funds and tax-exempt money market funds (see Figure 2.3):

1. Government securities money market funds
2. Taxable securities money market funds
3. U.S. Treasury money market funds
4. National *tax-exempt securities* money market funds
5. Single-state tax-exempt money market funds

Securities Investor Protection Corporation (SIPC) a government-sponsored, private corporation that provides limited protection for customers if their broker/dealer goes bankrupt.

ex-SIPC insurance literally excess SIPC insurance, this is insurance coverage beyond that provided by the government-sponsored Securities Investor Protection Corporation (SIPC).

Brokerage firms, mutual fund companies, banks, insurance companies, and other financial services companies sometimes create their own trademarked names for these accounts.

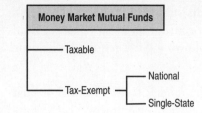

Type of Money Market Mutual Fund	Tax Status of the Interest Income
Taxable[1]	
Government Securities Money Market Fund	• Subject to federal taxes • May be exempt from state and local taxes
Taxable Money Market Fund	• Subject to federal, state, and local taxes
U.S. Treasury Money Market Fund	• Subject to federal taxes • Exempt from state and local taxes
Tax-Exempt[2]	
National Tax-Exempt Money Market Fund	• Subject to state and local taxes • Exempt from federal taxes
Single-State Tax-Exempt Money Market Fund	• May be subject to local taxes • Exempt from federal and state taxes for residents of the state

[1]Taxable means the income from the mutual fund is subject to federal taxes. State and local taxes may or may not apply.
[2]Tax-exempt means the income from the mutual fund is exempt from federal taxes. State and local taxes may or may not apply.

FIGURE 2.3 Types of money market mutual funds. This chart shows the five most common types of money market mutual funds. It also presents the tax status of the interest income from each type of fund.

tax-exempt security
a term frequently used to describe a municipal bond or note whose interest payments are exempt from federal taxes.

Taxable Money Market Funds

Government Securities Money Market Fund This fund invests in U.S. Treasury bills (T-bills), Treasury notes (T-notes), Treasury bonds (T-bonds), and other debt obligations issued or guaranteed by the U.S. government with 60 days or less to maturity. Depending on the securities in the portfolio, the income earned in this fund will be subject to federal taxes but may be exempt from state and local taxes. Because of the safety of U.S. government and *agency securities* purchased by the fund, this (and the U.S. Treasury money market fund discussed later) is considered one of the safest types of money market funds.

Taxable Money Market Fund   This fund invests in bank obligations (negotiable CDs), short-term and long-term corporate debt, and other short-term debt obligations traded between institutions. Income earned in this fund is subject to federal, state, and local taxes.

U.S. Treasury Money Market Fund   This fund invests only in U.S government securities issued directly by the U.S. Treasury with short-term maturities. Agency securities (e.g., those issued by the Government National Mortgage Association (GNMA) and other government agencies) are not included. The income earned is subject to federal taxes, but is exempt from state and local taxes.

Tax-Exempt Money Market Funds

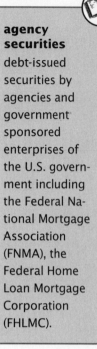

agency securities
debt-issued securities by agencies and government sponsored enterprises of the U.S. government including the Federal National Mortgage Association (FNMA), the Federal Home Loan Mortgage Corporation (FHLMC).

National Tax-Exempt Money Market Fund   This fund invests 75 percent of its assets in high-quality debt securities issued by any municipality. As with most market money funds, the securities in the portfolio mature within 60 days or less. The interest income earned is exempt from federal income taxes, but is subject to state and local taxes.

Single-State, Double Tax-Exempt Money Market Fund   This fund invests in municipal securities issued by a single state. The interest income from these funds is exempt from federal and state taxes for the residents of the state, but may be subject to local taxes.

Other Variations

While these are the basic types of money funds, there are other variations available. There are money market accounts that invest in only investment grade corporate debt—commercial paper, *debentures*, mortgage bonds, and equipment trust certificates (ETCs). Others invest in dollar-denominated short-term debt issued within and outside the United States by foreign corporations and governments.

debenture
a long-term, unsecured corporate bond backed by the full faith and credit of the issuer.

    As an individual mutual fund investor, your choice of money market accounts at a particular brokerage firm or mutual fund company depends of the value of

yield
the percentage
or rate of return
that an investor
makes on
capital invested
in a security or
in a portfolio of
securities.

hub and spoke
a mutual
fund that is
marketed and
sold through
different
organizations
(retail brokerage
firms, banks,
pension plans)
with each having
a different
amount of
expenses.

cash account
a brokerage
account in
which an
investor buys
securities and
pays for them
in full.

your account and your attitude toward paying taxes on the income. (Despite what happened with the Reserve Primary Fund, risk remains a small consideration.) The total market value of your account can affect the *yield* that you receive.

All money market accounts are no-load funds; however, there are other costs involved including management fees and trading commissions. (See Chapter 3, "Fees and Expenses.") Your schedule of charges depends on whether you open a regular money market account, a premium money market account, or an institutional money market account. The minimum required deposit or account balance is the only other significant difference among these accounts.

The Wall Street Journal, Barron's, as well as other publications and web sites, periodically publish a scoreboard of the best- and worst-performing money market funds. While there is little variation in the one-month returns, there is a significant difference in the 12-month returns. The difference is most likely due to the type of money market account (regular, premium, or institutional) and the expenses charged for each. The lower costs charged to the accounts requiring a high minimum balance results in more interest paid on the money market account; hence the higher yield.

In an increasingly commonplace arrangement, the cash from all of a mutual fund customers' accounts is invested in the same portfolio of money market securities (called the hub), but each account type (called the spoke) has a different schedule of fees. The lower your balance, the higher the expenses—therefore, the lower your yield. Another reason the yields might be different is that the manager purchases securities with either longer maturities or slightly higher risk. (Note: The *hub and spoke* arrangement is used for all types of mutual funds because it is more efficient and cost-effective for the mutual fund company.)

Most firms automatically "sweep" any cash that accumulates in your account into the money market fund that you choose. Other firms sweep funds only on designated days or only if the cash balances reach a specified minimum amount. If you purchase mutual funds in a *cash account* at a brokerage firm, bank, or other financial services company, then you should probably have your cash balances swept into a money market fund with some tax advantages. This is usually a tax-exempt money market fund. The reason for this choice is that you will pay no federal taxes at the end of the year on the interest earned. State and local taxes, however, may apply.

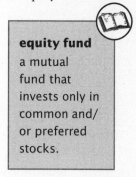

tax-deferred account
an account such as a retirement account in which interest, dividends, and capital gains build up tax free until they are withdrawn.

If you purchase mutual funds in a *tax-deferred account*—such as a 401(k), 529 plan, Individual Retirement Account (IRA), Keogh plan, 401(k), or Simplified Employee Pension (SEP) plan—then it is prudent to have the excess cash swept into a taxable money market fund attached to the account. The yield (or interest rate) is generally higher on this type of fund to compensate for the taxes you will pay on the interest income. Because you will pay no taxes on the money earned in the account, the higher yield means that you will earn more interest on the interest paid. This compounding results in a higher return over time. It is inappropriate to use a tax-exempt money market fund in a tax-deferred account. Regardless of the type of money market fund you choose, keep in mind that they are one of the reasonably safe (*not* absolutely safe) places to hold cash that will be needed in the short term.

Equity or Stock Funds

Equity funds invest primarily in *common stock*. (There are also equity funds that invest only in *preferred stock*.) All equity funds make money for their shareholders in two ways: (1) through the rise in the market value of the shares held in the portfolio, and (2) through dividend payments from those stocks. The way a particular fund makes money as well as the associated risks depend on the combined characteristics of the companies' common stock in the portfolio. And since common stock of different companies can have very different characteristics, a portfolio manager must look for those stocks whose profiles match the mutual fund's investment objective.

equity fund
a mutual fund that invests only in common and/ or preferred stocks.

The common stock of different companies is often categorized based on different features, such as dividend payment history, potential for capital appreciation, the size of the company, and reactions to the economy and business cycles. *Blue chip stocks,* growth stocks, and income stocks are examples of these groupings. Before you can understand and differentiate among

common stock
an equity security that gives the owner the right to receive dividends, vote on company issues, and vote for the board of directors of a company.

preferred stock
an equity security that is senior to common stock and has preference over common shares in dividend distribution and in claims on a company's assets in a liquidation.

the various investment objectives associated with equity funds, it helps to know a few of the basic categories of common stocks that mutual funds use in structuring their portfolios. These are defined next.

Stock Types

Blue Chip Stock   Named after the most valuable chips in a poker game at a casino, these are shares of the largest and most successful public companies—IBM, Johnson & Johnson, 3M, United Technologies, Merck, DuPont. These companies have shown the ability to maintain and grow profits, as well as increase dividend payments, over a long period of time and through different market conditions.

Established-Growth Stock   McDonald's, Microsoft, and Coca-Cola are classic examples of established-growth companies. Typically, stock issued by such a company has traded in the market for many years, but still shows steady increases in sales and earnings. As a result, the price of the stock has periods when it rises strongly and is expected to continue to do so. Many of the companies in this group pay small or no dividends. Investors make money from the price rise of the common stock and the resulting stock splits. The company is in a growth position because it continues to build and expand market share for its products, while at the same time introducing new products.

An established-growth stock and a blue chip stock share quite a few characteristics. Some analysts would argue that the difference is strictly in the eye of the beholder. However, one of the important differences between the two is price volatility. Blue chip stocks do not usually fluctuate as wildly in price as established-growth stocks. Blue chip companies show a steady, slow price rise as revenues and earning increase. Established-growth companies' stock prices tend to rise quickly when revenues are good, and drop equally fast when revenues prove disappointing.

Income Stock   Historically, utility company shares have been, for most investors, synonymous with the phrase "income stock." Today the term includes companies like Verizon, Wal-mart, and Kinder Morgan. These companies pay a high percentage of their earnings to their shareholders as dividends—and take pride in consistently doing so. In the old days, these shares were often called "widow and orphan" stocks—a reference to the once typical investors who would buy the stock for the reliability and size of the dividend payments. The conservative individuals who invest in these securities strongly adhere to the buy-and-hold philosophy. This results in income stocks being less volatile than the overall stock market.

Emerging-Growth Stock   This is the common stock of a company in an industry or a sector whose growth and earnings potential investors have only recently begun to recognize. These companies usually have no track record of steady growth of sales or earnings, and pay no dividends. They do, however, have an interesting, commercially viable product. If the product is successful, the result could be huge sales for the company and a thrilling increase in the stock's price. GT Solar is an example of an emerging growth stock.

Defensive Stock   This is the common stock of a company whose share price tends to be less adversely affected during declines in the overall economy or in a given sector; yet it still offers investors a reasonable (rarely, the top) rate of return during periods when the economy is doing well. In short, shareholders are somewhat shielded against the severe ups and downs of the economy or business cycle.

Capitalization   Also known as *market capitalization,* it is the current value of a public corporation determined by multiplying the total number of issued-and-outstanding common shares by the current price of a share. Companies are frequently described as *large-cap, mid-cap, small-cap,* or *micro-cap* according to the total dollar value of their capitalization:

> *Large-cap:* companies like Google, Microsoft, Walmart, and General Electric (GE), whose common shares have a total market value of $5 billion or more.

blue chip stock
a term used to describe securities issued by the well-established, senior, and most consistently profitable companies.

market capitalization
the total value of a company's outstanding common stock, computed by multiplying the market value of its common stock by the total number of shares outstanding.

large-cap
a company whose total market capitalization is $5 billion or more.

mid-cap
a company whose total market capitalization is between $1 and $5 billion.

small-cap
a company whose total market capitalization is between $300 million and $1 billion.

micro-cap
a company whose total market capitalization is less than $300 million.

Mid-cap: companies whose common shares have a total market value of between $1 billion and $5 billion.

Small-cap: companies whose common shares have a total market value of between $300 million and $1 billion.

Micro-cap: companies whose common shares have a total market value of $300 million or less.

It is important to understand that these are dynamic measures that change constantly and are often defined at different amounts by different research and information services companies. Many of the Internet and biotech companies, for example, were small cap companies when they initially issued stock to the public. However, shortly afterward, many became large cap companies because of the sudden and steep rise in the price of their outstanding common shares.

Small cap and micro cap companies usually are less liquid than other types of companies. Hence it may not only be difficult for a fund manager to buy or sell a large position in the shares, but it may cost more because of the direct effect the manager's activities will have on the price of the shares. In addition, there is often little research available on these companies. Because so few institutional investors own the stock, research companies, brokerage firms, and financial information services will be less likely to assign an analyst to follow the stock or issue an opinion about it.

IPOs   When companies raise capital by issuing common shares to the public for the first time, their initial public offerings (IPOs) are, more often than not, viewed as speculative securities. Because the company has no track record that analysts can use to reasonably predict its future performance, the movement of its share price in reaction to various market factors is uncertain. This means greater risk and volatility.

Equity Fund Objectives

Investment objectives of equity or stock mutual funds are listed in alphabetical order in Figure 2.4 and described in this section.

FIGURE 2.4   **Equity fund investment objectives.** This chart shows the most common types of equity mutual funds. Keep in mind that many of the basic objectives have been spliced (see Figure 2.1) to create mutual funds with more specifically targeted objectives.

Aggressive Growth   A mutual fund with this objective invests in the common shares of companies whose market price is expected to rise rapidly. The portfolio manager looks for and buys shares of emerging-growth, mid cap, and small cap companies. Because many of the companies with the investment characteristics the manager seeks are in new business areas, this fund frequently invests in initial public offerings (IPOs) and companies whose sales or revenues are expected to increase rapidly and strongly. An aggressive growth fund can invest heavily in a single sector or industry, and can sometimes use more speculative investment strategies, such as buying shares on margin and *selling short*. The speculative strategies that the manager can use must be specified in the prospectus.

> **selling short**
> a strategy, used to profit from an anticipated price decline, which involves selling securities that you have borrowed and promising to buy them back at a later date.

Many stocks in an aggressive growth fund's portfolio are described as highfliers. Their current market prices may be at a substantial premium (i.e., expensive) to the company's real value, but the portfolio manager buys the shares because he or she expects the price to continue to rise due to increasing sales, increasing earnings, or increasing demand for the shares themselves. Aggressive growth funds tend to provide impressively high gains during market rallies (especially when mid cap and small cap stocks are in favor with analysts and portfolio managers). They can also have steep price drops when the market declines. In short, aggressive growth funds are much more volatile than the overall stock market, sometimes unnervingly so.

Capital Appreciation   This type of equity fund is quite speculative. It seeks to make money by investing in common stocks whose prices are expected to rise. The reason for the expected rise can be due to any number of factors, from an increase in the company's earnings to the fact that everyone is buying the stock and driving the price higher. The time horizon of the price rise may be short-term or long-term. Managers of capital appreciation funds trade frequently. Hence the portfolio turnover is high and so are the associated transaction costs. The manager may employ speculative strategies (such as trading on margin and buying *options*). The adviser may also, under certain market conditions, maintain a large percentage of the fund's assets in cash. Price volatility is high with this type of fund.

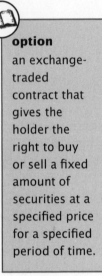

option
an exchange-traded contract that gives the holder the right to buy or sell a fixed amount of securities at a specified price for a specified period of time.

Equity Income   Funds with this objective try to provide current income for shareholders by investing the majority of their assets in income stocks, including preferred stocks. Some also invest in bonds. The portfolio will consist primarily of the common shares of large cap, blue chip companies and defensive stocks that pay a large portion of their earnings as dividends. Not only do these companies have long histories of paying dividends regularly, but they also frequently increase the amount of the dividend. Industry stocks that might be found in an equity income fund's portfolio include pharmaceuticals, utilities, and real estate.

Because of the capitalization of the companies in the portfolio, the volatility of an equity income fund tends to move in tandem with or be lower than that of the overall stock market. Another reason for the lower volatility, especially during a downturn in the market, is the stocks' high dividend payments. The fund's shareholders would be more likely to hold on to the fund because as the price of the fund goes lower, the amount of the dividend received represents a greater return on the value of the stock. In short, shareholders would be less likely to sell because the percentage of their return increases. This logic works during periods when the industries in which equity income funds invest are paying relatively high dividends. However, during periods when these industries are paying low dividends, there is less incentive to hold on to the fund—in terms of real money paid out as dividend. The volatility of equity income funds may increase, thereby eliminating some of the protection against volatility associated with this type of fund.

Growth   Funds with this objective invest in companies whose common shares are expected to increase in price. Dividend payments are decidedly a secondary objective, if considered at all. The growth fund's portfolio consists of large-cap and mid-cap growth stocks. There might also be a small percentage of emerging-growth companies and small-cap stocks in areas that the manager recognizes as having significant potential for growth.

The volatility among mutual funds classified as growth funds varies widely depending on two factors. The first is the types of securities that the prospectus defines as growth stocks. For one fund, the paradigm of a growth stock might be Coca-Cola; for another fund, it might be Urban Outfitters or Google. If the fund invests a large percentage of its assets in small-cap or emerging-growth stocks, then you can expect greater volatility. The second is the investment style employed by the manager of the portfolio. (See the discussion of investment styles in Chapter 5.) The more speculative the investment style (i.e., the greater the emphasis on profiting from short-term capital gains), the greater the volatility. The wide variations in what are called growth funds make it essential to read the prospectus before deciding which fund is suitable for your risk-to-reward tolerance.

Growth and Income   Capital appreciation and current income are equally important in a fund with this objective. The portfolio manager selects the income, large cap, and established-growth stocks in the portfolio based on their potential for a price rise and for their ability to pay steady and increasing dividends. A combination of an income fund and a growth fund, a fund with this objective has the potential to provide more capital gains than the former, yet is less speculative than the latter. The combination of securities results in price volatility that is equal to or less than that of the overall stock market. Therefore, your money invested is less at risk.

International/Foreign   Funds with this objective invest primarily in common stock companies located outside the United States. A foreign fund seeks to make money from the appreciation of the price of the common shares in the portfolio. Dividend payments are usually not a consideration.

The allure of gains in emerging foreign economies caused people to pour money into mutual funds investing in these markets. The reasons are as follows: Foreign stocks constitute a greater percentage of the value of the world's stock markets than do U.S. stocks. Because many of the country or regional economies are showing strong signs of economic development, there is substantial opportunity for growth and profit. Also, historical data show that many of the foreign markets have not always moved in tandem with the U.S. markets. If there were a downturn in the U.S. stock markets, some of these emerging markets might begin to rise. However, as the recent global recession has shown, sometimes all of the world markets move in the same direction. Nonetheless, if the market moves in different directions, the opportunity for gain in markets outside the United States could offset the temporary losses in the U.S. markets. With this point of view in mind, most asset allocation models recommend that some of every investor's money be placed in a foreign fund. The percentage recommended ranges from 5 percent to 20 percent.

Many investors have blindly followed the recommendations to invest in foreign funds without doing any research and without any understanding of the risks they face. Some mutual fund shareholders were lucky. If between 1990 and 1991 you had invested in a mutual fund that focused on Japan, you would have nearly doubled your money in one year. However, if you invested in the any of the Russia funds or some of the Far East funds in 1997 to 1998, then you learned firsthand (if a bit late) about the downside risks of investing overseas. And in 2008 to 2009, there were no safe havens in any investment markets as the recession spread around the globe. Investing in a foreign market requires careful analysis of the fund, especially its management. The important factors you must consider are explained in Chapter 5, "Evaluating Mutual Fund Performance."

Today foreign funds are spliced in many different ways (see Figure 2.5). As their individual names indicate, these more targeted funds focus on countries, regions, or types of securities within the international markets.

> *BRIC.* These funds get their names from the first letters of the countries in which they invest: Brazil, Russia, India, and China. Many people believe the economic develop and growth of these four countries is key to the world's future economic growth. These funds look for companies in these four countries that may deliver the hoped-for growth and investment returns.
>
> *Country/Regional.* These funds invest in equity securities trading primarily in a specific country or region of the world.
>
> *Diversified Emerging Markets.* This fund invests in equity securities issued by emerging markets worldwide, but does not usually concentrate its investments in any one region.

FIGURE 2.5　International/foreign fund investment objectives.

Europe Stock. This fund invests more than half of its total assets in equity securities of European companies.

Pacific Stock. This fund invests in equity securities of issuers located in countries in the Pacific Rim, including Japan, China, Hong Kong, Malaysia, Singapore, New Zealand, and Australia.

Sector/Specialty   Funds with this objective invest in the common shares of companies in a single industry, sector, or geographical area. The portfolio manager researches and selects companies within the stated, narrowly defined area, whose common stock prices are expected to rise. Capital appreciation, not dividend payments, is the primary consideration.

Sector funds permit individuals to focus their investment money in businesses or geographical areas that are expected to provide strong returns, usually over the intermediate term. This concentration can produce spectacular returns. For example, if you had bought one of the funds that specialize in data storage, technology, or e-commerce in the 1990s, your total return would have been considerably over 60 percent in one year! Such spectacular gains may lead you to ignore the fact that these high-flying funds are subject more to the volatility of that specific industry than to that of the overall stock market. Again, a technology or biotech fund provides a good example.

Suppose analysts release data showing that sales of both computers and computer chips are lagging and that there is a corresponding increase in the inventory among the industry's largest retail companies. In response to this news, investors (including mutual fund managers) decide to sell or decrease their holdings in these shares. The price of technology stocks and the net asset value of mutual funds that invest in them decline, perhaps sharply. Investor confidence in this sector is shaken. However, on the same day as the rout in technology stock occurs, the overall stock market— as measured by the *Dow Jones Industrial Average (DJIA)* or the *Standard & Poor's 500 index (S&P 500)*—may rise or stay relatively flat as investors buy shares in other sectors.

> **Dow Jones Industrial Average (DJIA)**
> the most widely quoted and narrowest measure of stock market movement, this is an average of 30 leading industrial stocks.

This scenario is not an uncommon occurrence in the stock and mutual fund markets. It illustrates that when you buy a sector or specialty fund, the money invested is subject to the potential rewards of such concentration, but equally subject to the specific risks associated with that sector. Sector funds can provide a particularly bumpy ride.

It is also important to read the prospectus of a sector fund to see exactly which stocks meet the sector fund's criteria in achieving its investment objective.

Standard & Poor's 500 index (S&P 500)
a capitalization-weighted index that includes the 500 large-cap issues that trade on the NYSE-Euronext and NASDAQ OMX.

You may discover that a stock you thought was associated with one sector, for example transportation, may be included in another, the natural resources sector for example, because the transportation company's products are major users of petroleum.

New sector/specialty funds are being created continually. As areas of the investment markets become hot or popular, mutual funds establish funds to give investors a way to profit from the growth in these areas. Some popular specialty or sector funds are:

Banking. Since the banks in the United States were bailed out by the government and the major brokerage firms converted to bank holding companies, many have shown a strong return to profitability, many people are interested in trying to profit from this sector which includes commercial banks, investment banks, brokerage firms, and other financial services companies that are similar to banks.

Communications. This fund invests primarily in equity securities of companies engaged in the development, manufacture, or sale of communications products or services.

Financial Services. This fund invests primarily in equity securities of financial services companies, including banks, brokerage firms, insurance companies, and mutual fund companies. While this fund benefits when the revenues and earnings of these companies increase, the bank stock in the portfolio have traditionally brought a more complex factor: interest rate sensitivity. Banks borrow and lend large amounts of money. As interest rates rise, a bank's cost of funds increases more rapidly than its income from its assets. At the same time, fewer businesses are willing to borrow at the higher interest rates. The cost increase combined with a drop in the demand for loans cause bank profits to decline. Hence the price of bank stocks declines. When interest rates go down, a bank's cost of borrowing money decreases and business borrowing increases. The bank's profits go up and its stock price rises. In summary, a high interest rate environment tends to be bearish for the price of bank stocks. Conversely, a low interest rate environment tends to be bullish for the price of bank stocks. (This is one of the underlying reasons that the Federal Reserve Board has kept interest rates so low in the U.S. as it seeks to stimulate economic growth.)

Health Care. This fund invests primarily in equity securities of health care companies, including pharmaceutical companies, drug manufacturers, hospitals, health insurance companies, and biotechnology firms.

Natural Resources. This fund invests primarily in the common stock of companies involved in the exploration, mining, distribution, or processing of natural resources.

Precious Metals. This fund invests primarily in the common stock of companies engaged in mining, distributing, or processing precious metals—gold, silver, platinum. The profitability and earnings of these companies are tied to the market price of the precious metal itself. As the price of gold, for example, moves up or down, the companies' common stock prices tend to move in a more exaggerated manner. This is due to the percentage by which the profitability of the companies increases and decreases as the price of gold changes. When the price of gold rises, a gold mutual fund may provide greater gains than could be made by purchasing the actual gold. This happens because the portfolio managers aggressively buy the companies' shares in anticipation of their increased profitability. During a price decline, however, a gold fund may show a more severe price drop than the actual metal. Selling by fund managers drives the share prices of the mining, distributing, or processing companies lower, which in turn prompts even more sales from other investors. In short, buying a precious metal mutual fund exposes an investor to greater price volatility than investing directly in the precious metal. Because precious metals tend to maintain their value better during a price downturn, many precious metal funds have the ability to invest directly in a precious metal or maintain large cash reserves during bearish periods.

Real Estate. Invested primarily in real estate-related equity securities, this fund tends to be particularly interest-rate sensitive. It does well during periods when interest rates are low (this is bullish for real estate) and the overall economy is growing.

Technology. This fund invests primarily in the common stock of companies engaged in the development, distribution, or servicing of technology-related processes, including companies that produce hardware and software.

Utilities. This fund seeks capital appreciation by investing primarily in equity securities of public utilities, including electric, gas, and telephone service providers.

Small Company Funds with this objective seek capital appreciation by investing primarily in stocks of companies with market capitalization of less than $1 billion. This includes small-cap and micro-cap companies. These shares are characteristically illiquid; hence they tend to be very volatile. Changes in their market prices are driven primarily by increases and decrease in earnings, sales or revenue growth, or market share growth. Exceeding analysts' expectations can cause the stock's price to soar. Failure to meet

special situation fund
a fund that invests in companies that are candidates for takeover or those that are emerging from bankruptcy.

expectations can cause portfolio managers to dump the stock fast and hard, driving the price of the stock way, way down.

Some small company funds—*special situation funds*—also invest in the common shares of companies that are in financial trouble, that may be the subject of a possible takeover, that may have filed for reorganization under bankruptcy laws, or that offer turnaround opportunities—where the company's management may be able to salvage the company and rebuild it. In all of these cases, the portfolio manager may decide, because of the fund's big stake in the company, to exert its influence either delicately or indelicately over the company's management. The objective of the intervention is to attempt to protect and save the fund's investment.

World/Global   Funds with this objective invest primarily in equity securities of issuers located throughout the world, while maintaining a percentage of assets (normally 25 to 50 percent) in U.S. companies. Many people think that this type of fund is a safer way to invest in or gain exposure to the international markets. This perception is based on two facts. First, because the U.S. multinational companies in the global fund's portfolio pay dividends in dollars, not in a foreign currency, the fund investor is somewhat shielded from the full effect of fluctuations in the exchange rate. Second, because the multinational corporations' shares trade on the U.S. stock markets, the performance of these securities closely follows the movement of the U.S. markets, not the market in the foreign country.

The seemingly beneficial effect of being shielded from the direct effects of the currency movement and volatility of the foreign market means that you are also shielded from the opportunities that such volatility offers. But keep in mind that the portfolio manager can have up to 75 percent of the portfolio invested in foreign markets. Depending on the mixture at any given time, a global fund's performance and volatility may closely track or move opposite to the U.S. stock markets.

Other Considerations

A type of fund that became popular for a while can be considered a subset of any of the stock fund objectives just described. It is called a *focused fund* or a select fund. The investment adviser concentrates the fund's assets and research, investing in the common stock of only 20 to 30 companies. The Janus 20 and the Oakmark Select funds are examples of this type of fund. Also, the manager can invest more than 10 percent of the fund's total net assets in the shares of one company. Therefore, it is not a *diversified fund*.

A variation on this concept is the *best ideas fund*. In this case, an adviser or a group of advisers construct a mutual fund portfolio that consists of their best investment ideas or picks from around the world. Many of these are foreign or world funds. The list of managers' best ideas is updated periodically, usually quarterly. At that time, the fund liquidates the old best ideas and buys the new ones.

Many investors are attracted to focused funds because they believe it is difficult for a manager to follow diligently the 100 or more stocks that make up most mutual fund portfolios. By concentrating in this way, it increases the adviser's chances of producing a return that beats a benchmark index, such as the S&P 500 index. The rewards from this strategy can be substantial. At the same time, investors must be aware of the added risk they face because of the portfolio's concentration in a few companies' stocks and the high percentage of its assets that can be invested in one company. If the price of one or two companies in the portfolio declines sharply, the impact on the fund could be pronounced. Focused funds are non-diversified, and are therefore less likely than larger diversified funds to cushion you from the day-to-day volatility of the market.

In reality, the distinction among some of the stock fund objectives discussed is not clear-cut. The actual stocks that constitute a specific mutual fund portfolio depend on the analysis and perspective of the fund's manager. Hence a generic investment objective (e.g., value, growth, income) can be interpreted and executed differently by different managers. One company's aggressive growth fund may look like another company's specialty fund, which may look like another company's world fund. It is important to read the fund's prospectus and review the list of its top holdings before making your final investment decision.

Today, mutual funds tend to be classified according to the size of the company (large cap, mid cap, small cap, etc.) and the basic type of investment strategy (value, growth, and core). These categories, although simple, seem too generic for a beginning investor. It's important to

focused fund
also called a select fund, a fund that invests in a small number of stocks, usually 30 or less (although some contain as many as 40) and more than 10 percent of the fund's net assets can be invested in one company.

diversified fund
a fund in which 75 percent or more of its assets are in a broad group of securities, with no more than 5 percent in any one issuer and holding no more than 10 percent of the voting stock of any one issuer.

best ideas fund
a type of focused fund in which the portfolio manager or managers invest in the companies that constitute their best investment ideas. The portfolio's holdings are reviewed periodically (usually quarterly) and changes are made when the manager comes up with his or her next best idea.

Federal Reserve Board (FRB)
the governing board of the Federal Reserve banking system, which sets the policies that affect the money supply and interest rates.

read the prospectus or summary prospectus so that you know whether that mid-cap growth fund is an aggressive growth fund or a focused sector fund.

Bond Funds (aka Fixed Income Funds)

Mutual funds that invest solely in bonds (Figure 2.6) have been less popular than those that invest in equities, particularly common stock. The primary reason is the return. Historically, bond funds produce lower returns than stock funds. The principal source of their return is the interest payments from the fixed income securities (i.e., bond, notes, etc.) held in the portfolio. There are also potential profits from capital gains. These, however, are usually quite small. The reason is that, unlike stock prices, the market prices of bonds do not increase as a company's sales and earnings grow. Instead, they are directly influenced by changes in interest rates. As rates decline, the market prices of bonds rise. Conversely, as interest rates rise, bond prices decline. Since the *Federal Reserve Board (FRB)* does not make substantial changes in interest rates often, bond prices remain relatively stable, thus offering little opportunity for significant gains. Hence, the possibility of cocktail-party-worthy story about a spectacular one-day killing in the bond markets is, in short, limited. This statement is especially true for high-quality bonds. However, the market price of low-quality bonds (see Figure 2.7) is much more affected by a company's performance. The added volatility means these high-yield or *junk bonds* offer a greater opportunity for capital gains.

Bond funds are considered to be safer than stock funds. This perception is partly due to the fact that issuers of bonds must pay interest when it is due. It is also partly due to the generally lower volatility of bonds, especially when compared to stocks. Because the net asset value of bond funds changes by smaller amounts, there is less likelihood that you—the investor—will lose all of your principal. Conservative investors with low risk tolerance are the primary purchasers of bond funds.

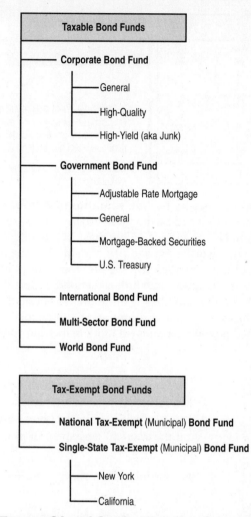

FIGURE 2.6 Types of bond funds. There are five major categories of taxable bond funds and two of tax-exempt funds. Each is classified according to the type of fixed-income securities in which the fund invests: corporate bonds, government bonds, world bonds, and so on. Within each of these major categories, a portfolio manager also considers other features of the bonds (such as default risk and time to maturity) when structuring the investment portfolio.

Bond funds and their investment objectives are defined using criteria different from that used for stock funds. These considerations include:

- The types of bonds in which the fund invests: corporate bonds, government bonds, world bonds, *Yankee bonds, Eurobonds,* and so on.

Moody's	S&P	Fitch	
Aaa	AAA	AAA	} Investment Grade Ratings
Aa	AA	AA	
A	A	A	
Baa	BBB	BBB	
Ba	BB	BB	} Junk or High-Yield Bond Ratings
B	B	B	(The bonds have speculative elements and their
Caa	CCC	CCC	future payment of interest and repayment of
Ca	CC	CC	principal cannot be assured.)
C	C	C	
	D	D	} Issuer has defaulted on a payment or has filed for bankruptcy.

FIGURE 2.7   Bond ratings by Moody's, Standard & Poor's, and Fitch.
This chart shows the scale used by the three organizations, respectively, to rate long-term bonds. The ratings reflect these independent companies' assessment of the creditworthiness and risk of default by the issuer and investment quality of the debt security. The first four ratings of the three companies are investment grade with little likelihood of default, although this isn't always true. Any bond rated below these grades is called a junk bond. Because this term has such a negative connotation in people's minds, these bonds are now called high-yield bonds—a more marketing-friendly phrase.

junk bond
also called a high-yield bond, a low-quality, speculative, long-term bond rated BB (by Standard & Poor's), Ba (by Moody's) or lower that pays a high interest rate.

- The bond rating (assigned by Moody's and Standard & Poor's) that evaluates the likelihood of the issuer's default on the bond's interest payments and the eventual repayment of principal.

- The average length of maturity of the bonds in the portfolio (e.g., short-term, intermediate-term, long-term).

- The taxation of the interest income from the bonds. If the interest income is subject to U.S. federal taxes, then the fund is described as a *taxable bond fund*. If the interest income is exempt from federal taxes, then the fund is said to be a *tax-exempt bond fund*. Keep in mind that the interest income from a tax-exempt bond fund may be subject to state and local taxes, depending on the bonds in the portfolio.

Taxable Bond Fund Objectives

Corporate Bond Funds   This group of mutual funds invests in bonds issued primarily by U.S.-based corporations. The funds may also invest in the debt securities of foreign companies. The long-term, fixed income securities include:

- *Debentures:* unsecured bonds backed by the full faith and credit of the issuer.
- *Mortgage bonds:* secured bonds backed by the real estate and property of the issuer.
- *Equipment trust certificates (ETCs):* secured bonds backed by the equipment of the issuer. Airlines are among the largest issuers of ETCs. They use the proceeds to buy airplanes.

Interest income from these securities is subject to all taxes—federal, state, and local taxes.

General Corporate Bond Fund. This fund buys investment grade bonds of primarily U.S.-based corporations. The first four rating by Moody's, Standard & Poor's, and Fitch shown in Figure 2.7 are considered to be investment grade.

High-Quality Corporate Bond Fund. The majority of this fund's total net assets are invested in corporate bonds rated A or better. However, the portfolio manager tries to maintain an average rating of AA (for S&P) or Aa (for Moody's) among all of the bonds in the portfolio.

High-Yield Corporate Bond Fund. The majority of the fund's total net assets are invested in corporate bonds rated BB (for S&P), Ba (for Moody's), or lower.

Government Bond Funds This group of mutual funds invests in long-term debt securities issued directly by the U.S. government or by Federal agencies, such as the Government National Mortgage Association (GNMA) and Student Loan Marketing Association (SLMA). While those securities issued directly by the United States (the first four in the following listing) are backed by the full faith and credit of the government, most agency securities are not. U.S. government securities are the safest in the world because the issuer has never defaulted on a loan.

Yankee bond
a bond, denominated in dollars, that is issued in the United States by a foreign corporation or government.

Eurobond
a bond issued in a country but denominated (both the principal and interest) in a currency different from that of the country in which it is issued and traded.

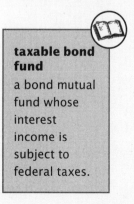

taxable bond fund
a bond mutual fund whose interest income is subject to federal taxes.

tax-exempt bond fund
a bond mutual fund whose interest income is not subject to federal taxes, but may be subject to state or local taxes.

investment grade bond
any bond rated from AAA to BBB by Standard & Poor's, or rated Aaa to Baa by Moody's. These ratings indicate bonds of the highest quality and least risk of default.

These securities, therefore, are rated triple-A. Among the agency securities, only GNMA is backed by the full faith and credit of the U.S. government. The others, including FNMA and FHLMC, are backed by the full faith and credit of the agency. And as the recent recession and housing crisis in the United States showed, the securities of the two mortgage agencies would have defaulted without the huge infusion of capital from the U.S. government.

The interest income from all securities issued by the U.S. government is subject to federal taxes, but exempt from state and local taxes. However, the taxation of income from agency securities varies. If the agency issues *mortgaged-backed securities (MBSs)*, then the interest income is fully taxable. All other agency securities have the same tax status as U.S. Government securities.

The long-term, fixed income securities (as well as some of the issuers) in which government funds invest include:

- **Treasury Notes (T-Notes).** These are U.S. government securities with more than one year to a maximum of 10 years to maturity. These securities are issued with a fixed rate of interest (called the *coupon rate*) and make interest payments every six months.

- **Treasury Bonds (T-Bonds).** These are U.S. government securities with more than 10 years to a maximum of 30 years to maturity. Like T-notes, T-bonds are issued with a fixed coupon rate, and makes interest payments semiannually.

- **Treasury STRIPS.** These securities are U.S. government *zero-coupon bonds* that make no periodic interest payment over their lives. Instead, they are issued at a discount and mature at par value ($1,000). The difference between the discounted price and par value is the interest received on the investment. The investor or fund receives this interest if the STRIPS are held to maturity. These are the most volatile U.S. government securities.

- **Treasury Inflation Protection Securities (TIPS).** First issued in 1997, *Treasury Inflation Protection Securities (TIPS)* are U.S. government Treasury bonds whose principal ($1,000) is adjusted upward or downward every six months by a percentage based on to the rise and fall of the Consumer Price Index (CPI). The bond's semiannual interest payment, which is a fixed percentage of par value, changes as the principal is adjusted. TIPS are designed to protect bond investors against purchasing power or inflation risk. This is the risk that the value of the money invested in a bond will be worth less due to the rise the amount the customer must pay for goods and services at the time the bond matures. At maturity, the bond-holder receives *the greater of* the adjusted principal amount (during an inflationary period) or the bond's face value (during a deflationary period).

mortgage-backed security (MBS)
the group name for the debt securities issued by companies like Federal National Mortgage Association (FNMA) that are backed by a pool of residential mortgages.

- **Government National Mortgage Association (GNMA).** Referred to as "Ginnie Mae," this agency issues debt securities (called *pass-through certificates*) that are backed by a pool of mortgages insured by the Veterans Administration (VA) and the Federal Housing Authority (FHA). This is the only agency whose securities are backed by the full faith and credit of the U.S. government because of the U.S. government entities that insure the underlying mortgages. GNMA certificates make monthly payments that consist of both interest and return of principal. As noted earlier, the interest income from these and other securities that are backed by a pool of mortgages is subject to federal, state, and local taxes.

coupon rate
stated as a percentage of the note's or bond's face value, the annual fixed interest rate paid to the bond holder.

- **Federal National Mortgage Association (FNMA).** Referred to as "Fannie Mae," this government sponsored enterprise (GSE) issues debt securities backed by a pool of two types of mortgages: insured mortgages (VA-insured and FHA-insured) and conventional home mortgages. These securities pay interest and principal monthly.

- **Federal Home Loan Mortgage Corporation (FHLMC).** Called "Freddie Mac," this government sponsored enterprise (GSE) issues debt securities backed by a pool of conventional home mortgages that it buys from banks. In short, it competes with FNMA. Like other mortgage-backed securities, its monthly payment consists of both interest and principal.

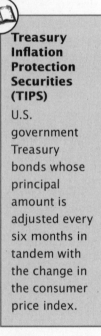

zero coupon bond

a bond that is issued at a deep discount, matures at face value, and makes no periodic interest payments over its life.

Treasury Inflation Protection Securities (TIPS)

U.S. government Treasury bonds whose principal amount is adjusted every six months in tandem with the change in the consumer price index.

- **Farm Credit Bank.** Part of the Federal Farm Credit System (FCS), this GSE issues bonds and notes with one to 10 years to maturity that are used to fund loans to farmer ranchers and agricultural cooperatives. This agency makes semiannual payments on its outstanding bonds.

- **Federal Intermediate Credit Bank (FICB).** Part of the Farm Credit System (FCS), this agency issues short-term bonds and notes with up to five years to maturity that are secured by loans made to farmers and ranchers. These loans are used to buy equipment, seeds, and so on.

Types of government bond mutual funds include:

Adjustable-Rate Mortgage Government Bond Fund. The majority of this fund's assets are invested in mortgage-backed securities (GNMA, FNMA, FHLMC) secured by a pool of adjustable-rate mortgages.

General Government Bond Fund. This fund invests in the T-notes, T-bonds, STRIPS, TIPS, mortgage-backed securities, and other debt securities issued by the U.S. government, agencies, and GSEs.

Mortgage-Backed Securities Government Bond Fund. This fund invests the majority of its assets in securities issued by GNMA, FNMA, and FHLMC. Most of the mortgage-backed securities are secured by a pool of fixed-rate mortgages.

U.S. Treasury Government Bond Fund. Virtually all of the fund's assets are invested in bonds and notes issued directly by the U.S. government. This is considered one of the safest mutual funds.

International Bond Funds   These mutual funds invest largely in debt securities issued by foreign corporations or governments that are denominated in and pay interest in foreign currencies. (Foreign exchange risk is therefore a significant factor.) The fund attempts to earn income from both interest payments and capital gains. Because of different interest rate and risk factors, the bonds of some foreign issuers are substantially more volatile than domestic debt; hence, there is a greater opportunity for capital gains.

Multi-Sector Bond Funds   This type of mutual fund invests in all types of long-term debt securities including government bonds, corporate bonds, *foreign bonds,* and Eurobonds. It can also invest in high-yield bonds issued by U.S.-based companies.

World Bond Funds   Like an international bond fund, a world bond fund buys the long-term debt securities of issuers around the globe. However, a large percentage of the fund's assets will be invested in *sovereign debt*—debt issue by foreign governments. Interest payments and, to a lesser extent, capital gains are the fund's primary sources of income.

Tax-Exempt Bond Fund Objectives

National Tax-Exempt Bond Fund   Also known as a National Municipal Bond Fund, this fund invests in the long-term municipal debt securities of town, cities, states, and municipal authorities from around the United States. This fund's income consists primarily of interest payments that are exempt from federal taxes. The interest is subject to taxation by the state (if the state has an income tax) and municipality that is your primary residence.

Single-State Tax-Exempt Bond Fund   The portfolio of this bond fund, also known as a Single-State Municipal Bond Fund, consists of debt securities issued by and within one state. New York and California, because of their size and the number of bonds they issue, are the two states whose securities have historically been used most frequently. The fiscal crisis in both these states and others has brought a significant amount of risk (default risk) to this type of fund. The interest income from this fund will be double tax-free—exempt from federal and state taxes—for residents of the single state. The interest may also be exempt from local taxes (and would be described as being *triple tax-exempt*) depending on the tax laws of the municipality that is your primary residence.

pass-through certificate
a debt security whose periodic payments consist of both interest and the repayment of principal.

foreign bond
a bond issued in a country that is not the primary domicile of the issuer. The bond is denominated in the country's currency where it is issued and is sold to that country's citizens.

sovereign debt
long-term bonds and notes issued by a foreign government.

**triple
tax-exempt**

a term used
to describe a
municipal bond
whose interest
payments are
exempt from
federal, state,
and local taxes.

**target bond
fund**

a bond fund
that invests
solely in zero-
coupon bonds,
especially
those
issued by
municipalities,
although it
can invest in
corporate and
government
zeros.

Target Bond Funds

Within each of the broad types of bond funds just discussed there is another type that is popular. They are sometimes called *target bond funds*. [Note: Do not confuse a target bond fund with a target-date fund which is explained in the section on hybrid funds.] These invest primarily in the zero-coupon bonds of municipalities, although some invest in U.S. government and corporate zero-coupon bonds. Because zeros, as these bonds are widely called, pay no periodic interest over its term or life, the fund makes money in one of two ways. First, if the price is very low, the manager may buy the zero-coupon bonds and hold them to maturity. By doing this, the adviser captures the yield that is reflected in the difference between the low market price and the bond's face value ($1,000) at maturity. This interest is only realized at maturity. Second, the manager may purchase the bonds, anticipating a drop in interest rates. Depending on how low rates drop, the market price of the zeros could rise substantially beyond their purchase price. The manager would then capture the capital gain by selling the bonds. The innate volatility of zero-coupon bonds creates more opportunities for capital gains than would be available from funds that invest in coupon bonds that make regular, periodic interest payments. Hence, potential returns—and risks—from target bond funds exceed those of other types of fixed income funds.

Hybrid Funds

Hybrid funds invest in both stocks and bonds. They can also invest in convertible bonds and preferred stocks. Generally, they are thought to be less risky than stock fund, while providing a return better than you would receive from a bond fund. It would appear from this description that a hybrid fund is appropriate for a conservative investor with a taste for a little risk. The degree of risk associated with a particular hybrid fund depends on the mix of stock and bonds, and the portfolio manager's discretion in changing the mix. This flexibility depends on the type of hybrid fund. (See Figure 2.8.)

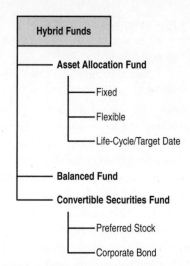

FIGURE 2.8   Types of hybrid funds. A balanced fund is the oldest type of hybrid fund. While the traditional portfolio mix has been 60 percent stocks and 40 percent bonds, each balanced fund can established its own percentages. Convertible securities funds are not as widespread, possibly because the risk-to-reward dynamics of these securities are more difficult to understand and because there are fewer issues available. Asset allocation funds, especially flexible asset allocation funds and target-date (or life-cycle) funds, are used more and more in retirement plans, like 401(k) plans, and in 529 college savings plans.

Asset Allocation Fund

The *asset allocation fund* is a variation on the balanced fund that invests in stocks, bonds, and *cash equivalents.* There are two types of asset allocation funds: fixed and flexible. A *fixed asset allocation fund* maintains a fixed percentage of its assets in each of the three asset classes: stocks, bonds, and cash-equivalents. This type is therefore quite similar to a balanced fund (discussed next) except that the fixed percentages differ. One of the common allocations used in these types of funds is known as the robot mix: 55 percent in stocks, 35 percent in bonds, and 10 percent in cash equivalents. In order to maintain these percentages, periodic adjustments are made as the fund's assets change value. This is known as re-balancing the portfolio. If stocks outperform bonds, the manager must periodically sell the stocks and buy more bonds to restore the fixed percentages. While the

asset allocation fund

a mutual fund that allows the manager to shift among the various types of securities, or maintains a fixed percentage of the fund's assets in each of the different classes of securities.

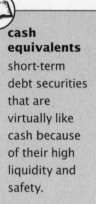

cash equivalents
short-term debt securities that are virtually like cash because of their high liquidity and safety.

fixed asset allocation fund
a fund whose manager must maintain a fixed percentage of the portfolio's assets in stocks, bonds, and cash.

fund manager cannot change the percentage, he or she does select the securities within each group in which the fund will invest.

A *flexible asset allocation fund* adjusts the mix of its assets in response to changing market conditions and investment opportunities. The manager who believes small cap stocks are about to rise after a long period in the doldrums can invest heavily in this type of stock. If the advisor thinks the market is about to peak, he or she can sell some securities in the portfolio and maintain a large portion of the assets in cash or short-term, fixed income securities. This flexibility is this fund's major advantage. The disadvantage, however, is that its success depends almost entirely on the fund manager's skill in predicting or "crystal balling" the overall market as well as the future investment potential of various business sectors and types of securities. Given investors' desire to get the highest return possible (at a relatively low risk) and their recognition that investment opportunities change constantly, many people are willing to bet on the flexible asset allocation manager's ability to predict the market's next hot investment area, whether its in stock, bonds, or both.

A *target-date fund (originally called a life-cycle fund)* is an asset allocation fund that adjusts the mix of securities in the portfolio, becoming more conservative and emphasizing preservation of capital as the fund moved toward a specified year that is part of the name of the fund. An example is the Vanguard Target Retirement 2020 Fund (VTWNX) which is for people who will retire in 2020. These funds are designed as a one-size-fits-all retirement planning fund for people who don't have sufficient amounts of money to do proper asset allocation or who don't want to take the time for personally manage their retirement investment portfolios. They have become a widely offered and very popular choice in corporations' 401(k) retirement plans. A target-date fund is often the default option in 401(k) plans that automatically enroll all employees in the defined-contribution plan under the Pension Protection Act.

It's important to understand that as good as these funds may sound, they have been subject to criticism, especially after the severe market decline in 2008 when some of the funds lost up to 40 percent of their value. Some target-date funds fail to explain clearly what percentage of their assets will be shifted to more conservative assets as the target date nears. Many maintain large percentages in stocks even as the target date nears, making them subject to the unpredictable volatility (and loss) associated with investing in stocks.

[Note: At the web site for the Vanguard Target Retirement 2020 Fund, a graph shows how the mix of assets—domestic stock, international stock, normal bonds, inflation-protection bonds, and cash—in the portfolio will change as the fund approaches the 2020 retirement date.] Additionally, some target-date funds have high expense ratios. These costs seem excessive (some would argue exploitive) given that the typical investor in these funds is the average working person who is probably not earning a six-figure salary. Some mutual fund companies lowered their expense ratio in response to this criticism; however, some did not. It is therefore, important to read and understand the target-date fund's prospectus or summary prospectus (especially the expense ratio) before investing your money. Remember: the lower the expense ratio, the more of the investment return that ends up in the investors account.

Finally, today there is a subtle difference between a target-date fund and a life-cycle fund (sometimes called an age-based fund). Typically, a life-cycle fund does not have a set date in the title. Therefore it's important for the investor to determine if the fund's current and future asset allocation mixes match your time horizon, risk tolerance, and need for preservation of capital.

Balanced Fund

This hybrid fund emphasizes preservation of capital as a main objective and invests set percentages in stocks, bonds, and/or cash. Many balanced funds maintain 60 percent of the fund's total net assets in blue-chip, dividend-paying stock and 40 percent in high-grade bonds. This is often called the "traditional mix" for a balanced fund. Others use what is called the "robot mix": 55 percent in stocks, 35 percent in bonds, and 10 percent in cash equivalents. Each fund sets it own fixed percentages and discloses them in the investment objective stated in the prospectus. Balanced funds are rarely the leading performers, but they are almost never the worst performers among all mutual fund groups. For a more conservative investor who wishes to have some exposure to the bond markets (and the greater degree of safety they afford compared to the stock market), balanced funds can be an appropriate choice.

flexible asset allocation fund
a fund whose manager can change the amounts of the fund's assets invested in stocks, bonds, and cash based on changing investment opportunities.

target date fund
designed for investors planning to retire in a specific year or period, a mutual fund that changes how its investments are allocated among cash, stocks, and bonds, becoming more conservative as the specific date nears.

Convertible Securities Fund

This mutual fund invests in corporate bonds and preferred stocks that can be converted into common stocks. The majority of the bonds and preferred stock in the portfolio are investment grade securities (see Figure 2.7). A small percentage of the fund's assets may be invested in nonconvertible corporate bonds, U.S. government securities, foreign securities, and common stock.

This type of fund is not well known or particularly popular. Part of this is due to the difficulty of understanding the investment characteristics of convertible securities. Sometimes they act like a common stock and at other times they act like a bond. Analyzing these securities, and the funds that invest in them, is not nearly as straightforward as a common stock fund or a bond fund.

Index Funds

Also called tracker funds and unmanaged funds, *index funds* seek to replicate the performance of a designated index (e.g., the S&P 500, the Russell 2000, the Dow Jones Industrial Average, the Wilshire 5000, customized indices), the overall stock market (e.g., a Total Market Fund), or of a particular segment of the investment market (e.g., long-term bonds, emerging markets). The fund accomplishes this by investing in virtually the same securities or a representative sample (determined using mathematical models) of the same or similar securities that make up the specific index.

index fund called a tracker fund in Europe, a mutual fund that seeks to replicate the performance of a particular index, such as the S&P 500 index, by investing in the securities that constitute the index.

Unlike other types of funds discussed in this chapter, index funds must be fully invested at all times. This means that they hold very little (if any) of their assets in cash. As more people buy shares of the fund, the management company must buy shares of companies in the index. When the money available is insufficient to buy the exact number of shares, the fund invests an amount in each stock based on its relative value in the index. This is the primary source of transactions-related expenses for these funds. Other trading costs are incurred when the composition of the index changes. The funds must buy the securities that have been added and sell those that have been removed.

The Vanguard Group was a pioneer in creating index funds. Its Index 500 Fund was one of the first in the industry and attracted huge amounts of investors' money. This success spurred the company and other mutual fund companies to create index funds that track other indexes, such as the long-term bond, emerging markets, the total stock market, and small-cap stocks. Each fund tracks a specific index, which is disclosed in the prospectus.

The success of index funds is directly attributable to the fact that a substantial majority of mutual fund managers (stock fund managers, in particular) produce returns that lag behind the S&P 500 index. Also, the often high expenses charged by actively managed funds further decrease a fund's performance. In contrast, index funds are not actively managed. The mix of securities changes only when there are changes in the benchmark index. Some indexes are altered several times during the year. Other indexes make changes only once a year. As a result, index funds' fees and trading costs are substantially lower.

The growth of assets invested in Vanguard's Index 500 Fund, in particular, not only prompted many mutual fund companies to create their own such funds, it has also led to more splicing of index funds' objectives. The seven most common types of index funds are listed in Figure 2.9.

Emerging Markets Index Fund

Many of these funds seek to replicate the performance of the MSCI Emerging Market Free Index, which invest in over 20 countries in Asia, Europe, Latin America, Middle East, and Africa. The fund may hold shares of hundreds of

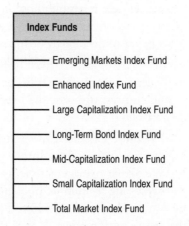

FIGURE 2.9 Types of index funds. Index funds are designed to track the performance of a particular group of securities—long-term bonds, small-cap stocks, the total stock market—or a particular market such as emerging markets. Sector-specific index funds are also popular, often based on customized indices. Mutual fund companies are constantly creating new index funds to meet the increasing demand for this group of products.

different companies. Many of the securities in these developing markets are difficult to buy and sell because the markets are illiquid. This means that the fund's administrative costs, trading costs, and other fees will be higher than those for a domestic index fund. Foreign exchange risk and political risk are significant factors in this type of fund.

Enhanced Index Fund

The *enhanced index fund* is a managed index fund that seeks to beat the performance of its benchmark index by at least 0.1 percent but no more than 2 percent. (If the index fund's performance were to exceed this 2 percent cap, it would then be considered a stock mutual fund.) The manager tries to accomplish this enhanced performance in the way he or she constructs the fund's portfolio. There are several approaches a manager may take.

enhanced index fund
an index fund in which the fund manager tries to beat the performance of the benchmark index by at least 0.1 percent but no more than 2 percent.

1. The manager may buy all of the securities in the index, but give more *weighting* to favorite stocks or sectors within it that are expected to outperform the index.

2. The manager may buy many (not all) of the same stocks contained in the index and then buy substitute stocks whose capitalization and investment characteristics closely resemble those in the index. These substitute securities are those in sectors that are viewed as being undervalued, or in areas where the manager expects there to be substantial price appreciation.

3. The manager may invest in derivatives, such as options and futures, to boost the overall performance of the portfolio.

weighting
a method for determining the worth of each company's stock relative to the value of the overall index.

Because enhanced index funds are managed, they have more expenses than unmanaged index funds. These include higher management fees and greater transactions costs resulting from more frequent trading in the portfolio. These additional costs have a direct effect in lowering the fund's performance. If they are excessive, the higher expenses could reduce the fund's return to below that of its benchmark index.

Large Capitalization Index Fund

This remains the most common and popular of the index funds. The majority of these funds seek to track the performance of Standard & Poor's composite index of 500 stocks—called the S&P 500 Index. This is an index of 500 large cap companies that trade on the NYSE-Euronext and NASDAQ OMX. The S&P 500's performance, like that of all indexes, assumes that all dividends paid by the stock in the index are reinvested.

Long-Term Bond Index Fund

This one of a growing number of index funds that focuses on bonds. This fund seeks to represent the yield on long-term bonds (those with 20 to 30 years to maturity) as measured by the Barclays Capital Aggregate Bond Index.

NASDAQ OMX
a fully electronic stock exchange that facilitates the trading of Nasdaq-listed securities and disseminates current price quotes for those securities.

Small Capitalization Index Fund

This index fund tracks the performance of companies with a capitalization of less than $1 billion. The benchmark index for these securities is the Russell 2000 index. Once a year (usually in July), the fund's creator, the Frank Russell Company, reconstitutes the index, adding and deleting companies based on changes in their individual capitalization. At the same time, the index fund sells those securities that have been deleted from the index and adds the new ones to its portfolio. It is only at this time that the fund realizes capital gains or *capital losses.*

capital loss
the loss that results when the proceeds from the sale of a security are lower than the price at which the security was purchased.

Total Market Index Fund

A *total market index fund* seeks to replicate the performance of the broadest measure of the U.S. stock market performance, the *Wilshire 5000 Index.* This is an index of a little over 4,000 common stocks that are listed and traded on the NYSE-Euronext, American Stock Exchange (which is owned by the NYSE) and NASDAQ OMX. While the name suggests there are only 5000 companies in the index, there is actually no set minimum or maximum. The number varies from year to year. Because the index is so broad, it is less influenced by the stability of large-cap, blue chip stocks. Therefore, the total market fund's performance more closely tracks the returns of mid-cap and small-cap stocks because there are more of them in this index.

Fund of Funds

As the name denotes, a *fund of funds* is a mutual fund that invests in a group of top-performing mutual funds. These may be managed or unmanaged funds. Mutual fund companies have tried to make these popular with investors. Indeed, the idea is appealing. Instead of having to research and select the few funds in which you want to invest from among the many types and investment objectives available, the manager chooses the best of the best for you. Not only is it like one-stop shopping, but the fund of funds usually provides instant diversification and asset allocation among different industries, different countries, and different classes of assets. However, the seeming advantages—and potential returns—of the ideas are not assured. In reality, when you invest in a fund of funds, you may get hit with two sets of fees: first, the management fees and other expenses that your fund assesses you, and second, the same expenses that the best-performing funds in the portfolio charge your fund. This double whammy is disclosed in the fund's prospectus and can have an adverse effect on a fund of funds' performance. Some mutual fund companies avoid the double charges by creating a version of this product using the best-performing within their own family of funds. Historically, the performance of funds of funds have varied widely, mostly due to their expenses and fees. This shows that the seemingly best idea does not guarantee the best performance.

Several mutual fund companies have spliced the fund of funds idea in an interesting way. These companies have created a group of mutual funds in which the eight or ten top-performing investment advisers from the funds that are part of the fund family or fund supermarket, each choose one or two stocks that will make up a specific fund's portfolio. In essence, this is a *fund of best or top fund managers.* A benefit this approach is that it eliminates the double layer of charges typically associated with a fund of funds. While it would seem that bringing together the best stock-selection talent to choose the securities in a fund's portfolio would assure stellar performance, the results have not been as positive as

total market index fund
an index fund that seeks to match the performance of the broadest measures of the market, the Wilshire 5000 Index, which consists of approximately 4,000 stocks listed and traded on the NYSE-Euronext, AMEX, and NASDAQ OMX.

Wilshire 5000 Index
considered the broadest measure of the overall stock market, this index consists of over 4,000 issues that are listed and trade on the NYSE, AMEX, and NASDAQ.

expected. Given the new technology and portfolio modeling tools that are available to day, this idea may eventually achieve better results and hence, become attractive to the public.

Summary

The specific investment objective indicates the primary type of security in which the portfolio manager invests as well as the primary way he seeks to make money for the shareholders. A particular fund manager may interpret the same objective quite differently from a manager at another fund. He or she may also use different criteria for analyzing and selecting the securities in which to invest. As a result of these differences, you may look at the prospectuses for a large-cap fund and a mid-cap fund and discover that both portfolios contain many of the same securities. Or you may examine the prospectuses for two biotechnology sector funds and find that the two portfolios contain totally different stocks. The manager's investment style or philosophy (discussed in Chapter 5) contributes significantly to which securities are bought and sold in portfolio.

fund of funds
a mutual fund that invests in the shares of the top-performing mutual funds.

fund of best or top fund managers
a mutual fund whose portfolio consists of the stock picks of the company's top fund managers.

With nearly 40 investment objectives available, achieving diversification or specificity among the funds has become easier. If you are looking for the lowest-cost mutual fund that will perform at least as well as the overall market, then an index fund is probably most appropriate. If you believe that a particular sector of the market—such as the banking, technology, financial services companies, or biotechnology companies—will be the next hot area of the market, you can buy a sector or specialty fund instead of having to research and determine which specific stocks in this sector have the greatest potential for capital appreciation.

Remember that the risks associated with a specific mutual fund correspond to the collective character of the securities in the portfolio. Before you invest in a mutual fund, ask yourself those questions that will help you define your investment objective, risk tolerance, time horizon, and desired return given the risk you are willing to accept. Then review the fund's objectives, associated risks, and portfolio of securities to see if they are suitable for your goals.

Fees and Expenses: Load, No-Load, and Pure No-Load Funds

Research has shown that fees and expenses have the greatest impact on the return investors earn from all kinds of mutual funds. This is especially true of index and target date funds. It's essential for an investor to pay attention to a fund's ongoing cost when evaluating it for purchase. At the bottom line, as an investor you want as much of the fund's return as possible to end up in your account, as opposed to coffers of the company that creates or sponsors the mutual fund.

Low transaction costs are one of the advantages of investing in mutual funds. Compared to the commissions that most investors pay when buying individual stocks or bonds, the cost of purchasing the same number of fund shares is usually much lower. The specific fees and expenses included in the phrase "transaction costs" or "expense ratio" are unclear to many investors. This confusion generates many questions, such as:

- Are management fees and sales loads different names for the same charges?
- Do mutual funds charge commissions?
- What are the differences among a *load fund,* a no-load fund, and a pure no-load fund?

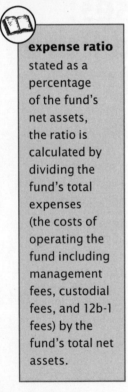

load fund
a mutual fund
that charges
its purchasers
a sales charge
when they buy
or sell (redeem)
shares of the
fund.

expense ratio
stated as a
percentage
of the fund's
net assets,
the ratio is
calculated by
dividing the
fund's total
expenses
(the costs of
operating the
fund including
management
fees, custodial
fees, and 12b-1
fees) by the
fund's total net
assets.

- What are the differences among the various classes of mutual fund shares, and which one is the best choice?

- Are there mutual funds that charge low fees or that specialize in no fees?

- Are high fees associated with particular types of funds?

- Is it true that a no-load fund always provides a better return than a load fund?

- What costs are included in the *expense ratio* and what does it really mean to the return on my investment?

Traditionally, mutual fund expenses and fees have been differentiated in the following way. Expenses were on-going costs that the fund deducts a little each day when it computes its net asset value (NAV) per share. Fees, also called sales loads or *sales charges,* were one-time costs typically incurred when an investor buys or redeems shares of a fund. Today, the distinction between expenses and fees is no longer clear-cut. In fact, some of the "fees" charged by mutual funds are treated more like expenses, especially in the way they are assessed and deducted. Today, the term "fees" is used widely to mean all of the costs, one-time and ongoing, associated with investing in a mutual fund.

Operating Expenses

At the end of each business day, a mutual fund is required to compute its net asset value (NAV) per share. In reality, a fund's custodian bank calculates and disseminates the price to the public and media via various information services. To calculate the NAV, the custodian bank totals the value of all cash and securities held in its portfolio. (The securities' value is based on that day's closing prices.) It then deducts from this total a small portion of the ongoing, annual costs associated with the fund's daily operations. The items included in the category of operating expenses are discussed next.

Management Fee

Also called an advisory fee, this is an ongoing, annual fee that a portfolio manager or investment adviser charges for supervising the research and selection of the securities that the manager will buy into and sell out of for mutual fund's portfolio. Typically, the individual or team that makes these decisions is employed by an *investment advisory service* that is a division of a fund's sponsor or is an outside company that specializes in this area. It is usually to this business entity (*not* to an individual) that a fund pays the management fee. Additionally, the fund may also agree to pay the investment adviser other fees to handle certain financial management services, such as tax filings.

This fee (and any other) is stated as an annual percentage of the fund's average daily net assets. The actual amount is computed by multiplying the stated rate by the value of the fund's net assets. The following example shows how this calculation applies for an individual investor. If you own a mutual fund with a management fee of 0.75 percent, then you will pay $7.50 annually for every $1,000 [$1,000 × 0.0075] of assets you have in the fund. Remember, this fee is not deducted all at once; instead, it is deducted a little each business day when your fund computes its NAV.

Many mutual funds' management fees are reduced to preset percentages as the average daily net assets increase. For example, a fund's annual charge may be 0.75 percent on the first $250 million of assets; then 0.675 percent on assets over $250 million, up to and including $1.5 billion; and 0.6 percent on all assets over $1.5 billion. A fund sets its own declining management fee schedule. The effect of the reduction is to lower each investor's expenses as the size of the fund increases.

Management fees (especially if they are high) can be particularly detrimental to the performance of a mutual fund, but especially of a new mutual fund. A new fund usually has a small amount of net assets, has no performance history, and, at the same time, is trying to attract new investors. To lessen the fee's impact on a fledging fund, its investment adviser may agree, either voluntarily or under a written agreement, to waive part or all of the management fee, or refund some of it during the first few years after the fund is launched. The terms of this agreement are disclosed in the fund's prospectus.

sales charge
the percentage of a fund's price that many mutual funds charge when an investor buys mutual fund shares or redeems the shares shortly after purchasing them.

investment advisory service
SEC-registered company or individual who, for a fee, provides investment advice or money management, usually in specific types of investments.

A new fund benefits in two ways from the waived or refunded management fee. First, the fund reports a higher total return than it would if the full fee were being deducted. The waived or refunded fees are said, in industry jargon, to "goose up"—that is, improve somewhat artificially—the fund's performance. And second, this higher return helps attract investors, especially those who are interested in funds with low expenses. Investors should never expect this expense savings to continue. As soon as the fund's total assets reach a certain level (usually specified in the contract), or the fund can absorb the fee without any significant adverse effect on its return, the investment adviser begins charging the full annual percentage.

The management fee is always (and must be) disclosed in the fund's prospectus. By law, the annual percentage must be clearly presented in a table labeled "Summary of Fund Expenses" or "Expense Summary" near the beginning of the prospectus. Within the table, the percentage is in a section called "Annual Fund Operating Expenses." Figure 3.1 shows an example of the table.

Any waiver, refund, or schedule of lower fees is detailed in footnotes to this table. In the annual report, the same information is explained in footnotes to the *financial statements*, specifically the Statement of Operations. (See Figure 3.2.)

Here the total dollar amount of the management fee for the fund's fiscal year is itemized, along with other expenses. Any relevant details about the components of the management fee would be revealed in the footnotes.

An investor must answer the following important question *before* buying a mutual fund: "Is the fund's management fee excessive?" Prevailing wisdom has long held that a management fee is excessive if it exceeds 1 percent per year ($10 for every $1,000 invested in the fund). This guideline is really meant to apply to equity funds that invest in U.S.-based companies. Like many terms or measurements in the investment world, *excessive* is relative. And evaluating what is an excessive management fee is not as simple as the 1 percent guideline suggests.

The percentage of the management fee varies depending on the type of fund. Those that invest in international securities or that focus on particular sectors or industries tend to have high management fees. Funds that invest in U.S. securities usually have lower fees. Domestic bond funds have among the lowest, with an average management fee of a little over 0.50 percent. Index funds have among the lowest management fees because there is no management of the portfolio. Also, some mutual fund companies (Vanguard being a notable example) keep their management fees low as a matter of policy.

The average management fee among all types of funds has crept up steadily during the past decade. Even during the economic downturn many mutual fund companies raised their fees. Currently, the average for a domestic equity fund is significantly more than 1 percent.

Expense Summary

	Class A Shares	Class B Shares
Shareholder transaction expenses		
Maximum sales charge imposed on purchases (as a percentage of offering price)	4.75%	None
Maximum sales charge imposed on reinvested dividends	None	None
Maximum deferred sales charge (as a percentage of the lower of original purchase price or redemption proceeds)[1]	None	5.00%
Redemption fee	None	None
Exchange fee	None	None
Annual fund operating expenses (as a percentage of average net assets)		
Management fee	0.40%	0.40%
12b-1 fee[2]	0.25%	0.75%
Service fee	0.25%	0.25%
Other expenses	0.37%	0.37%
Total Fund Operating Expenses	1.27%	1.77%

Examples

Your investment of $10,000 would incur the following expenses, assuming a 5% annual return:	1 Year	3 Years	5 Years	10 Years
Share Class				
Class A shares[3]	$600	$860	$1,140	$1,940
Class B shares:				
assuming complete redemption at the end of the period[4, 5]	$700	$890	$1,190	$1,950
Assuming no redemption[5]	$180	$560	$ 960	$1,950

[1]The maximum deferred sales charge on Class B shares applies to redemptions during the first year after purchase; the charge generally declines by 1% annually thereafter (except in the fourth year), reaching zero after six years. (See contingent deferred sales charge schedule, Figure 3.4.)

[2]Long-term shareholders in mutual funds with 12b-1 fees, such as Class A and Class B shareholders, may pay more than the equivalent of the maximum front-end sales charge permitted.

[3]Assumes deduction at the time of purchase of the maximum sales charge.

[4]Assumes deduction at the time of redemption of the maximum applicable deferred sales charge.

[5]Ten-year figures assume conversion of Class B shares to Class A shares at the beginning of the ninth year after purchase.

FIGURE 3.1 An example of the Expense Summary table from a mutual fund prospectus. The annual percentage of the management fee is the first item revealed under the section "Annual fund operating expenses." If the fund has different classes of shares outstanding, the chart provides the management expenses for each class separately. It always covers the fund's most recent fiscal year, unless the class of shares has not been outstanding during the past year.

Statement of Operations For the Year Ended December 31, 201X		
Investment Income		
Interest	$9,000,000	
Dividends	3,000,000	
Total investment income		$12,000,000
Expenses		
Investment management fee	35,000,000	
Distribution and service fees	18,000,000	
Shareholder account services	11,000,000	
Shareholder reports and communications	1,000,000	
Registration	1,000,000	
Custody and related services	1,000,000	
Auditing and legal fees	100,000	
Directors' fees and expenses	70,000	
Miscellaneous	100,000	
Total expenses		67,270,000
Net investment loss		(55,270,000)
Net realized and unrealized gain (loss) on investments		
Net realized gain on investments	900,000,000	
Net change in unrealized appreciation of investments	(100,000,000)	
Net gain on investments		800,000,000
Increase in net assets from operations		$744,730,000

FIGURE 3.2   An example of the Statement of Operations as it would appear in a mutual fund prospectus.

The management fee is typically the largest single expense of a mutual fund. The higher these fees are, the less money a shareholder earns. Comparing two funds with different management fees illustrates this point. Again, our example is based on $1,000 invested in the fund. If Fund A has a management fee of 1.45 percent, it costs the investor $14.50 [$1,000 × 0.0145] per year. If Fund B has a management fee of 0.75 percent, an investor pays $7.50 [$1,000 × 0.0075] annually. Let's assume that both funds provide the shareholder with a gross annual return of 15 percent. This would be approximately $150 [$1,000 × 0.15]. After deducting the appropriate amount for the annual management fee, the investor in Fund

A would have $135.50 [$150 − $14.50] left, while Fund B investor would have $142.50 [$150 − $7.50] of his return left. In this example, Fund B clearly provides the higher net return to the investor based solely on its lower management fee.

Contrary to a widely held misperception, mutual funds *do not* hide their management fees or report their returns without deducting these fees. The fee has already been deducted when a fund calculates both its NAV and its total return. While an excessive management fee should be a concern, the degree of the concern depends on (1) the fund's total return and (2) the type of fund. If a fund with a high management fee reports a better return than another with a low management fee, the net result may be that the investor makes more money in the former fund. For most stock funds, investors would be wise to focus on total return (see Chapter 5) and overall expenses, instead of just the percentage of the management fee. (Remember that in the investment community, there is never a free ride or a free lunch!)

financial statements
the generic name for the balance sheet, income statement, statement of changes to retained earnings, and flow of funds statement that a company must file with the SEC and send to investors regularly.

Investors in bond funds, particularly tax-free bond funds, must pay close attention to the management fee. Its impact on the fund's return can be significant. A bond fund invests in fixed income securities. Its primary source of investment income is the bonds' fixed interest payments. While there is some potential for capital gains with an intermediate or long-term bond fund, the likelihood for significant capital gains is much lower than with a stock fund. Therefore, an excessive or high management fee can substantially lower or drag down the fund's return.

While no investor likes to incur high investment costs, the importance of the percentage of management fees is closely tied to a fund's total return. If a fund's portfolio manager delivers a top return and charges a high management fee, an investor will still earn more money than if the same dollars were invested in a low-performing fund with a more modest management fee. If a portfolio manager delivers a top return *and* charges a low management fee, then a mutual fund investor has probably found the best possible combination.

Other Operating Expenses

Each of the remaining expenses presented in this section is seldom listed as a separate line item in a mutual fund's prospectus. Instead, they are grouped together in the "Other expenses" line in a prospectus' Expense Summary table. However, a mutual fund's annual report often lists the actual dollar amount of each of the expenses separately in the Statement of Operations, one of the fund's audited financial statements. Keep in mind that, like the management fee, all of the expenses discussed in this section are deducted a little each day when a fund's net asset value (NAV) is computed.

Administrative Services Fees These fees cover the rent, salaries, benefits, equipment, and other overhead expenses of running and maintaining the offices of the investment adviser and/or management company. Like the management fee, the administrative services fee is stated as an annualized rate based on the fund's average daily net assets. It can also be tiered, declining to predetermined percentages as the amount of the fund's average daily net assets increase to specified amounts. A new fund may have an agreement with its investment adviser that certain administrative costs are waived or limited for a period of time after the fund is launched.

Administrative services fees are disclosed in the fund's prospectus. The annual percentage rate may be listed as a separate line item or it may be included in a grouping of expenses in the "Expense Summary" or "Summary of Fund Expenses" table in the first few pages of a prospectus. (In Figure 3.1, these costs are included in the item titled "Other expenses.") Any waiver or schedule of lower percentages is noted in the footnotes to this table. In the annual report, the same information is explained in the footnotes to the "Statement of Operations."

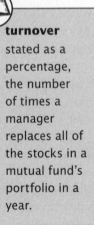

turnover
stated as a percentage, the number of times a manager replaces all of the stocks in a mutual fund's portfolio in a year.

Brokerage Fees Also called *turnover* costs and portfolio transaction fees, these are the trading costs resulting from the buying and selling of securities by the fund's portfolio manager. The more frequently the manager trades or turns over securities in the portfolio, the higher these fees will be. The total brokerage fees are not disclosed in the fund's prospectus. Instead, they are itemized in the fund's *Statement of Additional Information (SAI)*, which is available upon request.

The itemized dollar amount may not, however, reveal all of the costs of the manager's trading activities. On some securities transactions, the fund pays a commission. The amount of the commission is always disclosed as a separate item on the trade confirmation. Therefore, the total dollar amount of all commissions paid can be calculated. On other securities transactions, the fund pays a markup or a markdown. (This is especially true for many over-the-counter stocks, foreign securities, and certain types of bonds.) When a *dealer* executes the portfolio manager's trades by selling the securities out of or buying them into its own inventory, it adds a markup to the execution price of a portfolio manager's buy order, or it subtracts a markdown from the execution price of a sell order. The actual dollar amount of a markup or markdown on many over-the-counter securities transactions may not be disclosed separately on the confirmation; hence it may be impossible to break out all these costs. As a result, a mutual fund's actual costs of trading (i.e., brokerage fees) may be considerably higher than the total stated in the Statement of Additional Information.

Brokerage fees have a direct impact on a fund's return. The more a manager trades, the greater the profits must be in order to compensate for the higher costs. Certain types of funds (e.g., growth funds) generally have higher portfolio turnover rates than others (e.g., income funds or index funds). In the case of a growth fund, the manager hopes to make money primarily through the rise in the price of the stocks in the portfolio. He or she will tend to trade more often in order to realize the gains. In contrast, an income fund's manager looks for securities that pay high, regular dividends. Its investment strategy tends to be "buy and hold." Therefore, its turnover rate and brokerage fees are usually much lower. In general, brokerage fees tend to be high for those mutual funds whose objectives are more speculative (e.g., aggressive growth fund, small-cap fund), and lower for income-oriented funds (e.g., stock and bond income funds) and index funds. An explanation of how to evaluate the turnover rate when analyzing a mutual fund's return is presented in Chapter 5.

Custodian and Transfer Agent Fees A mutual fund pays these fees to the custodian bank (whose primary responsibility is to safeguard the fund's assets and calculate the daily net asset value (NAV)) and to the transfer agent (who is responsible for keeping an accurate record of the fund's shareholders). A fund may hire a bank or trust company to act as its custodian and another entity to act as its transfer agent. Alternatively, the fund may set up its own. For example, the

Statement of Additional Information (SAI)
an addendum to a mutual fund's prospectus that provides more details about the fund—its investment strategies and restrictions, the investment adviser's contract and fees, and calculation of return.

dealer
also called a principal or a market maker, a dealer is a brokerage firm that buys and sells securities into and out of its own inventory.

Putnam Funds' custodian is the Putnam Fiduciary Trust Company in Boston, Massachusetts. The same bank or trust may also act as both the custodian and the transfer agent, although many funds continue to use separate companies for these functions. Transfer fees are typically paid based on the number of shareholder accounts the agent handles. These fees sometimes reimburse the agent for certain out-of-pocket expenses.

Directors' Fees Also called trustee fees for mutual funds organized as trusts, these fees are used to compensate the members of the fund's board of directors for their work in monitoring the activities of the mutual fund adviser as well as all travel and entertainment expenses associated with attending board meetings.

Interest Fees A mutual fund can borrow an amount of money equal to one-third of its total assets. This provision allows a mutual fund to maintain liquidity through various market conditions. For example, during a severe market decline, a fund may experience an unexpected wave of redemptions. By being able to borrow to pay customers the money due them when they redeem shares, the mutual fund is not forced to sell stocks out of its portfolio. Today, many mutual funds maintain credit lines at banks so that they can access cash easily when it is needed. The interest costs of the borrowing and fees involved in maintaining the credit line are deducted as part of a mutual fund's operating expenses. These total annual charges are itemized in a fund's Statement of Additional Information.

Legal and Audit Fees The costs of required SEC and state-mandated filings as well as preparation of financial statements (audited and unaudited) are charged to the fund by its lawyers and accountants. These costs may also be itemized in the annual report as registration and filing fees.

Shareholder Service Fees These fees cover the cost for the customer service that a fund provides to its shareholders. Every time an investor telephones a fund's toll-free number to ask a question, check prices, place an order, get performance information, make a transfer or exchange, or have information mailed, the mutual fund charges for providing these services. Even services provided over the Internet cost money. Sometimes the expenses associated with printing and distributing fund communications (semiannual and annual reports, proxies, etc.) to shareholders are included in these fees, although they can be itemized separately. (See the itemization in Figure 3.1 under "Annual fund operating expenses.")

Shareholder service fees are paid to the fund's shareholder servicing agent. This entity may be a division of the fund's sponsor or management company, or it may be an outside organization. The fee, stated as an annual percentage rate, is based on the average daily net assets of the fund's shares held by customers serviced by the agent.

An outside shareholder servicing agent may impose restrictions or limitations on a fund's customers that are stricter than or different from those that the fund itself would have. For example, the servicing agent may require a higher minimum initial investment or it may charge its own fees for certain services. If new fees or restrictions are imposed by the agent, the fund's shareholders must receive sufficient notice (usually 30 days) before the changes take effect.

An agent may also elect to waive part of its shareholder servicing fee. This is often the case with a new fund, especially when the agent is a division or affiliate of the fund's sponsor or management company.

Miscellaneous Expenses   The expenses just discussed are those that are common among all mutual funds. In reviewing a fund's financial statements, you may find other expenses listed, such as professional fees, organizational expenses, and miscellaneous fees. These may vary among mutual funds, and their specific details, if any, are disclosed in the footnotes to the financial statements.

Some funds with cost-conscious management will sometimes reduce the expenses on their funds in order to make them more attractive to investors. The impact of this reduction on shareholders depends on how the stock and bond markets are doing. During a period of double-digit returns, the impact is minimal. However, once returns drop to single digits or are negative, investors become more sensitive to expenses and their direct impact on returns.

Fees, Charges, and Loads

While many of the costs discussed in the previous section are called fees (e.g., shareholder serving fees, directors' fees, custodian fees), they are more accurately categorized as expenses because they are the costs of running all aspects of a fund. In the mutual fund industry, the category termed *fees* has traditionally included the charges an investor incurs when buying or redeeming mutual fund shares. These include front-end sales loads, contingent deferred sales charges (CDSCs), back-end loads, and redemption fees. As mentioned earlier, some of the charges now included under the general heading of "fees" are treated as if they are expenses; 12b-1 fees are the prime example. All of these fees and the manner in which they affect a fund's net asset value (NAV) and its *public offering price (POP)* are explained in this section.

public offering price (POP)
for mutual funds, the price at which an investor purchases a mutual fund share, which may include a front-end sales charge.

All purchases of mutual fund shares are executed at a fund's public offering price (POP), also called the offer price or asked price. All redemptions are executed at a fund's net asset value (NAV). A fund's POP may be greater than its NAV, or it may be equal to its NAV. A mutual fund's public offering price can *never* be lower than the fund's net asset value. The relationship between a fund's POP and its NAV depends on how the fund's sponsor or management chooses to structure certain sales loads or sales charges associated with buying, redeeming, and holding mutual fund shares. While these fees are usually determined when the mutual fund is created, they can change or be amended if the majority of the shareholders vote for the change.

Net Asset Value (NAV)
the price at which an investor redeems or sells shares of a mutual fund and applicable fees are deducted

front-end load
a sales charge that is applied when an investor buys mutual fund shares. A front-end load is incorporated into a mutual fund's public offering price.

Front-End Load (Also Called Front-End Sales Charge)

A *front-end load* is a sales charge that is incorporated into a mutual fund's public offering price (POP) when an investor buys a fund's shares. Therefore, when a mutual fund charges a front-end load, its POP will be higher than its NAV. Importantly, when shares of a front-end load fund are purchased through a *dividend reinvestment plan,* the sales charge does not apply. These shares are purchased at their net asset value. All new money invested in the fund is subject to the sales charge.

To many investors, the sales charge or load is a commission. While this is conceptually correct, the use of the word *commission* is actually incorrect. By definition a commission is a charge that is added to a security's purchase price, not included in that price. Notice that in defining the term *front-end load,* I have been careful not to say that the sales charge is added to the fund's NAV. Instead, the sales charge is defined as an amount that is *incorporated into* the fund's public offering price when a person buys fund shares. Why do I make this distinction? Because the FINRA-approved formula for computing a fund's sales charge actually calculates it as a percentage of the public offering price, *not* as a percentage of the net asset value (NAV):

$$\text{Sales Charge \%} = \frac{\text{POP} - \text{NAV}}{\text{POP}} \times 100$$

Note: If the sales charge were calculated as a percentage of a fund's NAV, the formula would be:

$$\text{Sales Charge \%} = \frac{\text{POP} - \text{NAV}}{\text{NAV}} \times 100$$

Industry regulation mandates that the prospectus of a mutual fund with front-end loads must contain a table near the front of the document showing the sales charge. In the Expense Summary in Figure 3.1, the sales charge is the first listing under "Shareholder transaction expenses." Here it is disclosed as a percentage of the fund's offering price. However, in the front-end load breakpoint schedule in Figure 3.3, the sales charge is shown as a percentage of the fund's public offering price and also as a percentage of the net amount invested.

FINRA sets the maximum sales charge on a mutual fund at 8.5 percent of the public offering price, or as low as 6.25 percent depending on other fees that a fund may charge. In the 1970s and early 1980s, many funds charged the maximum percentage. Today, few front-end load funds charge the maximum. Increased competition among mutual funds combined with investors' reluctance to buy funds with high loads have caused mutual fund companies to reduce the front-end sales load and the number of funds that have them. Today, the typical sales charge percentage of a mutual fund with a front-end load ranges from 3 percent to 5.75 percent.

Breakpoints If a mutual fund has a front-end load, industry regulations mandate that under certain circumstances the fund must offer *breakpoints* to investors. A breakpoint is the dollar level at which an investor qualifies for a reduction in a mutual fund's front-end load. In short, it is a quantity discount—the more you buy, the lower the charge. While mutual fund regulations mandate a minimum breakpoint schedule, each front-end load fund has its own breakpoint schedule. Figure 3.3 provides an example.

dividend reinvestment plan
a plan whereby shareholders of a mutual fund can choose to have their cash dividends and capital gains distributions automatically reinvested in additional shares of the fund.

breakpoint
a reduction in the percentage of the sales charge on a front-end load for specific dollar amounts invested in a mutual fund.

Front-End Load Breakpoint Schedule		
	Sales Charge as a Percentage of	
Amount of Purchase	*Offering Price*	*Net Amount Invested*
Up to $49,999	4.75%	4.99%
$50,000–$99,999	4.00%	4.17%
$100,000–$249,999	3.50%	3.63%
$250,000–$499,999	2.50%	2.56%
$500,000–$999,999	2.00%	2.04%
$1,000,000 or more	0	0

FIGURE 3.3 Example of a breakpoint schedule for a mutual fund with a front-end load. Contained in a mutual fund prospectus, this schedule shows the reduced sales charges as both a percentage of the offering price and a percentage of the net asset value. Like many mutual funds, this schedule shows that investments of $1,000,000 or more are subject to no initial sales charge.

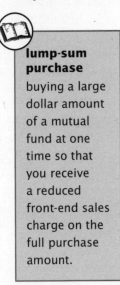

lump-sum purchase
buying a large dollar amount of a mutual fund at one time so that you receive a reduced front-end sales charge on the full purchase amount.

Front-end load funds usually reduce their sales charges to investors in two situations:

1. Lump-sum purchases.

2. Purchases made under the right of accumulation.

Using the sample breakpoint schedule in Figure 3.3, an investor who makes a lump-sum purchase of $60,000 of the fund's shares would be entitled to a reduced sales charge of 4 percent on the entire amount. Under the right of accumulation, when *the greater of* either (1) the total amount of an investor's purchases, (2) the total market value an investor's mutual fund shares, or (3) a combination of the two reach a breakpoint, all subsequent purchases receive the lower sales charge. For example, the total current market value of an investor's shares in a mutual fund is $47,000. She is about to invest $5,000 in the same fund. Her sales charge for this purchase will be 4 percent. The reason: The total of both the current market value of her holdings ($47,000) and the amount of the purchase ($5,000) equals $52,000. This places the value of her account above the $50,000 breakpoint.

Breakpoints are not only available for a single mutual fund; they can also apply when you buy funds within a family of funds. If you own several funds within the same family and the total amount of your collective holdings equals a dollar amount specified in the breakpoint schedule, you receive the lower sales charge on the purchase of any single fund that is part of that family.

By offering breakpoints in a fund family, the fund company attempts to give shareholders an incentive to keep all of their money invested under one roof. As an investor expands the types of funds in which he or she invests, by staying within the same fund family he or she can still take advantage of the declining front-end load schedule. This feature makes buying shares in a fund that is part of a large family much more attractive than investing in a small mutual fund company.

Some mutual funds are described as a *low-load fund*. These charge a front-end sales charge of 3 percent or less. Many of these offer breakpoints only on large lump-sum purchases of, for example, $1,000,000 or more.

A front-end load mutual fund may not stay that way forever. The board of directors of a fund may vote to reduce or to eliminate entirely the front-end sales charge. This may be done for two reasons. First, it is a small benefit for individuals who buy the fund shares directly from the fund itself, instead of through a broker. And second, it may increase sales because a cost-conscious investor will be more attracted to a fund with no up-front charges.

The elimination of a front-end sales charge does not necessary adversely affect a mutual fund's profitability for its sponsor. Most mutual funds earn the largest part of their revenues from the management fee and other fees (discussed in the previous section) that are charged annually based on the fund's total net assets.

right of accumulation
a reduction in a front-end load fund's sales charge on all subsequent purchases when the value of an investor's shares or the total money invested reaches a specified dollar amount.

low-load fund
a mutual fund whose front-end sales charge is 3 percent or less.

Back-End Load (Also Called a Contingent Deferred Sales Charge or CDSC)

Instead of imposing a fee when you purchase mutual fund shares, many funds assess a sales charge when you redeem your shares within a relatively short period of time (usually from one to six years) after purchasing them. This charge is commonly called a *back-end load*. However, within the mutual fund industry, it is also known as a contingent deferred sales charge (CDSC) or contingent deferred sales load. It applies to all shares purchased with new money

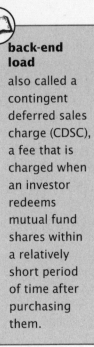

back-end load

also called a contingent deferred sales charge (CDSC), a fee that is charged when an investor redeems mutual fund shares within a relatively short period of time after purchasing them.

invested in a fund. No CDSCs apply when shares are sold that were purchased through a fund's dividend reinvestment plan.

The percentage of the CDSCs decreases the longer an investor holds the mutual fund shares. Therefore, these charges are subtly designed to encourage you to be—and reward you for being—a long-term, buy-and-hold investor. Figure 3.4 illustrates a typical declining back-end load schedule. (Also see footnote 1 in Figure 3.1.) It shows that the charge begins at 5 percent and then declines by 1 percent per year, except in the fourth year when the percentage repeats. If you hold shares of this fund for seven years or more, then you will not be assessed a load when you redeem them. Many funds have back-end load schedules that eliminate the load after five years.

When you redeem shares of a mutual fund that has a back-end load, the charge is calculated based on the number of shares sold. The applicable percentage is multiplied by *the lesser of* the original purchase price you paid for the shares or net asset value of the shares at the time you redeem them. The following example illustrates how this convention applies. Imagine that you bought 200 shares of The Financial Security Growth Fund at $15 per share (total investment: $3,000). The fund has no front-end sales charge

Back-End Load Schedule	
Redemption During	Contingent Deferred Sales Charge
First year since purchase	5%
Second year since purchase	4%
Third or fourth year since purchase	3%
Fifth year since purchase	2%
Sixth year since purchase	1%
Seventh year (or later) since purchase	None

FIGURE 3.4   Example of a contingent deferred sales charge or back-end load schedule. The contingent deferred sales charge schedule is detailed in a mutual fund's prospectus. Some funds also publish it as part of the Expense Summary table at the front of the prospectus, usually as a footnote. Others show the schedule further inside the prospectus, usually when explaining the shares to which the CDSCs apply.

but does have a back-end load whose schedule is the same as that illustrated in Figure 3.4. Three years after the purchase, the shares' NAV has risen to $26. You decide to sell (i.e., redeem) 50 of those shares. Given the period that you have held the shares (3 years), the 3 percent back-end load applies. Your CDSC would be calculated on the shares' original purchase price because it is less than their current market price. Your CDSC would be $22.50 [$15 × 50 shares × 0.03]. The amount of the charge would be deducted from the sales proceeds received after you've redeemed the shares. In this example you would receive total cash proceeds of $1,277.50 [(50 shares × $26) − $22.50].

On the other hand, if the shares' NAV had declined to $11 during the three years, then your back-end sales charge would be calculated on the current NAV because it is lower than your original purchase price. Your CDSCs would be $16.50 [$11 × 50 shares × .03]. You would receive a total cash payment of $533.50 [(50 shares × $11) − $16.50].

To keep your back-end sales charges as low as possible when you redeem shares, a mutual fund will first redeem any shares in your account that have no CDSCs. These will be either shares held beyond the time the CDSCs apply or shares bought through the fund's dividend reinvestment plan. If there are not enough of these shares to meet the full amount of the redemption, then the fund will choose those shares that have the lowest CDSCs (i.e., those held for the longest period of time).

Whether a fund charges a front-end load, a back-end load, or both, the maximum percentage of the sales load or sales charge cannot exceed 8.5 percent of the shares' public offering price. Under certain circumstance detailed in the prospectus, a mutual fund may waive its CDSC.

Redemption Fee

A *redemption fee* is often confused with a contingent deferred sales charge or back-end load. They are not the same. Many traditional and online publications use the term *redemption fee* to describe a back-end load. This usage is inaccurate and confusing. A redemption fee is a flat fee (e.g., 0.5 percent) deducted any time a customer redeems mutual fund shares. Unlike a back-end load or CDSC, a redemption fee does not decline the longer you hold your shares. Historically, funds have charged back-end loads instead of redemption fees. However, this has changed. Some investors try to "trade" hot mutual funds like short-term speculative stocks. Several funds impose redemption fees on shareholders in order to discourage such activity.

redemption fee

a flat fee that some mutual funds charge investors any time they redeem part or all of their shares.

12b-1 fee
named after the 1980 SEC rule, a fee that a mutual fund charges existing shareholders for the advertising expenses and costs associated with attracting new investors to the fund.

12b-1 Fee

Named for the 1980 SEC regulation that created it, there are two types of *12b-1 fees*: asset-based and service-based.

Asset-Based 12b-1 Fee Generally speaking, a 12b-1 fee is an expense that the mutual fund company deducts from the value of existing investors' shares in order to recoup a portion of the costs associated with attracting new shareholders to the fund. Costs included under this regulation are certain marketing and advertising expenses. A 12b-1 fee is also called a distribution fee or a marketing fee. The Financial Industry Regulatory Authority (FINRA) sets the maximum annual asset-based 12b-1 fee at 0.75 of 1 percent of the fund's average annual net assets. (In the securities industry, this is referred to as 75 *basis points*.) The following example translates this fee into real money. If you have invested in a mutual fund that charges the maximum asset-based 12b-1 fee per year, for every $1,000 you have invested, $7.50 [$1,000 × 0.0075] will be deducted as a 12b-1 fee. Remember that the total annual fee is deducted a little each day. Some companies reduce the percentage of the 12b-1 fee as the value of the fund's assets increase.

Unlike the other fees examined in this section, a 12b-1 fee is not a transaction-related charge. Instead, it is an ongoing cost, deducted for as long as an investor holds the fund's shares. In short, it never goes away. A 12b-1 fee is assessed against the total value of a customer's assets in a particular mutual fund portfolio. Hence, that is why it is referred to as an asset-based 12b-1 fee.

One of the curious aspects of a 12b-1 fee, and the mutual fund industry's reliance on it as a revenue stream, can be noted when a highly popular fund closes to new investors. Since the fund is no longer trying to attract new investors, it seems logical that the 12b-1 fee would be terminated or at least reduced. Neither occurs. These so-called marketing or distribution fees continue despite the fact that their original purpose no longer applies.

Service-Based 12b-1 Fee Because of its name, this fee is sometimes confused with the shareholder service fee discussed under expenses. They are not the same. This charge is ongoing compensation to the bank, brokerage firm, insurance company, or mutual fund supermarket that maintains and services the accounts of the shareholders who bought the fund. Some of this fee may also be allocated to the broker or financial adviser who recommended the fund and who periodically reviews your holdings. A service-based 12b-1 fee is an ongoing expense. The organization or individual continues to earn this 12b-1 compensation for as long as the investor remains in the fund. The maximum annual service-based 12b-1 fee is set by the FINRA at 0.25 of 1 percent (or 25 basis points) of the fund's average annual net asset value. For every $1,000 you have invested in a fund with a service fee, a total of $2.50 [$1,000 × .0025] would be deducted over the course of a year.

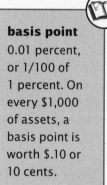

Figure 3.1 shows the percentages of a fund's "12b-1 fee" and "service fee" disclosed on separate lines in the prospectus' "Expense Summary" under the heading "Annual fund operating expenses." This separate disclosure is not standard. Many companies group both fees together under the heading "12b-1 fees" And within the industry the distinction between the different uses of the fees has been blurred. In such a case, you may see a fee of 1 percent, for example. This would be the combined maximum of the asset-based 12b-1 fee (0.75 percent) and the service-based 12b-1 fee (0.25 percent) permitted by FINRA. A footnote to the table should specify the specific percentage of each fee.

basis point
0.01 percent, or 1/100 of 1 percent. On every $1,000 of assets, a basis point is worth $.10 or 10 cents.

Like all ongoing charges, the ultimate effect of both types of 12b-1 fees is to reduce the total return an investor receives from a mutual fund. Because the percentages of these fees seem relatively small, most investors pay no attention to them at all. However, their impact on the investment return from a portfolio may surprise many investors. Remember, these are not onetime charges like a front-end load or a back-end load. They are on-going fees, deducted from the value of the investor's holdings during the entire time you own the shares. If you buy a fund that charges these fees and hold the shares over a long period, the cumulative total percentage of the ongoing 12b-1 fees may exceed the maximum FINRA-mandated sales charge of 8.5 percent. Currently, the SEC requires that this fact must be clearly stated in the fund's prospectus: *"Long-term shareholders may pay more than the economic equivalent of the maximum front-end sales charge."* (See footnote 2 in Figure 3.1.) Clearly, the drag on the fund's performance becomes more and more pronounced over time.

In July 2010, the SEC decided, after several failed efforts, to propose a cap on 12b-1 fees and to give them a new name. Asset-based 12b-1 fees would be renamed "ongoing sales charges." The percentage charged over the time an investor holds the shares could not exceed the maximum percentage of the front-end load on any classes of shares (see Figure 3.5) issued by the same fund. If, for example, a fund offers front-end load shares with a maximum sales charge of 3 percent, then the total asset-based 12b-1 fees on another class of shares without a front-end load by the same fund could not exceed 3 percent. Once the maximum percentage is reached, the fund would have to convert the shares to class that charges no "ongoing sales charges." Service-based 12b-1 fees would be renamed "marketing and service fees." The maximum would remain at .25 percent, but there would be no limit on the amount that could be charged during the time an investor holds the fund. Both types of fees would have to be more clearly identified and disclosed to the customer in plain English in the fund's prospectus, trade confirmations, and periodic shareholder reports.

Additionally, broker-dealers would be allowed to set their own sales charges on any sponsor's mutual funds that they sell to investors. Currently the mutual fund itself sets the sales charges, but would no longer be able to do so under the proposed regulatory change. In reality this would make a mutual fund sales charge function like a commission on a securities transaction. In theory, firms could charge different amounts based on the type of fund and level of service provided as well as competition.

No-Load and Pure No-Load Funds

no-load fund
a mutual fund that has no front-end sales charge and no back-end load, but can have a 12b-1 fee if it does not exceed 0.25 percent.

pure no-load fund
a mutual fund that charges no front-end load, no back-end load, no 12b-1 fees, and no service fee.

When the SEC permitted mutual fund companies to charge shareholders 12b-1 fees, it also redefined how the term *no-load fund* can be used. Traditionally, a no-load mutual fund charged no front-end load, no back-end load, no 12b-1 fees, and no service fee. Today, a "no-load" fund can have a 12b-1 fee (asset-based or service-based) as long as the annual percentage does not exceed 0.25 of 1 percent of the fund's average net assets. A fund that has no front-end load, no back-end load, no 12b-1 fees, and no service fee is now referred to as a *pure no-load fund* or total no-load fund.

Many mutual fund companies specialize in creating no-load and pure no-load funds. A large percentage of funds that call themselves no-load charge the maximum (or close to it) 0.25 percent 12b-1 fee permitted by FINRA. This is especially true for many of the no-load funds advertised and sold through the mutual fund supermarkets. Schwab and Fidelity do not sell other companies' funds for free. You, the investor, pay for this one-stop shopping convenience through the 12b-1 fees that many of these fund companies charge. They then pay part of this fee to the sponsor of the mutual fund supermarket. The names of low-load, no-load, and pure no-load funds are available through a variety of newsletters, or can be found online at specialized web sites by searching for no-load mutual funds.

Classes of Mutual Fund Shares

Until the early 1980s, each mutual fund issued only one class of share. It would have a front-end sales charge or a back-end load, or it would have no sales charges. Those simpler days disappeared when mutual fund companies went through what's often called a period of "fee madness" and became more savvy at marketing the same fund to investors with differing tolerances regarding costs and differing time horizons. Today, these mutual fund, referred to as multi-class funds, offer several classes of shares—Class A, Class B, Class C, and an institutional class (sometimes called Class D or Class I shares)—all backed by the same or a substantially similar portfolio of securities. Each class has a different cost structure designed to appeal to different investors and, subtly, to make certain expenses less obvious.

> **multi-class fund**
> a mutual fund that offers several different classes of mutual fund shares, each with a different fee structure, all backed by the same portfolio of securities.

The major difference among the various classes is how the front-end load, back-end load, and 12b-1 fees (asset-based and service-based) are allocated. Figure 3.5 and the discussion that follows illustrate some of the general differences among the four most common classes. Keep in mind, however, that a specific fund may choose to slice and dice these fees in different ways and percentages to appeal to a particular group of investors.

Class A shares usually have a low to moderate front-end sales load, no contingent deferred sales charge, and low (or no) 12b-1 fees. If Class A shares do have 12b-1 fees, it is usually 0.25 percent or less. These shares are targeted at individuals who don't mind paying their cost up front when purchasing securities. Investors buying Class A shares can also take advantage of a fund's breakpoints (lower sales charges based on the total amount of money being invested).

Class B shares generally have no front-end load. Instead, they typically have contingent deferred sales charges (that decline over a period of four, five, or six years), and moderate to high 12b-1 fees (near the maximum 1 percent, which includes both asset-based and service-based fees). These shares are designed for the investor who wishes to avoid paying any up-front charges and who plans to hold the shares long enough for the CDSC to decline to zero. While the transaction fees on B shares are low, the ongoing costs (12b-1 fees, and expenses) are much higher than A shares. Over the long term, these costs will not only lower the mutual fund's return, but they may also exceed even the initial front-end sales charges the investor was attempting to avoid. Also an investor purchasing Class B shares cannot take advantage of a fund's breakpoint schedule.

CLASSES OF MUTUAL FUND SHARES AND THEIR FEE STRUCTURES

| | | | Fee Structure | |
| | | | 12b-1 Fees | |
Class of Share	Front-End Load	Back-End Load	Asset-Based	Service-Based
Class A	Low to moderate (3%–5%)	None	Low (0.25%) or none	None or low
Class B[1]	None	5% in the first year, scaled down (at 1% each year) to 0% over six years	High (near the maximum 0.75%)	High (near the maximum 0.25%)
Class C[2]	None or low (1%)	Typically 1% on shares sold within one year of purchase	Moderate (higher than for A shares)	High (near the maximum 0.25%)
Class D or I[3] (Institutional)	None	None	None	None or low

[1] Most funds' Class B shares automatically convert to Class A shares when the back-end load reaches 0% or after a fixed number of years.

[2] This class is usually sold through a financial adviser or planner, or a mutual fund wrap account. The adviser, planner, or broker receives a large part of the service fee. The more assets invested in the fund, the greater the adviser's ongoing compensation.

[3] These shares are available only to individuals who invest in the fund through their employer's pension plan, such as a 401(k) plan, in which the mutual fund is one of the investment choices. These are also available to investors with high-net-worth accounts.

FIGURE 3.5 Classes of mutual fund shares and their fee structures. This table shows the four most common classes of mutual fund shares and the fee structures generally associated with each. This chart is designed to provide an overview only. A mutual fund company may have more classes (a few funds have five), may give its classes different names (e.g., Class I, Class II), and may combine the fees in different ways or different percentages. In Figure 3.6, for example, the Financial Security Growth Fund uses the A, B, D classification.

Virtually all mutual funds with Class B automatically convert to Class A shares when the back-end load or CDSC has dropped to zero (usually six year) or after a set number of years (usually eight). Every firm has its own method of making this change. The conversion is a benefit to the customer. The expenses deducted from an investor's holdings would decline because 12b-1 fees are lower on Class A shares than on Class B shares.

Class C shares have a low front-end load, a low back-end load, as well as moderate to high 12b-1 fees. The 12b-1 fees are slightly higher than those for a fund's A shares. The shares are often sold through a financial planner or a *financial adviser* who charges the customer an annual fee based on the total amount of assets under management. In addition to the annual fee that you—the customer—pay the adviser, the mutual fund also pays the adviser for as long as you hold the fund. This second fee, sometimes called a trailing commission, is paid out of the service-based 12b-1 fee the fund charges. Class C shares never covert to another class.

> **financial adviser**
> an individual or company who receives compensation for providing advice to investors about the advantage or disadvantage of investing in specific securities.

Class D or Class I (institutional) shares are no-load or pure no-load shares that are available only to institutions or through an employer-sponsored retirement plan, such as a 401(k) plan. In an attempt to acquire a greater percentage of individuals' retirement money that is captured in corporate retirement plans, many mutual funds market their services to these companies. One fund group (or more) establishes an agreement with a corporation to offer all or a select group of its most popular mutual funds through the company's retirement plan. The fund also arranges to handle much of the reporting (i.e., sending statements to employees), record keeping, and customer service for the employer. In effect, the employer outsources these responsibilities. Interestingly, funds that are closed to new investors are not closed to new employees of a company that offers the same mutual fund as part of a 401(k) or other qualified pension plan.

The fee structures of the different classes of shares make it difficult for an investor, particularly a beginning investor, to decide which shares to purchase. Usually, however, you don't have much choice. Unless you are buying shares directly from the fund itself, you are only offered the class of shares that your particular bank, brokerage firm, or financial adviser has chosen to sell to all of its clients. Nonetheless, when most investors are asked to choose between Class A and Class B shares, for example, most immediately select the B shares because there is no initial cost. All of the money you invest immediately goes to work for you. And generally speaking, buying a security without paying an up-front sales charge is a better deal. However, as revealed by the past controversy surrounding the deliberate and inappropriate selling of B shares because of the compensation brokers received, an old adage comes to mind: "Cheap is dear."

If you plan to hold the shares for the long term, it may be better to buy the Class A shares than Class B shares, particularly if the B shares do not convert to A shares. Indeed, with A shares the front-end load is immediately deducted and the remainder of the money is invested for you. The fund's performance will first have to recover the percentage of the initial charge in order for you to break even on your investment. To use the jargon of Wall Street, your investment is already "under water." However, the high 12b-1 and service fees on B shares lower this class's performance significantly over time.

Notice that the B shares shown in Figure 3.6 have a lower net asset value and lower returns over time compared to the same fund's A shares. The longer you hold the B shares, the greater the cumulative effect of the 12b-1 fees will be. And their total may, over time, exceed the amount of the up-front sales charge.

If, however, the B shares eventually convert to A shares in a relatively short amount of time and the A shares have a significantly lower expense ratio, then you may want to buy the fund's B shares. You get the benefit of avoiding an up-front sales charge, thereby putting all of your investment money to work at once, and you will have lower expenses after the shares convert. If the fund produces a good return over the long term, you are a winner all around. But remember you cannot

NAV	Net Chg	Fund Name	Inv Obj	YTD Return (%)	4Wk Return (%)	Total Return 1 yr	3 yr	5 yr	Max Init Chrg	Exp Ratio
Financial Security Growth Fund										
25.87	+0.07	Growth A	LG	+11.3	−1.3	+30.1 C	+24.7 C	+32.9 A	4.75	1.53
24.35	+0.06	Growth B	LG	+11.0	−1.3	+29.0 D	NS	NS	0.00	2.28
24.33	+0.06	Growth D	LG	+11.0	−1.3	+29.0 D	+23.7 D	NS	0.00	2.28

FIGURE 3.6 Comparison of returns of different classes of shares from the same fund. Financial Security Growth Fund A shares have one expense ratio, while its B and D shares have a higher expense ratio. Each fund can slice and dice its expenses as it wishes in order to market the fund more effectively to its targeted group of investors. Thus the expense ratio can vary, sometimes significantly. A mutual fund listing sometimes shows all of the different classes of shares under the fund's name. If you examine Financial Security Growth Fund's different classes of shares (Growth A, Growth B, and Growth I), you see that Class A shares have an NAV of $25.87, while B shares have an NAV of $24.35. Also note that the year-to-date (YTD) gains are different as well: 11.3 percent for the A shares and 11 percent for the B shares. This difference is due in large part to the B shares' higher ongoing 12b-1 and service fees.

take advantage of a fund's breakpoints when you buy B shares. So a careful analysis of the costs of holding the different classes of shares is important.

Class C shares, depending on the fund, may have an NAV equal to or lower than that of the B shares. Again, the additional expenses and fees are the key differential. When buying any of the classes of shares that mutual funds create to further "slice and dice" the fees, it is necessary to read the prospectus and, most important, to be keenly aware of the time horizon for your investment.

Not all mutual fund companies believe that offering multiple classes is a positive development for investors. Some firms believe that instead of clarifying the basic features and benefits of mutual fund investing, it only makes it more confusing. These funds typically offer low-load, no-load, or pure no-load funds, and they also try to keep the other fees and charges relatively low.

Expense Ratio

The expense ratio is one of the most important measurements for understanding the workings of a mutual fund. Generally speaking, it measures how efficiently the fund is managed. The formula for a fund's expense ratio is:

$$\text{Annual Expense Ratio} = \frac{\text{Total Operating Expenses}}{\text{Total Net Assets}}$$

In order to understand the expense ratio, you must first know what items are included in its total operating expenses. In the previous sections, we differentiated between a fund's expenses and its fees. One would naturally assume that all of the items categorized as expenses would be included in the operating expenses and that the transaction-related fees (front-end load, back-end load, redemption fee) would not. As the following list of operating expenses used in the calculation shows, some ongoing expenses are not included.

- Management fees
- Administrative service fee
- Custodian and transfer fees
- Shareholder service fees
- Directors' fees
- Legal and audit fees
- Interest costs
- 12b-1 fees

Notice that brokerage costs (commissions and other portfolio trading-related costs) are excluded when calculating a fund's total operating expenses.

The reason is simple. They are treated as a transaction related expense, not as a predictable, ongoing cost. The amount of brokerage costs varies depending on how frequently the manager buys and sells securities in the fund's portfolio. Similarly, the amount of a front-end load varies with the fund's breakpoint schedule and the amount of a back-end load depends on how long you hold the shares. Neither of these costs is included when calculating expense ratio.

An examination of the "Expense Summary" in Figure 3.1 shows how the operating expenses are calculated for a fund with two different classes of shares. The items included in the "Total Fund Operating Expenses" (under the section labeled "Annual fund operating expenses") are the management fee, 12b-1 fee, service fee, and other expenses. For Class A shares the total operating expenses are 1.27 percent, while for Class B the total is 1.77 percent. Class B shares' higher expense ratio is due to their higher 12b-1 fees. They are at the maximum 1.00 percent, which includes the service-based 12b-1 fee (called the "service fee").

The expense ratio is always disclosed in the fund's prospectus and is always available on mutual fund web sites and in various publications. What is most interesting about the expense ratio is to examine the different percentages among a small sampling of funds. The difference between a fund with the lowest expense ratio and a fund with the highest is quite wide.

The lower the expense ratio, the greater the percentage of the return from the portfolio will go to its shareholders. The higher the expense ratio, the lower the return for the shareholders. Given the economies of scale associated with mutual funds, it is logical to assume that the expense ratio would decline as the assets in a fund grow. Indeed, many funds do reduce their expenses and consequently their expense ratios, but not by as much as one might expect. The expense ratio does not decline in direct proportion to the growth of the mutual funds assets. In fact, in quite a few funds the ratio remains the same or creeps up ever so slowly as net assets grow. It is the responsibility of the fund's board of directors to monitor the expenses to make sure they are not excessive.

The more dollars deducted for expenses—especially for the management fee, which is typically the largest expense of a fund—the lower your return will be. If your fund has an expense ratio of 1.5 percent and your fund achieves a gross annual return of 25 percent, your net return is 23.5 percent [25% − 1.5%]. In this case, the expense ratio represents a 6.4 percent [1.5% ÷ 23.5%] of net total return. If, however, the same fund achieves a gross annual return of only 9 percent, then your net return is 7.5 percent [9% − 1.5%]. In this case the ratio represents 20 percent [1.5% ÷ 7.5%] of your net return. Clearly, the impact of the expense ratio increases as a fund's performance declines.

What do the total annual operating expenses cost you in real dollars, instead of percentages or basis points (which are not easy to understand)? To help you understand the fund's expenses in real dollars, FINRA requires each mutual fund to summarize all of its expenses and fees in a uniform table near the front of the prospectus. Figure 3.1 is an example of this table. Notice that near the bottom of the table (just before the footnotes) there is a FINRA-mandated example based on a hypothetical $10,000 investment in the fund. The example shows how much a shareholder's expenses would be in real dollars if he or she had invested $10,000 in the fund and held the shares for one year, three years, five years, and ten years. The amount of the expenses shown assumes a 5 percent annual return with all dividends reinvested. Both the time periods covered and the annual rate of return used in the table are mandated by FINRA. After the example, the following statement or something similar must be printed in boldface or italic type:

> *The example should not be considered a representation of past or future expenses. It is for comparison purposes only. Actual expenses may be greater or less than those shown and the 5 percent return used in this example is a hypothetical rate.*

If a mutual fund's expense ratio is unusually high in a given year, the reason must be explained to the shareholders. This information is disclosed in the fund's Statement of Additional Information, specifically the "Statement of Operations" and its accompanying footnotes.

Notice in Figure 3.1 the expenses incurred by the A shares and the expenses incurred by B shares (assuming no redemptions) gradually converge over time. The large difference in the early years reflects the fact that the A shares have a front-end sales load resulting in higher initial expenses when the fund is purchased, while the B shares do not. The difference narrows over time because the B shares have much higher 12b-1 fees. In the 10th year, there is a projected difference of only $10 between the expenses of the A shares and the B shares. Footnote 5 reveals the reason. In the ninth year after you purchase the Class B shares, they convert to Class A. This reduces your ongoing costs because the A shares have a lower expense ratio. The conversion of B shares into A shares after a period of time, usually when the B shares' contingent deferred sales charges have declined to zero, is a common feature among funds that offer multiple classes of shares.

Market research has shown that investors are much more tolerant of high mutual fund expenses during periods when the market and funds are producing double-digit returns. People who began investing in the late 1980s and in the 1990s saw this type of return; so, they tended to turn a blind eye to the costs associated with their mutual fund investments. An industry professional has estimated that given the amount of money most people have invested in mutual funds, the cost of maintaining the investment (i.e., the ongoing fees and expenses) is probably the third or fourth largest expense in most American households. In 2000 and 2007 to 2008, when funds began producing negative or single-digit returns, investor awareness of expenses increased because the effect on the amount the investor makes and loses is more apparent.

Now that you understand (1) the operating expenses of a mutual fund, (2) the transaction-related fees of a mutual fund, and (3) the importance of a fund's expense ratio, here are some practical points to keep in mind:

- Always read the footnotes accompanying the tables that disclose this information in the prospectus. Most importantly, look for any agreements between the advisers and the fund that temporarily limit or waive the expenses that are charged to the fund. In one prospectus that I looked through while writing this book, the fund showed total annual operating expenses of 1.2 percent on its A shares and 1.9 percent on its B shares. However, upon reading the accompanying footnotes, I discovered without the advisers' agreement to limit expenses, the total annual expenses would have been 7.07 percent for the A shares and 7.77 percent for the B shares. Not a small difference! In the future when the limits are no longer imposed, your return from such a fund could be adversely affected.

- The terms *no-load* and *pure no-load* do not mean that a mutual fund has a low expense ratio. No-load funds can have high expenses because of both the management fee and the service-based 12b-1 fees. Pure no-load funds can have high expense ratios primarily due to high management fees.

- Some mutual fund companies specialize in creating funds with low expense ratios. Also, certain types of funds, such as index funds and government bond funds, and target-date funds typically have very low expenses. The low costs mean more of the investment return ends up in your pocket.

- A low expense ratio is always an attractive feature of a mutual fund. It is an especially important consideration when you're looking to invest in a bond fund where the returns are relatively low or a passively managed fund (such as an index fund). A high ratio would devour a large percentage of your return. It is also an important feature to look for with stock funds, especially during periods when stock funds are yielding low or negative returns. In the case of target-date funds, research has show that high expenses are a significant contributing factor to below-average returns.

Finally, at any time and for any type of fund, buying a mutual fund with low expenses is an obvious, risk-free way of increasing your return. To paraphrase Benjamin Franklin, 1 percent saved is 1 percent earned.

Chapter

4

Buying, Redeeming, and Exchanging Mutual Fund Shares

While watching one of the financial news channels or checking the markets online, you learn that the stock market is in a steep decline. Newscasters are using phrases like "panic sell-off," "market rout," and "flash crash." You anxiously call your broker or mutual fund company, or you go online in the middle of the day and place an order to sell your fund shares before the market goes any lower. You do not want to lose all the gains you made over the past few years.

Or, perhaps you view the market's decline as a long-term buying opportunity. You believe that at some point during the day, stock prices will become so low that it is a good time to buy some mutual fund shares or add to existing holdings before the market rebounds. You place an order to buy shares of a mutual fund in the middle of the day when stock prices seem to be at their lowest point.

Many new investors see buying and selling mutual fund shares as the equivalent of buying and selling shares of stocks. This comparison is inaccurate for two basic reasons: (1) Mutual funds are redeemable securities, not tradable securities. Shares can only be bought from and redeemed with the mutual fund company itself or through one of its authorized selling group members. (2) The daily purchase price and the redemption price of mutual funds are determined in a completely different way from that of a corporation's common stock.

Forward Pricing

The method by which the purchase and sale (redemption) prices of mutual fund shares are determined is known as *forward pricing*. Each mutual fund (or more accurately, the fund's custodian bank) computes and reports its shares' net asset value (NAV) only after the stock markets close each day. There is no continuous intraday pricing of fund shares. Therefore, when you place an order to buy or sell a fund's shares, your order is executed based on NAV calculated at the *end* of that day, no matter what time you place the order during the trading day. On the other hand, if you call in the middle of a business day to get the price of your fund shares, the price quoted to you is the previous day's NAV because that was the last time the fund calculated and reported this value.

Forward pricing, instead of continuous pricing, is used in the mutual fund market because of several dynamic characteristics of the basic product. The prices of the securities in the fund's portfolio are changing constantly during the day, and the fund is taking buy orders and redemption requests throughout the day. As a result of this last feature, the number of shares outstanding for each mutual fund can change every trading day. After the close of the trading day (4:00 P.M. Eastern Standard Time), each fund takes these steps:

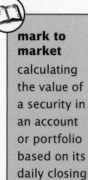

forward pricing
the calculation of a mutual fund's net asset value at the end of each trading day after the securities markets close.

1. *Marks to market* its portfolio—that is, it calculates the total value of securities and cash equivalents held in the portfolio based on their closing prices.

2. Subtracts any ongoing expenses, fees, overhead costs, and trading costs from this total.

3. Divides the net amount by the number of fund shares outstanding (based on the number of buy orders and redemption orders received that day).

mark to market
calculating the value of a security in an account or portfolio based on its daily closing price.

This resulting number is the fund's net asset value (NAV) per share. Each mutual fund must report this value to FINRA by 5:30 P.M. Eastern Standard Time each trading day. It is then distributed to the public via various market data services and Internet sites. It is also published in the next day's newspapers and business periodicals on their web sites.

If the published NAV is always the previous day's, then what benefit is it to you, the investor? It is the dollar amount that you (and the mutual fund company) use to

NAV	Fund Name	Type	YTD Return	Total % Return				Max Initial Chrg	Exp Ratio
				1 Yr	3 Yr	5 Yr	10 Yr		
Financial Security Funds									
20.45	Grln A p	LG	+7.8	+13.3	+20.1	+17.0	+15.5	5.75	0.86
20.20	Grln B t	LG	+7.7	+12.5	+19.2	+16.1	NS	0.00	1.61

Note: **p** indicates the fund charges 12b-1 fees (also called distribution fees).

t indicates the fund charges a back-end load as well as 12b-1 fees.

NS indicates the fund did not exist during this period of time.

FIGURE 4.1 Typical weekly, monthly, or quarterly mutual fund listing in a financial publication or on a web site. Each line is a snapshot of a mutual fund, its current NAV, its name and investment objective, its year-to-date performance (i.e., since January 1, the beginning of the calendar year), its total return over a number of years mandated by the SEC, its maximum initial sales charge (if any), and the fund's expense ratio. Some listings also show the number of years the current management has been in place, the fund's annual turnover, and other useful information.

determine the market value of your holdings on any given day. By comparing this value with the price at which you bought the shares, you can calculate the amount of unrealized gain or loss on your holdings.

You can also think of the NAV as the approximate liquidation value of your shares. Since all redemptions are executed at a fund's NAV, the dollar amount is the approximate money per share you would receive (less any applicable back-end load and redemption fees) if you chose to sell your shares, thus realizing the gain or loss.

Importantly, forward pricing is nothing more than an industry convention that determines when a fund's NAV is calculated and disseminated to the public. It is not a tool for determining when to buy and sell a fund's shares. Such decisions are based on other factors—such as your investment objective, the time horizon of your investment, and your intermediate-to-long-term expectations for the fund's and the market's performance. (This last factor is discussed in Chapter 5.)

Purchasing Fund Shares

When you place an order to buy shares of a mutual fund, your order is executed at the fund's public offering price (POP). This is also called the fund's offer price or asked price. If you are buying shares of a no-load fund or pure no-load fund, then the fund's public offering price (POP) and net asset value (NAV) will be the same. If, however, you are buying a fund with a front-end load, the POP will be greater than the fund's NAV. The difference between the prices is the fund's sales charge or sales load.

Note in Figure 4.1 that a fund's public offering price is never published or distributed. Because the price at which various investors can buy the same front-end load fund is affected by different factors (explained in this section), the POP can therefore vary by customer. Each fund, therefore calculates, a customer's appropriate public offering price after the close of the trading day on which the buy order is entered.

Each front-end load must compute its public offering price using its NAV at the close of that business day and the appropriate sales charge percentage taking into account any breakpoints the customer may be eligible to receive. The formula used to calculate the POP of a front-end load fund is:

$$\text{Public offering price} = \frac{\text{Net asset value}}{100\% - \text{Sales charge }\%}$$

Using Financial Security Growth and Income Fund's Class A shares (NAV = $20.45) listed in Figure 4.1 as an example, you can compute the fund's public offering price, assuming you are being charged the maximum initial sales load (5.75 percent) shown in the second column from the right.

$$\text{Public offering orice} = \frac{\$20.45}{100\% - 5.75\%} = \frac{\$20.45}{.9425} = \$21.70$$

If you invest $1,000 in this front-end load fund, you would buy 46.082 shares [$1,000 ÷ $21.70]. By comparison, if this were a fund with no front-end load, so that you could buy the shares at their NAV, then you would purchase 48.90 shares [$1,000 ÷ $20.45]. In addition to showing you which type of fund would enable you to buy more shares, the two examples show you how much of your $1,000 will immediately begin to work for you. In the case of the fund with no front-end load, all of your money starts working for you immediately. In the case of the fund with the front-end sales charge of 5.75 percent, only approximately $942.50 is invested in the fund. The approximately $57.50 [$1,000 × 5.75%] difference is deducted up front from your $1,000 investment by the fund as its sales charge.

Most front-end load funds offer quantity discounts on the sales charge called breakpoints. (These are discussed in detail in Chapter 3.) If the amount of money you want to invest reaches a stated amount in its breakpoint schedule, the fund calculates your public offering price using the appropriate lower sales charge. If, for example, you deposit enough money to qualify for a 3 percent sales charge on the purchase using a hypothetical breakpoint schedule for the Financial Security Growth and Income Class A shares, then your offer price would be:

$$\text{Public offering price} = \frac{\$20.45}{100\% - 3.00\%} = \frac{\$20.45}{.97} = \$21.80$$

Investing $1,000 in the fund with a reduced sales charge of 3 percent results in your buying 47.438 shares [$1,000 ÷ $21.08] of the Financial Security Growth and Income Class A shares. Of the $1,000 you deposit, $970 would be invested immediately after the fund deducts its $30 [$1,000 × 0.03] sales charge.

Breakpoints enable you to buy more shares in a front-end load fund. However, the dollar amount required in most breakpoint schedules to get the reduced sales charges is much higher than that used in the example. (See Figure 3.3.) The arbitrary $1,000 investment amount is used in all three situations so that you can make a clear comparison of the effects on your investment dollars.

Mutual fund investors can take advantage of breakpoints in one of two ways:

1. Making lump-sum purchases—that is, investing a large amount of money in a mutual fund at one time).

2. Purchasing shares under the fund's right of accumulation provisions.

Continuing with the example using the Financial Security Growth and Income Class A shares in Figure 4.1, you can make a lump-sum purchase in the fund that entitles you to receive a sales charge of 3 percent on the entire amount invested. Or under the right of accumulation, you will receive the lower sales charge when *the greater of* one of the following reaches a breakpoint: (1) the total amount of an investor's purchases, (2) the total market value of an investor's mutual fund shares, or (3) a combination of the two. All subsequent purchases would be assessed the lower sales charge. (See Chapter 3 for a detailed example.)

Breakpoints are not only available for a single mutual fund; they also apply when you buy funds within a family of funds. Usually one breakpoint schedule applies to the total combined amount you have invested in any number of funds in the same family. This benefit makes buying shares of a fund that is part of a large family attractive.

Many front-end load funds permit you to take advantage of a breakpoint when the money you are investing is approaching a breakpoint. It is illegal for a fund to sell you a dollar amount of shares that is just below a breakpoint

Letter of Intent (LOI)

an agreement that permits a mutual fund purchaser to take advantage of a reduced sales charge by investing a fixed amount of money over a fixed amount of time.

and thereby earn a higher sales charge for itself. The fund company or its representative must tell you when you are approaching a breakpoint and must offer you the opportunity to purchase shares at the lesser sales charge. This is accomplished with a *Letter of Intent (LOI)*. An LOI permits you—the customer—to receive a reduced sales charge on all purchases you intend to make within a fixed period of time. The total of the intended purchases must meet or exceed the dollar amount specified in the breakpoint schedule in order to receive the lesser sales load.

An example best illustrates this point. Imagine that you are about to invest $5,000 in a front-end load mutual fund, and over the next year you plan to invest another $50,000. The sales charge on your $5,000 purchase is 4.75 percent, but the fund offers a breakpoint—a reduced sales charge—of 3 percent at the $50,000 level. You can sign a Letter of Intent with your mutual fund company that lets you receive the lower (3 percent) breakpoint on all purchases during a stated period of time. The maximum life of an LOI is 13 months. You therefore have 13 months from the date of the original purchase to invest the additional $50,000 in the fund. During the 13-month period the $50,000 of shares bought under the terms of the Letter of Intent are held in a separate account where they accrue all benefits as if you actually owned them. The shares are credited fully to your account when you pay for them, thus fulfilling the terms of the Letter of Intent.

If, however, you do not fulfill the terms of the Letter of Intent by the designated date, the shares that have not been paid for and all the benefits they have accrued in the separate account revert to the mutual fund company. The appropriate higher sales charge on the original purchase amount is immediately deducted from your account.

A Letter of Intent can also be backdated for up to 90 days. If you choose not to sign the LOI when it is offered and then, within 90 days of that day you change your mind, you can go back and sign the letter. (Perhaps your financial situation has changed.) The maximum life of the LOI is still 13 months, including the 90-day backdate period. Many low-load funds do not offer a Letter or Intent to shareholders. No-load funds do not have breakpoint schedules for obvious reasons and thus there is no need for an LOI.

Today all funds offer an *automatic investment plan* to make investing easier, whether or not there's on LOI. This service is arranged with your bank through your mutual fund company. Once you sign the proper documents (given to you by the mutual fund) to set up the plan, money is automatically debited from your bank account on a pre-determined date and immediately invested in a mutual fund you have chosen. You select whether you want the automatic debit to be made monthly or quarterly. However, the minimum dollar amount of the debit is set by each fund.

Dollar-Cost Averaging

By setting up an automatic investment plan and sticking to it over the long term, you can potentially benefit from one of the much-touted advantages of this disciplined investment approach. This is called *dollar-cost averaging*. To achieve its benefit, you must invest the same amount of money in a mutual fund at regular intervals, typically biweekly or monthly. You buy shares without considering the fund's offering price on the date of each purchase. The regularity of your periodic investments and the consistency of the amount you invest are essential contributors to the long-term result.

Dollar-cost averaging works on the following simple principle: If a fund's purchase price has declined on the date that you invest, the purchasing power of your money expands—that is, you buy more shares for the fixed amount invested. If the fund's purchase price has risen on the day you invest, the purchasing power of your money contracts and you purchase fewer shares for the same fixed amount invested. If you invest over the long term, buying shares at different prices as a fund's value characteristically moves up and down, you will find that the *cost* of each share is lower than the share's *average price* during the same period. This is the beneficial effect of dollar-cost averaging.

At first reading, this explanation of dollar-cost averaging sounds like a form of investment alchemy. After all, how can shares bought over a period of time cost less than their average price? The example in Figure 4.2 illustrates the mechanics and benefits of dollar-cost averaging.

In this example, you invest $250 (either by automatic investing or with a check) on the same day each month in a mutual fund. Characteristically, the market price of a fund fluctuates every day as the closing prices of the securities in the portfolio change. Your $250, therefore, buys a different number of shares each time based on the fund's public offering price on the date of the purchase. As Figure 4.2 shows, you buy a total of 121.225 shares over the 12-month period.

automatic investment plan
a method of investing in a mutual fund where you arrange with the fund to have money automatically debited from your bank account and immediately used to buy shares.

dollar-cost averaging
investing the same dollar amount in a mutual fund at regular intervals without regard for the fund's price fluctuations.

Month	Dollars Invested	Offer Price per Share	Number of Shares Purchased
1	$250	$25	10.000
2	$250	$22	11.364
3	$250	$20	12.500
4	$250	$26	9.615
5	$250	$19	13.158
6	$250	$18	13.889
7	$250	$24	10.417
8	$250	$28	8.929
9	$250	$31	8.065
10	$250	$35	7.142
11	$250	$30	8.333
12	$250	$32	7.813
Total Number of Payments	Total Amount Invested	Average Purchase Price per Share	Total Number of Shares Purchased
12	3,000	$25.83 ($310 ÷ 12)	121.225

FIGURE 4.2   Example of dollar-cost averaging over a 12-month investment period. This table illustrates the benefit of dollar-cost averaging if you invested $250 per month in a mutual fund during a period when the price of the fund was somewhat volatile. When the fund's price declines on the purchase date (e.g., payment #6), your $250 buys more shares. The purchasing power of your investment dollars expands. When the price of the fund rises on the purchase date (e.g., payment #10), your $250 buys fewer shares. The purchasing power of your money contracts.

The average price per share is computed by adding up the prices at which the shares were bought and then dividing this total by the number of months in the period.

$$\text{Average price per share} = \frac{\$310.00}{12} = \$25.83$$

The average cost per share is computed by dividing the total amount of money invested by the total number of shares purchased over the period of time.

$$\text{Average cost per share} = \frac{\$3000.00}{121.225} = \$24.75$$

Comparing the two results, you see that each share costs $1.08 [$25.82 – $24.75] less than the average price per share during the 12-month investment period. Given that the price of a mutual fund always fluctuates—it almost never moves straight up or straight down—dollar-cost averaging virtually guarantees that your average cost will always be lower than the average price per share over time.

The fact that the average cost is lower than the average price does not mean that you have a guaranteed gain. Such a guarantee would indeed be more than investment alchemy; it would probably qualify as an investment miracle. If, for example, a fund's price steadily declines over an investment period, the average cost will still be lower than the average price. However, you will have an overall loss on the value of the fund. An examination of the first six months of the period illustrated in Table 4.1 demonstrates this point. The fund's POP at the beginning of the period is $25. In the sixth month, it is $18, a decrease of $7 per share. The average price per share during the six months is $21.67 [$130 ÷ 6 months]. The average cost per share during this same period is $21.27 [$1,500 ÷ 70.526], $0.40 lower than the average price. This result is in keeping with the principles of dollar-cost averaging. However, if you were to redeem the shares at the end of the sixth month, assuming the fund is a no-load fund in which the NAV and the offer price are the same, you would have a realized loss of $3.27 [$21.27 – 18.00] because the market value of the shares is lower than their average cost.

Dollar-cost averaging works in both a declining market and a rising market, and its benefits are enhanced when it is combined with the reinvestment of dividends and capital gains distributions from the fund. (This is discussed in the next section). However, the strategy offers no guarantees that you will make a profit on the investment or be protected against a loss.

There are several disadvantages to dollar-cost averaging. First, it can limit your profits during a rising market. If the price of a mutual fund increases sharply with only small reversals or declines, then the average cost per share will most likely be higher than the fund's price when the strategy was started. In this case dollar-cost averaging limits your gain. You would have had a greater profit by investing all of the money in the mutual fund at one time.

This disadvantage is of minimal concern to most investors for two reasons. First, the typical mutual fund investor does not have bags of money to invest all at one time. Instead, he or she is a working person with modest amounts to invest periodically (usually at each pay period) and wealthbuilding is usually this person's long-term investment goal. Dollar-cost averaging is therefore an "invisible perk" that encourages the individual to continue investing during the inevitable rallies and declines of the stock market. And second, the relationship between the initial purchase cost and the average cost varies according to the price fluctuations during the investment period. For each investor, the specific benefits of dollar-cost averaging will differ, depending on the specific fund's price changes during that period of time and the amount of money invested.

Automatic Reinvestment of Dividends and Capital Gains

People invest in a mutual fund expecting to see the value of the shares appreciate over time and to receive payments in the form of dividends and capital gains. Unless you are retired and living off this income, there is little or no reason for you to receive "in your hands" these periodic distributions from a fund. Instead, you may want to have them automatically reinvested in the fund. In doing this, you increase the number of shares that you own without adding any new money. You now own more shares that will, hopefully, increase in value over the long term.

Most mutual funds allow their shareholders to have their dividends and capital gains automatically reinvested at the fund's NAV. No front-end or back-end sales charge applies to shares bought through a dividend reinvestment plan. While there is no legal requirement to offer this benefit to shareholders, most funds do so in order to make themselves more attractive to shareholders. Also, there are some legal restrictions on the maximum sales charge percentage a front-end load can impose if it does or does not offer dividend reinvestment. The limitations are specified in SEC legislation.

A few front-end load funds permit their shareholders to reinvest dividends, but *not* capital gains, at the fund's NAV. Instead, the gains are reinvested at the fund's higher POP, which includes a front-end sales charge. Many investors consider this a decidedly undesirable feature of a fund. Usually, they interpret it as a sign of the greediness of the fund's management and advisers.

Although taxes are discussed in Chapter 5, one widespread point of confusion must be clarified here. When you sign up for automatic reinvestment of dividends and capital gains, you must still pay taxes on these distributions. In order for you to have the dividends and capital gains to reinvest, the fund pays them out to you. While you have not received the money "in your hands," it has nonetheless been credited to your mutual fund account and immediately used to buy more shares. These distributions are subject to taxation in the calendar year they are paid out, whether you—the investor—keep the cash or reinvest it in the mutual fund. The only way to avoid paying current taxes on these distributions is by holding your mutual fund shares in a tax-deferred account, such as an Individual Retirement Account (IRA), a SEP (Simplified Employee Pension plan), a Keogh plan, your employer's 401(k) plan, a nonprofit organization's 403(b) plan, or a 529 college savings plan. In these accounts, you will pay taxes on the gains only when you begin to withdraw the money for your retirement, or make premature withdrawals prior to retirement age.

Redeeming Mutual Fund Shares

When you place an order to sell mutual fund shares, you are, in reality, redeeming the shares with the mutual fund itself or one of its authorized sales agents—a brokerage firm, bank, insurance company, mutual fund supermarket, and so on. (Remember: Mutual fund shares are considered redeemable securities, not tradable securities.) All mutual fund shares are redeemed at the fund's NAV, which is calculated after the stock market's close and then widely published throughout the financial markets, media and Internet. For funds with no contingent deferred sales charges and no redemption fee, the redemption process is quite straightforward. The fund simply buys back all of the shares you wish to sell at the NAV and then distributes the proceeds to you. However, if a firm has any type of back-end load or redemption fee, then redemption becomes more complicated.

When you redeem shares of a mutual fund with a back-end load (or CDSC), the amount deducted from your proceeds is calculated based on the number of shares sold. The applicable percentage is multiplied by *the lesser of* (1) the original purchase price of the shares or (2) the net asset value of the shares at the time you redeem them. The following example illustrates how these fees are calculated and deducted. Suppose you originally bought 1,000 shares of the Financial Security Growth and Income Class B shares at an NAV of $13. (See Figure 4.1.) The fund has a back-end load that begins at 5 percent and declines by 1 percent each year to 0 percent by the sixth year. It is now three years since the purchase. You place an order to sell 50 shares of your holdings. The NAV of the shares is now $20.20. The applicable back-end load is 3 percent. Your 50 shares would be redeemed at the fund's NAV for a total of $1,010 [50 shares × $20.20]. From these gross proceeds, a back end-load of $19.50 would be deducted. This charge is calculated by multiplying the number of shares being redeemed by their original purchase price, and then multiplying that sum by the applicable 3 percent load [50 shares × $13 × 0.03]. Your net proceeds from the sale of 50 shares of the Financial Security Growth and Income Class B shares would be $990.50 [$1,010 – $19.50].

On the other hand, if the shares' NAV had declined to $12 over the three years, then your back-end sales charge would be calculated on the current NAV because it is lower than your original purchase price. Your CDSC would be $18 [50 shares × $12 × 0.03]. You would receive a total cash payment of $582 [(50 shares × $12.00) – $18].

To keep your back-end sales charges as low as possible when you sell shares, a fund company first redeems any shares in your account that carry no CDSCs. These will be either shares held beyond the time the CDSCs apply or shares bought through the fund's dividend and capital gain reinvestment plan. A back-end load does not apply to mutual fund shares purchased through an automatic reinvestment program. If there are not enough of these shares to meet the full amount of your sell order, then the fund will sell those shares with the lowest CDSCs (i.e., those held for the longest period of time). If a fund charges a flat percentage redemption fee, then that amount would be deducted from the sales proceeds.

Redeeming mutual fund shares is a taxable event. You will have to pay taxes on the gains in the calendar year in which the redemptions occur unless the transaction occurs in a tax-deferred account. If the redemption results in a capital gain, you will have to pay taxes by the filing date for that tax year. If the sale results in a capital loss, it can be used to offset, in part or in whole, a capital gain on another security.

Many mutual fund companies with front-end load funds also permit shareholders to reinvest in the same fund at its NAV if they repurchase the fund within a fixed period of time, usually 60 or 90 days after the initial redemption. This is a benefit that recognizes that sometimes people have temporary emergencies and may need access to the money they have invested.

Exchanging Mutual Fund Shares

Instead of receiving a cash payout when you redeem shares, you can use the money to buy shares of another fund in the same family. This is called an *exchange.* Most mutual funds permit investors to exchange their shares in one fund for an equal dollar amount of shares in another fund at no additional cost as long as both funds are in the same family. If a fund has different classes of shares (A shares, B shares, C shares, or I shares) you can exchange your current holdings only for the same class of shares in the new fund. If the fund does not have the same class of shares, then you cannot perform an exchange. The acquisition of the new fund's shares in this case would be considered a new purchase.

exchange
redeeming
mutual fund
shares and
using the
proceeds
to purchase
shares of
another fund
in the same
family.

Exchanges are always executed at both funds' NAV. If the new fund you are buying has a front-end load, then you do not pay the sales charge. All of your money goes to work for you at once.

Mutual fund exchanges give investors the flexibility to switch their holdings to different funds should their investment objectives or their outlook on a particular asset class or sector of the market change. If, for example, you expect stock prices to be bullish over the long term, you might switch from a bond fund to an equity fund within the same family. Parents who have invested money in a bond fund to pay for a child's education may switch to a stock fund during a period when interest rates are low in order to potentially earn a higher rate of return. An investor who is approaching retirement and wants to preserve capital while generating steady income may switch from a growth fund to a stock or bond income fund within the same family.

The word *exchange* confuses many mutual fund investors. It is frequently interpreted to mean that the shares have been swapped, and therefore no sale and purchase has occurred. This is incorrect. An exchange always involves the redemption of one fund's shares and the purchase of the same class of shares of another fund within the same family. Depending on the type of account (e.g., non-retirement or retirement) in which the exchange occurs, there may be tax consequences for the customer similar to those discussed in the section on redemptions. It is prudent to check with your investment adviser or accountant before exchanging shares. Additionally, a fund can charge administrative fees of up to 1 percent and trading fees of up to 3 percent on all exchanges. All applicable restrictions and charges for exchanges are detailed in each fund's prospectus.

The actions of some mutual fund investors caused many fund companies to place restrictions on their exchange privileges. A number of investors began to exchange mutual funds within a short period after purchasing them. These individuals are essentially trying to time the market—get in and out of a fund after some quick gains (or losses). No doubt many see this as a way of "trading" mutual fund shares. In reaction, some mutual fund companies reserved the right to limit, modify, or temporarily suspend exchange privileges for a specific shareholder as well as all shareholders for a period of time. A perusal of several prospectuses reveals that some funds limit each shareholder to no more than four exchanges per year. If a person exceeds this limit, the fund may temporarily suspend that customer's privileges and then further restrict or eliminate all future exchanges. In a not-so-subtle way, mutual fund companies are reminding these shareholders the mutual funds are designed to be long-term investments, not short-term trading vehicles.

Deciding Which Shares to Redeem

Redeeming mutual fund shares is a taxable event, unless the transaction occurs in a tax-deferred account. If the redemption results in a capital gain, you will have to pay taxes by the filing date for the tax year in which the transaction occurred. If the sale results in a capital loss, it can be used to offset, in part or in whole, a capital gain on another security.

Before you begin redeeming or exchanging some of the shares you own in a specific fund, you must choose which shares of your holdings will be sold. It is important to think this through carefully because it will (1) determine the cost basis of the current sale as well as all future sales, and (2) subsequently determine the amount of taxes that you will pay. The three methods for select-ing the shares that will be redeemed are:

1. *First In, First Out.* Referred to by the acronym FIFO, this directs the firm to sell the shares in the sequence in which they were purchased. In short, the securities purchased first will be those that will be redeemed first.

2. *Average Cost.* The fund computes the average purchase price of the shares being sold and that becomes the cost basis used to calculate your capital gains or loss on the redemption.

3. *Specific Shares.* When you place the order to redeem your holdings, you tell the fund or its representative the specific shares you want to sell according to their cost basis.

You should consult your accountant or tax planner before you begin to redeem. Once you have decided one of the three methods, you must always sell using that same selection. You cannot change. If, however, you liquidate your entire holdings at one time, then the three choices are a moot point.

Whether you invest in mutual funds through a financial adviser, through a broker, or online, it helps to know (1) how the purchase and redemption prices of a fund are calculated, (2) how the various fees are calculated and deducted, (3) the mechanisms available to you for investing in and redeeming mutual fund shares, and (4) some factors you must consider when you buy and sell. This knowledge is important in helping to make you—the mutual fund shareholder—a better investor. How you use this information not only affects the return that you can potentially earn, it is also important for tax purposes.

Chapter

Analyzing Mutual Fund Performance

"**H**ow much money can I make by investing in a particular mutual fund?"

"Could I make more money by purchasing another type of fund?"

"What important measures must I examine and understand in order to choose the fund that's right for me, given my risk tolerance and time horizon?"

"Are there any web sites, information services, or newsletters that provide easy-to-understand, objective evaluations of mutual funds and their performance?"

These are perhaps the four questions most frequently asked by virtually every person trying to decide which mutual fund to buy. Figuring out the answers can be a bit bewildering and frustrating. The information you need to make (and feel comfortable with) your decision is typically presented in tables with lots of numbers. (See Figures 5.2, 5.3, and 5.4.) The density of data can be intimidating. What you really want to know is which of these numbers are critical to understanding and evaluating a mutual fund and its potential future performance. In spite of all the charts, tables, and analysis available, no single measure of a fund's potential performance exists. Arguably, the four most important factors are:

1. Total return.

2. Investment style and risk.

3. Portfolio composition.

4. Turnover and taxes.

In addition to understanding the fund's expenses and fees, you must examine combinations of these four factors to be able to understand the specific characteristics of a given fund. It is important to know how these measures are computed and how to interpret them. You can then use them to properly evaluate a particular fund relative to others with the same or a different objective, and relative to other types of investments.

Also keep in mind that examining these four factors reflects only how a mutual fund has performed in the past. Such performance may not continue in the future. After all, "past performance is no guarantee of future performance." This notice (or warning) must be printed on every mutual fund summary prospectus and statutory prospectus. Proper analysis gives you a better understanding of a fund and the risks associated with investing in it, and suggests returns that one might reasonably hope for in the future.

Total Return

When you invest in a mutual fund, you can make money in three ways:

1. Dividend distributions.

2. Capital gains distributions.

3. Increase in the fund's NAV through unrealized capital gains.

investment income

the dividends (from stocks) and interest (from fixed income securities) paid by the investments held in the mutual fund portfolio.

Taken together, these three ways of making money constitute your total return. Each is explained in the sections that follow. Their importance in calculating and understanding a fund's total return is discussed afterward.

Dividends

Also called *investment income*, a mutual fund's dividends include two types of cash payments from the securities in the fund's portfolio: (1) *cash dividends* paid by stocks (common and preferred), and (2) interest payments made by bonds and other fixed income securities. (See Item 5 in Figures 5.2, 5.3, and 5.4.) When, for example, Johnson & Johnson or United Technologies pays a cash dividend quarterly on its outstanding common stock, or Verizon makes its semiannual interest payment on its outstanding bonds, this money goes into the portfolio of the mutual fund holding these securities. The fund, in accordance with its own distribution schedule—monthly, quarterly, semiannually, or annually—then pays this money to its shareholders. You can choose to take your payments as cash or to have them automatically reinvested in the fund at its NAV. This choice is yours and depends on your financial needs.

A fund holds undistributed dividends (and capital gains) in cash-equivalent securities (i.e., a money market fund) until their regularly scheduled payout date. On the day a fund distributes its investment income, the NAV per share declines by an amount equal to the cash paid out per share. This makes sense because the distribution results in fewer assets in the fund. The date on which the NAV is reduced is known as the fund's *ex-dividend date*. This date is set by the fund's board of directors. This reduction in price on the distribution date is the most significant effect the accumulated dividends and interest have on the NAV of a fund's shares.

> **cash dividends**
> part of a company's after-tax earnings, which its board of directors decides, usually quarterly, to distribute to individuals and mutual funds holding its common and preferred stocks.

Distribution of Realized Capital Gains

Capital gains are the profits resulting from the rise in the price of a security that a mutual fund has purchased for investment. Capital gains are described as unrealized or realized. The following examples illustrate both. Suppose a fund buys shares of Johnson & Johnson (JNJ) at $50 and the price rises to $90. If the fund continues to hold the shares, then it has an *unrealized gain* of $40 per share. If, however, the fund sells the securities at $90, it realizes the $40 gain. *Realized gains* are any capital gains on securities the manager has sold out of the fund's portfolio.

Tax laws permit a mutual fund to distribute capital gains only once a year. During the year, the fund keeps a record of its accumulated realized capital gains and realized capital losses. In actuality, it is the net capital gains (realized capital losses have already been deducted) that are distributed only once a year to mutual fund shareholders. (See Item 6 in Figures 5.2, 5.3, and 5.4.) Many funds pay out these gains near the end of their fiscal year. (A fund's fiscal year is rarely the same as a traditional calendar year.) When the capital gain distributions

> **ex-dividend date**
> the day on which the net asset value of a mutual fund is reduced by the dividend amount per share being paid out by the fund.

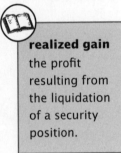

unrealized gain
the profit resulting from an increase in the value of a long security position or a decrease in the value of a short security position that is still being held.

realized gain
the profit resulting from the liquidation of a security position.

have been made, shareholders can elect to receive them as cash or have them automatically reinvested in the mutual fund, usually at the fund's current NAV.

Net Asset Value Increase through Unrealized Capital Gains

As the Johnson & Johnson example in the last section illustrated, an unrealized gain is the appreciation in the price of a security that is still being held in the fund's portfolio. The investment manager has not sold the security. As the market price of these securities rises, the net asset value (NAV) of each mutual fund share also increases. These gains are referred to as a fund's paper profits. The manager decides when the best time to realize these gains is.

Any unrealized losses are also reflected in the fund's NAV when the market price of each security still in the fund's portfolio is marked to market at the end of each business day based on the closing price of the stock of bonds. If the majority of the securities have decreased in value, the fund may have a paper loss reflected in a lower NAV.

It is the total amount of the fund's distributions— investment income (i.e., dividend and interest distributions) and net capital gain distributions—combined with the increase or decrease of the fund's NAV due to unrealized capital gains and losses that constitute an investor's total return from a mutual fund for a given period of time. When measured over a number of years, the total return is one of the most important factors used to gauge the possible future performance of a given mutual fund.

Measures of the Growth of Your Investment

Total Return   This is the most frequently cited and comprehensive measure of a mutual fund's performance. Total return reflects: (1) a fund's distributed investment income from dividend and interest payments, (2) its distributed realized capital gains, and (3) its unrealized capital gains (or losses) reflected in the change in the fund's NAV over the period of time being measured. Importantly, this calculation also assumes that all distributions of investment income and capital gains are reinvested in the fund instead of being paid directly to the shareholder. The total return is always computed for a given period of time—year-to-date (YTD), one year, three years, five years, ten years, and so on (some time from the inception of the fund)—as mandated by the Securities and Exchange Commission (SEC). See Item 2 in Figures 5.2, 5.3, and 5.4.

The formula for total return is:

$$\text{Total Return} = \frac{\text{ENAV} - \text{BNAV} + \text{DIST} + \text{DIV}}{\text{BNAV}}$$

where: ENAV = the fund's NAV at end of the period

BNAV = the fund's NAV at beginning of the period

DIST = the total capital gains distributed during the period

DIV = the total investment and/or interest income distributed during the period

[Note: The amounts of the distributions from a mutual fund are itemized on a tax form (Form 1099-DIV) distributed to the customer by the mutual fund or brokerage firm shortly after December 31 each year. The dividends and capital gains flow through the fund to you, the investor, untaxed. This feature is called *conduit tax treatment* and it is one of the benefits of mutual funds. Investors are taxed only once on the money made from a mutual fund. It is the investor's responsibility to report and pay the taxes.]

conduit tax treatment
an IRS regulation that permits a mutual fund to distribute virtually all of its net investment income untaxed to its shareholders.

Total return is a relatively simple concept, especially when the period of time being covered is one year or less (e.g., the year-to-date return). However, applying the concept to a period of several years (e.g., three-year, five-year total return) can prove confusing because the one-year total return idea evolves into a concept known as the annualized total return or the average annualized total return. This far more complicated calculation incorporates the compounded returns you would have made on the reinvested dividends and capital gains over the years involved. While (thankfully) you will never have to perform this calculation, it is good to have an overview of what the annualized total return means mathematically.

An easy way to understand the average annualized total return is to add the total return of each year in a given period and then divide that sum by the number of years in the period. (See the yearly total return in the row that

load-adjusted total return
the total return adjusted for any sales charges or redemption fees that the fund would assess a shareholder who bought or sold the fund.

includes Item 2 in Figures, 5.2, 5.3, and 5.4.) This simplified formula is only an approximation. It may overstate or understate the actual return depending on the market's fluctuations during a given period. Nonetheless, this calculation is only designed to help you understand the basic concept, not perform the actual calculation.

Importantly, because ongoing expenses (e.g., management fees, custodial fees, directors' fees, 12b-1 fees) are deducted each day when the fund computes it NAV, their costs are already factored into the numbers used in the total return calculation. No separate deduction is needed. A fund's sales load (front-end and back-end) and any applicable redemption fees, on the other hand, are not usually included in the calculation. When the total return is adjusted to incorporate the effect of these sales charges and redemption fees, it is known as a *load-adjusted total return*. (See Item 7 in Figures 5.2, 5.3, and 5.4.) When this return is presented, it must be clearly labeled as such in the mutual fund prospectus and other regulatory filings, and the specific adjustments are usually disclosed in a footnote or in an explanatory note in the performance report or in an advertisement highlighting the returns. Because load-adjusted returns result in lower performance figures, they are not widely published by mutual fund companies. Some web sites, newspapers, and magazines report them because they recognize they are a more accurate measure of return.

Mutual funds do not deliberately try to confuse investors about these returns by using different formulas in different documents and advertisements. SEC regulations mandate the formulas that must be used as well as how the mutual fund company must present the information to the public.

The importance of each component of a fund's total return varies with the type of fund. Because of their focus on capital appreciation, growth funds, world funds, foreign funds, and high-yield (junk) bond funds are likely to show a greater change in their NAV from the beginning to the end of a given period. Hence their total return calculation may be strongly affected by unrealized capital gains and large capital gains distributions. Dividend distribution would have little or no effect on these funds' total return. Compare the amounts of Item 5 (income) and Item 6 (capital gains) in Figures 5.2 and 5.3.

On the other hand, bond funds (Figure 5.4, compare items 5 and 6), preferred stock funds, and equity income funds usually provide more investment income in the form of interest and dividend payments from the securities in the portfolio and less in capital gains (both realized and unrealized).

Therefore, investment income would be a dominant factor in these funds' total return.

Evaluating Total Returns When evaluating a mutual fund for possible investment, you must examine the total return in three ways:

1. Review the fund's return over three or more years to see how it has performed during various bull and bear market cycles.
2. Compare the fund's returns for the period to those of other funds with the same investment objective or in the same style category.
3. Compare the fund's returns to an appropriate benchmark index for the same period. (See Figure 5.1 for a partial list of the benchmark indexes for some of the most common types of funds.) The specific benchmark a fund uses is disclosed in its prospectus.

In the "Financial Highlights" section of its prospectus, each mutual fund reports its total return for several years (usually up to 10 years). This and other

Equity Funds	
Type of Fund	*Benchmark Index*
Large cap domestic stocks	S&P 500
Mid cap domestic stocks	S&P Mid-Cap 400
Small cap domestic stocks	Russell 2000
Total stock market	Wilshire 5000
International stocks, excluding Canada	MSCI EAFE Index
Bond Funds	
Type of Bond	*Benchmark Index*
Government, corporate, and mortgage-backed bonds	Barclays Capital (BarCap) Aggregate Bond Index
Investment grade municipal bonds	Barclays Capital (BarCap) Municipal Bond Index
Money Market Funds	
Type of Money Market Fund	*Benchmark Index*
All	IBC's Money Fund Report Averages

FIGURE 5.1 Benchmark indexes for the different types of stock and bond mutual funds.

important financial information is disclosed for each class of share separately. While this information must be labeled and presented in a tabular format as mandated by the SEC, the style of each fund's table differs.

Additionally, remember that with a managed mutual fund, the total return you earn is the work of the portfolio manager. So you will want to check the tenure of the fund's portfolio manager or advisor. How long has the manager or team been in charge of the fund? (See Item 9 in Figures 5.2, 5.3, and 5.4. Note that Value Line provides a percentage ranking of the managers.) Was the manager or team in charge of the fund during its good or bad years? Has the manager been in charge of the fund during a bear market and how did his performance compare to that of similar funds? Check to see how the performance ranks with other fund managers.

Locating this information from among these columns and rows of numbers in the prospectus can prove a bit daunting. Morningstar and Value Line publish mutual fund performance summary sheets with the same information presented more concisely. (See Item 2 in Figure 5.2 and Figure 5.3 for the fund's total return.) Standard & Poor's publishes a similar, multi-page summary and evaluation of mutual funds. In addition to the fund's total return, the summary sheets also show the fund's performance relative to:

1. A standard broad index used to measure of the performance of the particular group or class of securities. (See Item 3 in Figures 5.2, 5.3, and 5.4.) This is called a benchmark index. For equity securities, the standard benchmark is the S&P 500 Index; for bonds, the Barclays Capital Aggregate Bond Index. Other indices closely aligned with the fund's investment objectives and portfolio composition may be included.

2. Its peers—all funds with the same investment objectives or investment style. (See Item 1 in Figures 5.2, 5.3, and 5.4.) The fund itself frequently includes its "star" or numerical ranking among its peers in the correspondence accompanying the semi-annual reports to shareholder—especially if its ranking is high (e.g., five stars or #1). It's also touted in the fund's advertisements.

Some mutual funds and information companies go even further. They provide the fund's performance relative to what has been determined to be the most appropriate benchmark index. This is called the Best Fit Index. (See Item 8 in Figures 5.2 and 5.4.) In all cases, the fund's return relative to the indexes and its peers is stated according to the percentage the fund underperformed or outperformed the index. For example, a benchmark performance reported at +3.25 percent means that the fund did 3.25 percent better than the index or its peers. If the performance is reported at –12.55 percent, it means the fund underperformed the index by 12.55 percent.

By comparing a fund's total return with that of a broad market index, a more specific benchmark index, and its peers, you are able to learn how well or poorly a fund has done and you can begin to understand its relative volatility over time. During a rising market, by what percentage did the fund outperform or underperform the benchmarks? During a falling market, did the fund decline in value more or less than its benchmarks? Understanding a fund's performance during a bear market is important, especially for most investors' emotions. You get a sense of how much downside risk or volatility you can expect from the fund. The Value Line Mutual Fund Survey sheet summarizes the bull market and bear market performance of the fund in a box labeled "Past Market Cycle Performance"—Item 10 in Figure 5.3.

When evaluating a fund's performance, risk usually refers to the consistency and growth of returns over the long term. A fund with relatively predictable returns through bull and bear markets is considered less risky than one that shows a Total Return of +35 percent one year, –10 percent the next year, and +3 percent the year after that. This fluctuation reflects the fund's volatility. Greater volatility means greater risk and greater potential reward. By examining these past fluctuations in total return (See Item 2 in Figures 5.2, 5.3, and 5.4), you can determine if the fund's risk profile is suitable for you.

Like all investors, you want to maximize your returns. Therefore you are looking for a fund whose total return is near the top of its group for the period examined, yet provides the lowest risk—not an easy requirement to fill. Both Morningstar and Value Line give you an historical snapshot of each fund's historical risk/reward profile. (See Item 13 in Figures 5.2, 5.3, and 5.4.) With the information you've learned in this section, you can now evaluate where you are on the risk scale. Are you willing to trade less volatility for lower, perhaps more consistent total returns? Or are you willing to live with more volatility (and risk) in order to maximize your return? Only you can answer these questions for yourself.

Income Return If you are investing in a fund to generate money for living expenses, *income return* is the most important factor to consider. Income return is a component of a fund's total return. It measures a fund's investment income (i.e., dividends and interest distributions) against its NAV. Morningstar and Value Line

income return
the amount of a mutual fund's total return that is being generated by dividends and interest payments.

report this percentage (Item 4) and the actual amount per share (Item 5) in the same section as the total return. Since bond funds and equity income funds can offer limited opportunity for capital appreciation, the major component of their total return comes from the interest payments on the bonds (and other fixed income securities) or dividend payments from the stocks in the portfolio.

A note of caution. Do not ignore a fund's volatility when you are investing for income. Often your accompanying (and unspoken) objective is preservation of capital. You do not want to see the money you've invested in a fund decrease in value. Given that a mutual fund's NAV changes daily as the market value of the securities in the portfolio fluctuates, a possible short-term decline in the fund's market value is inevitable at some point. You must decide how much of a decline in the value of your investment you can tolerate. If you don't want to risk losing *any* of your principal, then a mutual fund, even one that invests in bonds, may not be an appropriate product for you.

Total Return in Real Money   While reading this discussion of a fund's total return, you have probably been saying to yourself, "What I really want to know is how much money can I make if I invest in a particular fund? Knowing the total return percentages is okay, but tell me, in real money, how much I can make."

Both Morningstar and Value Line show you how much an investment of $10,000 would be worth if it had stayed in the fund over periods of time ranging from three months to 15 or 20 years, respectively. (See Item 12 in Figures 5.2, 5.3, and 5.4.) Importantly, the Value Line survey sheet shows the growth of the money in two scenarios: (1) you made a one-time investment of $10,000 and reinvested all the dividends and capital gains distributions, and (2) you invested $10,000 and then continued to invest $100 per month for the period shown, reinvesting all dividends and capital gains. The difference in the growth of the value of your money is impressive. Using the Value Line sheet, if you invested $10,000 (including reinvesting all dividends and capital gains), your initial investment in the Fidelity Contrafund Fund would have grown in 15 years to $35,302. If you had added $100 each month after making the initial investment, your money would have grown in value to $64,376.

This is a statement of return that everyone can understand. And it illustrates in real dollars the benefits of investing in a fund for the long term. By looking at the total return in combination with the growth of a $10,000 investment over your expected time horizon, you may be able to avoid focusing too much on a fund's short-term return.

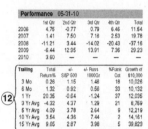

FIGURE 5.2 Morningstar Mutual Fund Evaluation Sheet for the Fidelity Contrafund. The numbered items highlighted are discussed in the text. For the most current version of the evaluation sheet as well as more detailed explanations about all of the information featured on the sheet, visit Morningstar's web site (www.morningstar.com). (Reprinted by permission of Morningstar, Inc.)

FIGURE 5.3   The Value Line Mutual Fund Survey Sheet for the Fidelity Contrafund. The numbered items highlighted are discussed in the text. The company regularly publishes new pages with updated information. Visit the company web site (www.valueline.com) for updated sheets and more detailed explanations about all of the information contained on the sheets. (Reprinted by permission of Value Line Publishing, Inc.)

Data through May 31, 2010

PIMCO Total Return D

Ticker PTTDX	Status Open	Yield 3.9%	SEC Yield 1.88%	Total Assets $227,893 mil

Mstar Category: Intermediate-Term Bond

Governance and Management

Stewardship Grade: B

Portfolio Manager(s)

Bill Gross and PIMCO's extensive team of analysts and traders, who jointly received Morningstar's Fixed-Income Manager of the Year honors in 1998, 2000, and 2007, are widely acknowledged to be among the best in the business. Gross most recently took honors as Morningstar's Fixed-Income Manager of the Decade ending December 2009.

Strategy

Manager Bill Gross couples PIMCO's long-term macroeconomic outlook with its take on short-term cyclical factors to determine this fund's sector weightings and duration (a measure of interest-rate sensitivity). Although Gross will focus heavily on certain sectors, he doesn't make huge interest-rate bets against the Barclays Capital Aggregate Index. (Such plays are typically plus or minus 20% of the index's duration.) However, he will occasionally invest in nonindex sectors of the market, such as high-yield, developed-markets international, and

Performance 05-31-10

	1st Qtr	2nd Qtr	3rd Qtr	4th Qtr	Total
2006	-0.61	-0.37	3.80	0.84	3.66
2007	1.62	-1.40	4.50	3.84	8.73
2008	3.23	-1.39	-2.15	4.89	4.48
2009	1.42	4.66	5.96	0.92	13.50
2010	2.90	—	—	—	—

Trailing	Total Return%	+/-BC Agg Bnd	+/-Barcap 5-10 Yr Gov	%Rank Cat	Growth of $10,000
3 Mo	1.67	-0.10	-0.71	45	10,167
6 Mo	2.99	0.91	0.46	42	10,299
1 Yr	11.86	3.44	-0.11	55	11,186
3 Yr Avg	10.10	3.22	2.34	1	13,346
5 Yr Avg	6.86	1.53	1.30	3	13,934
10 Yr Avg	7.53	1.01	0.14	4	20,668
15 Yr Avg	—	—	—	—	—

Tax Analysis	Tax-Adj Rtn%	%Rank Cat	Tax-Cost Rat	%Rank Cat
3 Yr (estimated)	7.64	2	2.24	92
5 Yr (estimated)	4.72	4	2.00	92
10 Yr (estimated)	5.34	6	2.04	88

Potential Capital Gain Exposure: 5% of assets

Morningstar's Take by Eric Jacobson 05-12-10

PIMCO Total Return may be more in sync with some new investors than others.

The pace of this fund's growth has been torrid. Roughly $52 billion poured in over the past 12 months ending April 30—or 16% of all taxable-bond fund flows. Anecdotal evidence suggests many investors have been shifting money to bonds from equities in the wake of the crisis, fearing they have been too heavily exposed to stock market risk. The sheer size of the flows here, though, also suggest that many may be looking at the fund's sheer historical returns, whether recent or longer term, in the expectation that manager Bill Gross will be able to replicate them in the future.

That could be a dangerous assumption. Gross himself has argued that bond returns overall will be lower in the future, and the double-digit gains of 2009 were clearly an anomaly. And while he's an excellent manager, one shouldn't look to him for alchemy. He works to beat the BarCap U.S. Aggregate Index while keeping risk at bay, but he

doesn't manage the fund to sidestep all pain. If the bond market were to broadly suffer steep losses, it would be fair to expect Gross to mute them in the fund, but it's almost certain the portfolio would still endure negative returns.

That said, Gross' current stance reflects concern about risk. PIMCO sees the global recovery as uneven and worries that growth may be countered by unemployment and the cessation of government stimulus. And while the fund recently had 36% in U.S. government debt, its stake in agency mortgages is as low as it's ever been. Gross did have bets on emerging markets (7%) and fiscally strong developed countries (13%) as of April, but his overall uncertainty has led to a profile intended to minimize risk relative to the fund's benchmark.

If history is any guide, the fund's excellent record suggests that Gross will either prove right or quickly adjust to keep it in the hunt. And while the fund's growth and now massive size deserve more scrutiny than ever, evidence has yet to surface that

Address:	PIMCO Funds, Stamford, CT 06902, 800-426-0107
Web Address:	www.pimco-funds.com
Inception:	04-08-98
Advisor:	Pacific Investment Management Co LLC
Subadvisor:	None
NTF Plans:	Fidelity Retail-NTF, Schwab OneSource

Minimum Purchase:	$1000 Add: $50 IRA $0
Min Auto Inv Plan:	$0 Add: —
Sales Fees:	No load
Management Fee:	0.25%, 0.50%A
Actual Fees:	Mgt:0.50% Dist:0.25%
Expense Projections:	3Yr:$296 5Yr:$515 10Yr:$1143
Income Distribution:	Monthly

Historical Profile

Return: High
Risk: Average
Rating: ★★★★ Highest

	1999	2000	2001	2002	2003	2004	2005	2006	2007	2008	2009	05-10	History
	9.90	10.39	10.46	10.67	10.71	10.67	10.50	10.38	10.69	10.14	10.80	11.10	NAV
	-0.61	11.73	9.14	9.85	5.19	4.81	2.56	3.66	8.73	4.48	13.50	3.91	Total Return %
	0.21	0.10	0.70	-0.41	1.09	0.47	0.13	-0.67	1.76	-0.76	7.57	0.20	+/-BC Agg Bnd
	2.27	-0.71	0.32	-3.18	-0.78	-0.49	0.73	-0.15	1.18	-0.58	7.00	-1.16	+/-Barcap 5-10 Yr Gov
	5.60	6.54	5.54	4.35	3.11	2.09	3.39	4.43	4.93	4.91	5.09	1.13	Income Return %
	-6.21	5.19	3.60	5.50	2.08	2.72	-0.83	-0.77	3.80	-0.43	7.81	2.78	Capital Return %
	26	11	14	17	34	19	12	68	2	13	47	35	Total Rtn % Rank Cat
	0.57	0.63	0.56	0.44	0.33	0.22	0.36	0.46	0.50	0.51	0.56	0.12	Income $
	0.00	0.00	0.30	0.35	0.18	0.33	0.08	0.04	0.07	0.49	0.11	0.00	Capital Gains $
	0.75	—	0.75	0.75	0.75	0.75	0.75	0.75	0.75	0.75	0.75	—	Expense Ratio %
	—	—	6.24	4.73	3.77	2.40	2.10	3.78	4.50	4.82	5.09	—	Income Ratio %
	154	223	448	445	234	273	470	325	257	226	300	—	Turnover Rate %
	64	174	530	1,323	1,703	2,208	3,106	3,748	4,410	7,222	14,490	16,906	Net Assets $mil

Rating and Risk

Time Period	Load-Adj Return %	Morningstar Rtn vs Cat	Morningstar Risk vs Cat	Morningstar Risk-Adj Rating
1 Yr	11.86			
3 Yr	10.10	High	Avg	★★★★★
5 Yr	6.86	High	Avg	★★★★★
10 Yr	7.53	High	Avg	★★★★★
Incept	6.87			

Other Measures	Standard Index Barcap Agg Bd TR	Best Fit Index LB. U.S. Univ. Bd
Alpha	3.3	3.8
Beta	0.94	0.90
R-Squared	68	73

Standard Deviation	4.71
Mean	10.10
Sharpe Ratio	1.77

Portfolio Analysis 12-31-09

Total Fixed-Income: 11670	Date of Maturity	Amount $000	Value $000	% Net Assets
US Treasury (Fut)	04-01-10	—	—	9.74
United States Treas Nts	11-30-11	7,600,618	7,553,418	3.74
Irs Eur R 6me/3.0 06/16/	06-16-15	6,632,400	6,604,062	3.27
US Treasury (Fut)	03-23-10	5,232,901	6,041,546	2.99
United States Treas Nts	10-31-11	5,259,344	5,256,255	2.61
United States Treas Nts	07-31-11	5,153,486	5,162,947	2.56
Irs Eur R 6me/3.0 06/16/	06-16-15	4,682,401	4,662,394	2.31
United States Treas Nts	09-30-11	4,318,149	4,318,320	2.14
Irs Eur R 6me/3.0 06/16/	06-16-15	3,478,500	3,463,637	1.72
BRAZIL NTN-F	01-01-12	5,696	3,176,719	1.57
United States Treas Nts	12-31-14	2,700,000	2,693,042	1.33
United States Treas Nts	11-30-16	2,547,771	2,453,623	1.22
Pimco Fds Private Accoun	06-01-10	206,041	2,062,886	1.02
United States Treas Nts	09-30-14	1,979,501	1,963,414	0.97
FNMA 5.5%	07-01-36	1,604,873	1,687,039	0.84
United States Treas Nts	08-31-11	1,536,553	1,537,815	0.76
FHLMC 5.5%	02-01-38	1,262,454	1,345,107	0.67
FNMA 5.5%	05-01-34	1,236,613	1,299,925	0.64
Sim Stud Ln Tr 2008-9 FR	04-25-23	1,283,469	1,273,351	0.63
United States Treas Nts	11-15-12	1,242,000	1,233,462	0.61

Current Investment Style

Duration: Short / Int / Long
Quality: High / Med / Low

Avg Eff Duration[1]	4.7 Yrs
Avg Eff Maturity	6.0 Yrs
Avg Credit Quality	AA
Avg Wtd Coupon	4.68%
Avg Wtd Price	99.21% of par

Coupon Range	% of Bonds	Rel Cat
0% PIK	0.0	0.0
0% to 6%	79.8	1.1
6% to 8%	13.0	0.6
8% to 10%	4.7	0.8
More than 10%	2.5	2.2

1.00=Category Average

Credit Analysis		% bonds 12-31-09	
AAA	66	BB	5
AA	4	B	1
A	13	Below B	1
BBB	9	NR/NA	0

Sector Breakdown — % of assets

US Treasuries	37
TIPS	0
US Agency	1
Mortgage Pass-Throughs	20
Mortgage CMO	7
Mortgage ARM	0
US Corporate	21
Asset-Backed	2
Convertible	0
Municipal	3
Corporate Inflation-Protected	0
Foreign Corporate	7
Foreign Govt	3

Composition - Net			
Cash	4.7	Bonds	90.1
Stocks	0.0	Other	5.2

Special Securities	
Restricted/Illiquid Secs	6
Exotic Mortgage-Backed	1
Emerging-Markets Secs	2
Options/Futures/Warrants	Yes

MORNINGSTAR® Mutual Funds ®

FIGURE 5.4 Morningstar Mutual Fund Evaluation Sheet for the PIMCO Total Return (D shares).

The numbered items highlighted are discussed in the text. For the most current version of the evaluation sheet as well as more in-depth explanations about all of the information featured on the sheet, visit Morningstar's web site (www.morningstar.com). (Reprinted by permission of Morningstar, Inc.)

Understanding Investment Style and Evaluating Risk

"I know the market can decline, but aren't my mutual fund investments protected by diversification?"

Indeed, a large diversified fund may cushion you against the decrease in the price of any single security or sector in the fund's portfolio. The degree to which a mutual fund's investors are cushioned, however, depends on the amount of money the portfolio manager has invested in a particular security or sector. Mutual funds do not protect their shareholders against market or *systematic risk*—the risk that the overall market may decline, as we saw in 2008 and 2009. The effect of an overall market decline on a particular fund will depend on the types of stocks, bonds, and other securities in the portfolio as well as how much money is invested in each, especially the fund's top 10 holdings or business sectors.

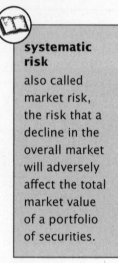

systematic risk
also called market risk, the risk that a decline in the overall market will adversely affect the total market value of a portfolio of securities.

As with all investments, mutual funds can decline significantly in value. The risks associated with a mutual fund are determined by two factors: The first is the fund's investment objective. As discussed in Chapter 2, some objectives are clearly more speculative than others. Those objectives that permit the manager to buy risky securities—high-yield (junk) bonds, low-priced stocks— and use speculative investment strategies (i.e., buying on margin, short selling, buying options) are clearly more volatile and risky.

The second factor is the portfolio manager's investment style. On what basis does the manager choose the securities that will enable him or her to achieve the fund's investment objectives? How does he or she analyze the securities before buying them? Is the manager's style—value, growth (including momentum), blend or core—currently not effective given the economic or market conditions? Will the style produce stronger returns when conditions change or improve?

Equity Funds

A portfolio manager employs one of three basic investment styles, either alone or in combination, when analyzing and selecting stocks to add to or sell out of a mutual fund's portfolio. They are value investing, growth investing, and core investing. A fourth style, called the blended style, combines value investing and growth. It will be discussed under growth investing.

Value Investing A portfolio value manager invests in the common stock of companies whose current market value appears to be below the company's real worth or earnings power, or below the value of comparable companies in the same business sector. In short, the shares are thought to be a bargain.

Managers use fundamental measures such as *price-to-earnings (P/E) ratio* and *price-to-book-value (P/B) ratio,* among others, to find such bargains. A company's P/E ratio is calculated by dividing the price of a company's common stock by its earnings during the past 12 months. A high P/E ratio indicates that investors are willing to pay more today to obtain the company's earnings growth because they believe in the firm's ability to increase its earnings in the future. A low P/E ratio can be interpreted in one of two ways. It may indicate that investors have less confidence in a company's ability to increase its earnings in the future. Or, it may indicate that the stock is undervalued relative to stocks in the same industry or sector and its market price may appreciate over time.

The price-to-book (P/B) ratio is calculated by dividing the current market value per share of a company's outstanding common stock by the company's book value per share. Book value is a company's total assets (not including intangible assets) minus its total liabilities. It is the amount a shareholder could reasonably expect to receive if the company's net assets were liquidated at their current value as shown on the company's *balance sheet.*

The P/B ratio is used to judge whether a company is undervalued or overvalued relative to the worth of its assets. A high P/B ratio may indicate that the market price of a company's stock exceeds the value of the company's net assets. The share price is trading at a premium and may be overpriced. A low P/B ratio may indicate that the stock's trading price is below the value at which the assets could be sold off. The price of the stock is at a discount to its real value and, therefore, may be a bargain.

price-earnings (P/E) ratio used to determine how expensive a stock's current market price is relative to its earnings, a ratio computed by dividing a stock's current market price by its annual earnings.

price-to-book value (P/B) ratio used to compare the market value of a company to the value of its net assets at the worth they are assigned on the company's balance sheet.

After determining what he or she believes the price of a company's common stock should be relative to its current earnings and earnings growth rate as well as other fundamental factors, the manager estimates the amount of the discount between this price and the current price. If the discount is deep

balance sheet
a financial statement that is a snapshot of a company's financial position, showing its assets, liabilities, and net worth at a specific moment in time.

enough, the manager may buy the security. Individual managers also establish fixed prices or percentages that serve as sell signals. When the stock becomes "fully valued" based on the same measures, the manager typically sells the stock out of the portfolio. Value investing is a buy-and-hold strategy with a medium-to-long-term time horizon.

Growth Investing   A portfolio manager who uses the growth investing approach selects a potential company based on expectations of strong growth in earnings. The underlying belief is that if a company's earnings growth meets or, more importantly, exceeds analysts' expectations, then the price of the common stock will appreciate.

The period leading up to a company's quarterly earnings report can be very volatile for a stock's price as expectations and reality meet. This volatility can be reflected in the price movement of growth funds. This is especially complicated because there are three earnings figures that determine the markets' and managers' reactions. The first two, which all public companies must report, are called the primary earnings per share (EPS) and the fully diluted EPS. The difference between the two is that the second (the fully diluted EPS) adds to the calculation all additional common stock that would be created if certain securities (stock options held by senior management and employees, for example) were converted. These are the estimated earnings numbers that analysts publish in their various reports and public documents. This is usually a conservative number, reflecting some contingencies surrounding the company or the sector. The third earnings figure is the so-called "whisper number." This is the unofficial number analysts expect the company to report if all of the contingencies were completely realistically evaluated. If the company's reported earnings exceed expectations and analysts believe growth will continue in the next quarter, then the price of the stock should rise. If the reported earnings are below expectations, the price of the common shares should decline. And if analysts project that the earnings or EPS growth will continue to slow or remain below annual projections, the stock's price will likely decline more steeply.

A portfolio manager who uses growth investing in a more aggressive way may include momentum investing as part of the strategy. In this case, the manager selects and invests in the common stock of companies whose market value he or she expects to increase rapidly. The manager ignores value measures when selecting a company's stock, which means the market price of a given stock at the time of its purchase may be overpriced or underpriced. A momentum manager believes that as long as there are strong buy recommendations from a majority of the analysts following the stock, or sales or earnings continue to grow strongly, exceeding expectations, then the market price of the company's shares will continue to rise.

This investment style tries to profit from the "herd mentality." If the herd is bullish on the price movement of a stock, then the portfolio manager joins the stampede and rides the stock's price upward. If the herd suddenly turns bearish, then the manager tries to sell all or a portion of his or her holdings quickly before the price decline occurs. The key for a successful aggressive-growth oriented manager using a momentum approach is the ability to sense when and in which direction sentiment about an individual stock's price or the overall market will move. In short, the manager is trying to "time the market."

A slightly more conservative approach that blends the growth and value styles is *growth at a reasonable price*, often referred to by the acronym GARP. The GARP manager looks for reasonably priced stocks (using the measures discussed in the value investing section) that promise above-average earnings growth.

> **GARP**
> acronym for *growth at a reasonable price*, an investment style that looks for reasonably priced stocks with significantly above average earnings growth.

Analysts may use another tool to measure potential growth—the sales-to-price per share ratio. Also called the revenues-to-price ratio, it is calculated by dividing a company's total annual sales per share by the market price per share of its common stock. This ratio is particularly useful for evaluating young companies in nascent, emerging-growth business areas. None of the traditional price valuation measures—earnings growth, P/E ratio, P/B ratio, dividend yield—are meaningful determinants of price movement for these companies because many have little or no tangible assets, earnings, or dividends. For companies with these features, sales or revenue growth can be a valuable measure of their overall future outlook and share price movement.

A portfolio manager does not consider the sales-to-price per share ratio in isolation. The momentum of the quarterly increases or decreases in the ratio for a specific company is interpreted in light of its peers, business sector, and the economy. Basically, as sales increase, the sales-to-price ratio increases. If the percentage or momentum of the increase is strong (a subjective evaluation depending on the particular industry), the price of the company's stock should also increase. Managers buy the company's stock if they believe the sales momentum will continue. While some investment advisers hope sales growth will eventually lead to earnings growth, others simply buy the stock because they like the pace at which sales are increasing.

A slowdown or decline in sales or revenues can be quite devastating to such young companies' stock prices and the net asset value (NAV) of the fund that invests in them. This is particularly true if the decline is due to difficulties within the company (e.g., production and delivery delays) or problems within that particular business sector (e.g., increased competition, pressure to lower prices, a sector-specific economic downturn). This loss of sales momentum, even for a short period, typically results in massive dumping of the stock. The resulting price decline can be steep and last a long time before it reaches a bottom.

Investors in growth funds can experience very different amounts of price volatility. The mix of stocks in a portfolio is a key factor. Managers may see growth in different sectors and among companies with different capitalizations within that sector. The smaller the overall capitalization of the stocks in the portfolio, the greater the fund's price swings. Growth funds generally are more volatile than value funds.

Core Investing   The portfolio manager selects the majority of the securities that make up the mutual fund's holdings so that they are aligned with the performance of a specified index, such as the S&P 500 Index or the Russell 2000 index. Then the manager tries to produce total returns that exceed those of the specified benchmark index. The manager will use a mix of growth and value investment styles when selecting the securities that he or she hopes will help the fund to do better than its chosen index.

Other Considerations   While value, growth, and core are the three basic and most prevalent investment styles used by mutual fund managers, other considerations are sometimes combined with these. Two of the most widely known (though not necessarily used) factors are (1) socially responsible investing and (2) investing based on *insider* trading activity.

insider
an officer, director, or partner of a company; or any person with material, nonpublic information that may affect the market price of the security.

A *socially responsible fund* invests in companies that adhere to (or at least do not violate) particular health, environmental, or social issues stated in the fund's investment objectives. For example, some socially responsible funds will not invest in companies that pollute the environment, endanger certain animals, or sell alcohol or tobacco products. This type of fund is also referred to as a green fund, particularly when it focuses on environmental issues in its stock selection process. Other such funds will not invest in companies that exploit workers, especially children in foreign countries or do not promote diversity in the workplace. While many investors think of a socially responsible fund as a separate type of mutual fund, it is not. Any of the mutual fund objectives discussed earlier (e.g., income, growth, sector) can be a socially responsible fund. The specific social responsibility that is the fund's focus is stated with the investment objective in the fund's prospectus.

> **socially responsible fund**
> a fund that does not invest in any company whose products or policies may be damaging to human life, animal life, or the environment.

Regardless of the primary investment style, many mutual fund managers also track the trading patterns of those who own large numbers of shares or stock options in the company, such as a company's owner, senior executives, and members of its board of directors. These insiders are required to report all of their trading in the company's stock to the SEC by the 10th business day of the month *after* the month in which the activity occurred. Also, every week many web sites, online newsletters and financial newspapers report recent insider activity. A fund manager reviews the reports of insiders' purchases and sales, and interprets them as possible indicators of the insiders' beliefs about the company's future performance.

In general, growth and value investing are the two most widely used styles. Some fund managers use only one of these, while others use a blend. Others who use the core investments style will also employ elements of the growth or value styles to help boost the funds return. Momentum investing is characteristic of aggressive growth mutual funds that seek capital appreciation as the principal source of their returns. A fund's specific investment style is stated in its prospectus, although sometimes the specific details of the strategy are expressed in general terms or implied rather than stated explicitly.

Investment Style Matrices for Stock Funds To help you more easily understand a fund's investment style, Morningstar and Value Line have created matrices (see Figure 5.5) that encapsulate a fund's investment style more clearly than can be obtained from the prospectus. These are contained on each company's mutual fund survey sheet. (See Item 14 in Figures 5.2 and 5.3.)

Both matrices are simple and easy to understand. The columns indicate the investment style (value, growth, or blend) and the rows indicate the capitalization (i.e., size) of the companies in which the portfolio manager primarily invests. Morningstar uses a nine-square matrix, as show on the left in Figure 5.5, The darkened square tells you that the manager uses a growth investment style and primarily selects large-cap stocks for the fund's portfolio. Value Line uses a 16-square matrix. Its matrix is on the right side in Figure 5.5. It shows that the manager (of the same fund) buys large-cap stock and that his investment style is purely growth. The two matrices for the same mutual fund may

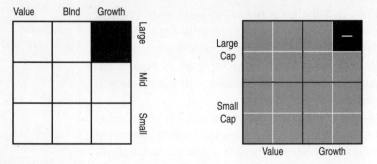

FIGURE 5.5 Investment style matrices of equity mutual funds.
The matrices, designed by Morningstar (left) and Value Line (right),
help investors understand the style of a particular mutual fund and the
likely level of risk associated with that fund. (Reprinted by permission of
Morningstar, Inc. and Value Line Publishing, Inc.)

not always be exactly the same as they are in this case. These two independent, third-party mutual fund evaluation companies will sometimes differ in their assessment of the investment style based on the types of securities they see in the portfolio and the amount of trading that occurs.

Both Morningstar and Value Line label the columns and rows of their matrices with their own standardized measures and terms. Neither company uses a particular mutual fund's definition because they can vary among funds. This standardization is an important feature. It makes it easier for investors to compare different funds with the same objective. Not surprisingly, there are many variations in the management styles and types of securities used among mutual funds to achieve the same investment objective. As a rule, funds whose investment style is in the upper left corner of both matrices (value investing using large-cap stocks) tend to be less volatile and less risky. As the style moves closer to the lower right corner of the matrices (growth investing using small-cap stocks), volatility and risk increase.

Special Considerations for Evaluating Foreign and Global Equity Funds

Foreign or global equity funds generally employ a combination of growth investing and value investing styles. The stronger emphasis is usually on growth. The manager invests in the stocks of companies in foreign markets whose prices are expected to appreciate as their local economies grow or improve. In addition to examining the fund's performance and volatility relative to the appropriate benchmarks and, importantly, the experience, tenure, and track record of the fund manager, there are two other important risk factors to keep in mind.

Currency Risk   Also called foreign exchange risk, this is risk resulting from the change in the value of a particular currency relative to the U.S. dollar (or any other currency). If the value of a currency declines against the U.S. dollar (that is, the dollar strengthens), it means that it takes more of that currency to equal (or buy) one dollar. If, for example, you are a U.S. citizen on vacation and buying foreign currency with your dollars, then your vacation becomes cheaper. However, if you are a mutual fund investor receiving capital gains or dividends in that foreign currency, then that money will be worth less when it is converted into dollars. If, on the other hand,

global fund
a mutual fund or closed-end fund that invests in the securities of corporations located in the United States and abroad.

the value of a currency rises relative to the U.S. dollar (i.e., the dollar weakens), it now takes less of that currency to equal one dollar. Any returns from these foreign or *global funds* will be worth more to an American investor when they are converted into U.S. dollars.

Currency risk affects (1) the value of the returns you receive from a mutual fund, and (2) the fund's volatility. Imagine that the price of shares in the local markets have remained flat. However, the local currency has depreciated in value by 10 percent relative to the value of the U.S. dollar. This means the value of returns from the foreign fund are now worth less solely on currency or exchange rate risk. The NAV of the foreign or global fund drops because of the decline in the value of the currency and, as a result, lowers the fund's total return. If the currency strengthens, however, this means the local economy is doing better. The value of the fund's shares rise, thereby producing gains, because of the improved economic conditions.

In each scenario used above, the NAV of the fund changes due to currency fluctuation, not because of changes in the fundamental value of the securities in the foreign or *international fund's* portfolio. Foreign funds do not reveal to shareholders how much of their return is due to currency fluctuations, although they sometimes mention it as a factor affecting the return.

international fund
a mutual fund or closed-end fund that invests in the securities of companies located outside the United States only.

Country Risk   This risk results from concentrating too much of a mutual fund's asset in a particular country. Such concentration increases a mutual fund's exposure to that country's currency fluctuations, economic risk, and political risk, all of which can cause the price of shares on the local stock exchanges to plummet or skyrocket. The percentage of a foreign fund's assets invested in a particular country is revealed in the prospectus. Keep in mind, however, that these percentages are not static. Many foreign fund managers can concentrate a significant percentage of the portfolio's assets in a small group of countries to try to profit from positive changes in the investment environment. As a result, the degree of risk associated with a particular country or economy is dynamic, and often higher than expected.

Bond Funds

To paraphrase the late Rodney Dangerfield, bond funds "get little respect" and, historically, even less money when compared to stock funds. This is partly because they are less sexy than stock funds, except in bad economic times when the stocks are down. In 2010 there was a substantial increase in investors putting money into bond funds as they sought safety from the volatility of stocks and tried to preserve their capital, including any gains they had made from a recent rally in equities. Rather than producing those flashy, moderate-to-high double-digit returns, bond funds tend to provide more predictable returns. Individuals who invest in them tend to be more conservative, seeking a safe haven—relatively speaking—for their money. While conservative means lower risk, it does not mean risk-free. In fact, the risks associated with bond funds are more complicated.

One complication arises from investors' perception that bond funds are managed differently from stock funds. Many investors imagine the investment manager buys bonds and, like individual investors who buy bonds, holds them to maturity. This misperception leads many to think they will eventually get back their original investment when the bonds in the fund's portfolio mature. This construct is completely incorrect. Bond fund managers can trade bonds into and out of the portfolio with the same discretion and frequency as those who manage stock funds. If the market value of a bond has dropped significantly, the manager can choose to sell the bond and realize the loss. He or she is not obligated to hold the bond until its maturity in order to recover its face value.

Some of the other factors that must be considered before buying a bond fund are the quality of the bonds in the portfolio and interest rate risk.

Bond Quality   The quality of bonds in which the fund will invest is identified in the fund's prospectus. Moody's, Standard & Poor's, and Fitch assess the default risk on bonds (see Figure 2.7) and assign them a rating. Investment grade bonds are the safest, offering the lowest yield. Bond funds that invest in debt securities issued directly by the U.S. government are among the safest. All U.S. government debt is rated investment grade. As a bond's quality declines (and the likelihood of default increases) among the ratings classified as investment grade, the bond is considered to be more risky and must pay a higher interest rate to investors who are willing to accept that risk in exchange for a possible higher return.

A more risk- and volatility-tolerant investor may choose to place his or her money in a high-yield (junk) bond fund, which invests in low-quality domestic and emerging market debt. This type of fund is among the most volatile. Its price swings tend to be similar to those of common stock. Also the risk of loss due to default is significant.

As shown on the Morningstar sheet for the PIMCO Total Return Fund (Figure 5.4, Item 10), the credit analysis section gives you the different ratings of the bonds and other fixed income securities in the portfolio. It also tells you the percentage of the total portfolio that is made of bonds with each specific rating. In the PIMCO Total Return Fund's portfolio investment grade bonds (rating from AAA to BBB) make up a total 96 percent of the holdings.

Interest Rate Risk   The market prices of bonds move opposite to interest rate changes. As interest rates rise, bond prices decline; as interest rates fall, bond prices rise. The amount by which the market price of a bond changes in response to interest rate changes varies depending on several factors, such as the length of time to maturity, the coupon rate, and the bond rating. For example, bonds with long-term maturities are more volatile than bonds with short-term maturities. If you invest in a long-term bond fund, it helps to have a strong constitution for volatility. A small rise in interest rates could result in a decline in the NAV of a long-term bond fund that negates all the investment income (interest) you have received for the year.

> **interest rate risk**
>
> the risk that an increase in interest rates will result in lower bond prices.

If safety of principal and liquidity are the reasons you are interested in a bond fund, then it is advisable for you to look at funds that focus on high-quality debt—that is, investment grade—with short-to-intermediate term maturities. Knowing how long you need to hold the money in the fund and how safe you want its value to be during this period are prime considerations in selecting a bond fund (Figure 5.4, Item 14, summarizes the bond fund's current investment style).

Portfolio Composition

What specific stocks or bonds are in the fund's portfolio? Morningstar, Value Line, Standard & Poor's, and mutual fund companies' web sites all list the 10 to 25 top holdings in the fund's portfolio as well as how the total holdings are divided among various types of securities—by sector, by length of time to maturity, or by asset class. A mutual fund's annual report lists all of the securities in the fund's portfolio at the time it was published. It is important to review this list because it indicates how a manager interprets a fund's investment objective. You may discover that the same stock is among the top holdings of several mutual funds that you own or are about to buy. For example, you might find Google in a large-cap fund, a growth fund, a technology fund, a telecommunications fund, and a computer fund. Or you may find Coca-Cola in the portfolios of growth and income funds, world funds, and large-cap value funds. For stocks it all depends on the key business areas of the company. For bonds, it depends on the source of interest income that the portfolio manager deems important when analyzing a security's future cash flows. If the portfolios of the funds are too similar, you may not be as diversified as you think. In fact, you may be too concentrated in a narrow group of stocks. This increases your risk that if these stocks decline, all of the different funds you own would be adversely affected.

Item 15 in Figures 5.2, 5.3, and 5.4 shows the top holdings in the fund's portfolios, the quantity of each, and the percentage each stock or bond represents of the fund's total portfolio. Another area labeled "Sector Weightings" or "Sector Breakdown" (Item 16) shows how the overall portfolio is divided among various sectors. Compare this information among the various funds you are researching to make sure there is no substantial overlap.

One of the problems with making accurate comparisons is that the funds do not report this information on a timely basis. Some only reveal their exact holdings in their annual report as required by the SEC. Some disclose the information semiannually or quarterly. And even fewer do so monthly. (Monthly updates of portfolio holdings can be found at some mutual funds' web sites or obtained from one of the information agencies—S&P, Morningstar, or Value Line—or web sites that track this information.) When making this comparison, get information that is as current as possible. If the same stocks are showing up in several of your mutual fund portfolios, it may be time to redeem some of those funds and diversify by adding new ones.

Turnover and Taxes

Turnover

The turnover rate measures how often an investment manager changes the total holdings in a fund's portfolio over a year. In short, it indicates how frequently a manager trades. A turnover rate of 100 percent means that the manager changes the entire portfolio of securities once during the year. A rate of 300 percent indicates the entire portfolio changes three times a year. In contrast, a 50 percent rate indicates that the manager changes only half of the portfolio annually.

A low turnover rate (less than 30 percent) is characteristic of a fund whose manager employs a buy-and-hold strategy. Stock funds that focus on large cap, value investing, and conservative bond funds report low turnover rates. (Some have rates as low as 5 percent or 10 percent.) A turnover rate of 100 percent or more indicates that the portfolio manager employs an active trading strategy or is investing in fixed income securities with short-to-intermediate term maturities. Equity funds whose styles are more oriented toward growth (especially when combined with momentum)—such as aggressive growth and capital appreciation funds—can have rates in excess or 300 percent or 400 percent. And as noted earlier, bond funds that focus on short-term or intermediate-term fixed income securities can also have a high turnover ratio. In Figures 5.2, 5.3, and 5.4, turnover is shown (see Item 17) in the section listing the historical performance of the fund. Note that the PIMCO Total Return Fund has a significant higher turnover ratio than the Fidelity Contrafund: 300 percent and 77 percent, respectively. This would indicate that the PIMCO manager probably focused on more short-term fixed income securities during the time when the outlook for the economy and the financial markets were uncertain.

Importantly, turnover costs are not included when a fund calculates its expense ratio. They are treated as separate costs. Higher turnover results in higher trading expenses—commissions and other fees. The fund's manager must produce returns that not only recoup the expenses of operating the fund, but also the cost of the trades. If they are not recovered, these added costs erode or lower a fund's return.

High turnover is not always bad. A fund's turnover rate should be considered in the context of its investment objective, its investment style, and the types of securities in which it invests. With some securities (small-cap stocks, emerging growth stocks, short-term fixed-income securities, and junk bonds, for example), it is necessary to use more active trading strategies in order to take advantage of short-term profit opportunities. If the fund manager is buying and selling the appropriate securities at the appropriate times, the fund can maximize its return regardless of a high turnover rate. If the fund's performance is poor and the turnover rate is high, it usually indicates a problem—usually with the manager's selection process.

During times when the stock market is charging upward, investors tend to ignore turnover and other costs because the high total return diminishes the impact of the trading costs and expenses. However, as we've seen in 2008 and 2009, when the market was flat or declining, these costs stand out more starkly. When they are deducted, it can result in a mutual fund's total return being significantly less than that of the benchmark index or the overall market.

Many people are attracted to funds whose managers trade frequently. They equate trading prowess and aggressive strategies with market savvy and intelligence. These are dangerous associations and their costs, in terms of both real dollars and risk, are much higher than most investors let themselves imagine.

Taxes and Tax Efficiency

In addition to high turnover causing the mutual fund to incur higher trading costs, it also results in the fund realizing more capital gains (and losses) on its investments. In accordance with Internal Revenue Service (IRS) and SEC rules, virtually all net capital gains (those from which capital losses have already been deducted) must be distributed to mutual fund shareholders once each year—usually near the end of the fund's fiscal year. An actively traded fund may produce huge capital gains distributions, and consequently its shareholders may have a huge tax bill to pay when they file their taxes.

In a truly worst-case scenario, the mutual fund in which you have invested produces a negative return for the year (in short, you lose money), yet you receive a large capital gains distribution on which you have to pay substantial taxes. This situation can happen to a fund that employs even a mildly aggressive trading strategy during a prolonged bear market or during a period when a specific fund is producing mediocre or negative results. If a fund is hit with a sudden wave of redemptions by disappointed or scared investors and the manager does not have a sufficient amount of cash or a credit line available to pay these sellers, he or she would be forced to liquidate (and realize the gains on) some of the portfolio's most profitable holdings in order to raise the needed cash. If you were one of the investors who held on to the fund's shares during this period of poor or negative performance, you would end up receiving a substantial net capital gains distribution at year-end. Paying the taxes on the distributed gain would further reduce the amount of the overall mediocre return that you would get to keep in your pocket. Such a scenario can be described as adding insult to injury.

A Mutual Fund and Its Taxes   Why, you may ask, does a mutual fund whose NAV has decreased—in effect, you have lost money—have to pay any distributions to its shareholders? In order for a mutual fund to avoid being taxed on all of the total net income from its investment portfolio, it must distribute 90 percent or more of its net investment income. The dividends and capital gains, therefore, flow through the fund to you, the investor, untaxed. This feature is called *conduit tax treatment* and it is one of the benefits of mutual funds. Investors are taxed only once on the money paid out by the fund. However, if a fund distributes less than 90 percent of its net investment income, then the fund itself is taxed on *all* of its net investment income. This legislation is designed to encourage funds to pay out their income and capital gains to shareholders. As a general rule, most funds distribute virtually all of their investment income, including capital gains.

A mutual fund can distribute the money it receives as dividends and interest from securities in the portfolio as often as it wishes during its fiscal year. (See Item 18 on Figures 5.2, 5.3, and 5.4.) The scheduled payment dates are disclosed in the fund's prospectus. Capital gains, however, can only be paid out once a year. (The annual amount is disclosed in Item 6 in Figures 5.2, 5.3, and 5.4.) Additionally, Figure 5.3 also gives the last capital gain payout date (just above Item 18.) A fund distributes this money near the end of its fiscal year.

During the year, as a fund trades securities in its portfolio, it keeps track of both the realized gains and losses. If the gains exceed the losses during the year, the gains are kept within the fund until the scheduled payment day. Such a fund is said to have an *embedded capital gain*. While this is a benefit to someone who has held the fund for a long period and has enjoyed its appreciation, it can be a decided liability for someone who buys the fund just after a substantial short-term rise in the fund's net asset value *and* just before the scheduled capital gains distribution date. On the distribution date, the new shareholder would see the NAV of the fund drop by the amount of the capital gains distribution (perhaps below what the investor paid for the fund) and would be obligated to pay taxes on the substantial distributed gain after being in the fund for only a short period of time. This situation highlights the importance of planning when to buy a fund.

> **embedded capital gain**
> a capital gain that a mutual fund has realized but cannot distribute until its once-a-year payout date.

A Mutual Fund and Your Taxes: Tax Efficiency The total amount of a fund's distributions is reported to its shareholders on Form 1099-DIV. This form is sent out by the fund shortly after December 31—the end of the tax year. The information on this form must be included in your tax filing. Dividend income and capital gains income are reported separately. As a shareholder, your dividend income and capital gains are taxable in the year you receive them, whether the money is paid out to you or reinvested in the fund.

The distributed capital gains qualify as short-term or long-term depending on the length of time the fund held the securities. Under current tax laws, if the fund holds a security for one year or less, the distributed gain is short term. If the holding period is greater than one year, then the gain paid out to you is long term. Form 1099-DIV clearly specifies which gains are short term and which are long term. (Consult a qualified accountant or tax planner on specific tax rules regarding these distributions.)

Many mutual funds are managed with an eye toward being tax-efficient for their shareholders. As part of the fund's investment strategy, a manager may try to minimize the amount capital gains the fund generates so that its shareholders will not have to pay a huge tax bill at the end of the year. How this is accomplished by a managed mutual fund can be complex and dependent on many factors. However, one of the simple ways a manager seeks to make a fund tax-efficient is to keep portfolio turnover low. The more frequently a manager trades, the more capital gains or losses the fund realizes. By trading less frequently, fewer profits are realized, and less is paid out.

If low portfolio turnover is a way of judging a fund's tax efficiency, index funds and funds that emphasize value investing are exemplars. Index funds are perhaps the best example because they sell securities from the portfolio (thereby realizing a capital gain or loss) only when there are changes in the composition of the index that they track. Large-cap value funds usually employ a buy-and-hold strategy that results in low portfolio turnover.

Tax efficiency is an important issue if you are buying mutual funds in a regular, non-tax-deferred account. In this account you pay taxes each year on the distributions you receive from the fund. If, however, you are buying mutual fund shares in any kind of tax-deferred account, such as your IRA or your company's 401(k) plan, then this is not an issue for you to worry about. You will pay taxes only when you begin to receive money from the plan at your retirement.

Summary

Evaluating a mutual fund for possible investment involves making comparisons.

- Is the fund's performance better or worse than that of the benchmark index over time?
- Does an index fund provide a better return at a lower cost and risk profile?
- Does the fund perform as well as, better than, or worse than its peers?
- How has the fund performed during bull market and bear market cycles compared to other funds in the same category?
- What funds have been performing best: value fund, growth funds, blends, or core funds?
- Are small-cap, mid-cap, or large-cap companies the type of companies in which you want your money to be invested, given the risks of each?
- What is the impact of turnover on the fund's returns?
- Are bond funds currently providing better and more consistent returns than stock funds?

- Are tax-exempt bond funds yielding more than taxable bond funds on a tax-equivalent basis?

- Are there opportunities for better overall investment returns by allocating some of your money for investment in the international markets?

By asking yourself these 10 questions you are making important comparisons among different types of funds, among different investment styles, and among a fund and its representative benchmark index and related indices.

You must always ask these and other questions in order to determine if you've selected the most suitable fund in which to invest. Given the vast number of sources of information about mutual funds, especially online, you could spend weeks or months gathering the information. You don't have to. A fairly complete picture can be formed using just a few good sources: Morningstar Reports, Value Line Surveys, Standard & Poor's Mutual Fund Reports, Barron's, and the fund's prospectus.

- The mutual fund's summary prospectus and statutory prospectus states the specific fund's objectives, details the costs in a fee table, and provides information about the fund's portfolio manager. Every investor should read the prospectus thoroughly. If you want even more detailed information, request a copy of the fund's Statement of Additional Information (SAI).

- Morningstar Reports, Value Line Survey reports, and Standard & Poor's Mutual Fund Reports provide objective, easy-to-use, third-party comprehensive analysis of a fund's performance, investment objectives, fees, turnover, portfolio contents, and an assessment of its portfolio manager.

- Various web sites help you to locate no-load funds, funds with low-expense ratios and high returns, and funds that are "green." Because mutual funds are the primary way that the majority of people invest in the stock market, there are many web sites that provide reliable, objective, and up-to-date information. Find those that work best for you and consult them regularly.

- Mutual Fund Supermarkets and many Web-based mutual fund newsletters publish select lists that help investors to focus on a smaller list of the best-performing funds with impressive long-term track records.

- The *Wall Street Journal* and *Barron's*, especially their web sites, are good sources for pricing, price changes, and news of significant events affecting the mutual fund markets. The *Wall Street Journal* publishes a

"Quarterly Review" that summarizes the return on mutual funds, contains articles covering some important issues, and lists the leaders and laggards by fund group.

Always keep in mind as you evaluate a mutual fund that all of the measures you are analyzing are based on past performance. Remember: Past performance is no guarantee of future returns. When you finally make your choice, you are in essence making an educated guess about what the fund's future performance will be, given its track record as well as that of its portfolio manager (or managers) and the team of analysts.

Chapter

Shareholder Services

Providing clients with services that make investing, record keeping, and preparing tax filing easier has always been an attribute of the mutual fund industry. However, as fund companies have sought to capture a larger percentage of each person's assets and as the number of funds competing for this money has increased, we have all been the beneficiaries of essentially copy-cat or "anything you can do, I can do better" services. This desire to keep you informed about your current investments, to make it easy to invest more money or change the amount of money invested in funds, to provide detailed research and performance data, and to distinguish themselves from other types of invest-ments has kept mutual fund companies working to expand the services they offer. (See Figure 6.1.)

Many of these services as well as in-depth research data are accessible online 24 hours a day. This is both good and bad. Access to this information certainly allows you to track your investments more easily, and to feel that you are more in control of your financial destiny. This is good. However, many people spend far too much time tracking their holdings each day. This obsessive attention to the daily change in your fund's NAV is not good. It causes some people to focus too closely on the day-to-day, short-term volatility of the market and lose sight of their long-term objective.

**Typical Shareholder Services
(in Alphabetical Order)**

Automatic investment

Check writing privileges

Dividend and capital gains reinvestment

Exchange privileges

Information via telephone or Internet

Investment help (sorting by fees, objectives, performance, etc.)

Low minimum investment amounts

Reinstatement privileges

Shareholder reports

Simplified record keeping

Systematic withdrawal plans

Tax-deferred retirement accounts

Web-based screening tools

Wire transfers

FIGURE 6.1   List of typical shareholder services. Not all mutual funds offer all of these. You must read the prospectus to find out which ones are available to you. Funds are continually expanding and improving their online services to include more market data and educational information to help investors make more informed decisions. Asset allocation models and tools to let you sort funds by various criteria are widely available.

The specific shareholder services that a fund offers are described in the prospectus. Not all funds will offer the same services, although competition among funds has resulted in a similarity of services.

Automatic Investing

You can arrange through your mutual fund company or mutual fund supermarket to have the money you want invested in a specific fund automatically deducted from your checking or savings account. The mutual fund provides you with an authorization form that you fill out. With this form, you must usually attach a blank check with "VOID" written across its front. This form authorizes the mutual fund company to automatically debit from your bank account each month an amount that you specify on a date that you set. This is an easy, painless, and flexible way to invest periodically in a fund. Usually with 30 days' notice, you can change the amount of the automatic deduction or stop it.

Each fund sets the minimum amount that it will deduct for its automatic investment plan. The usual amount for retirement accounts and for accounts targeted at beginning investors is $25.

Another method of automatic investing involves a contractual plan with a mutual fund. In this arrangement, you sign a letter promising to invest a fixed amount in the fund over a designated period of time. Usually, you cannot change the amount of the debit during the life of the contract.

Check Writing

Many money market funds and a few bond funds give shareholders the ability to write checks. Most set a minimum amount for which a check can be written—usually $100 or $500. While the amount may be high for most people's purposes, the real problem with using your mutual fund as a checking account is that each check you write forces the fund to redeem some of your shares. Keep in mind that each redemption, especially in a bond fund, is a taxable event. At the end of the year, you may have to pay taxes on interest and/ or capital gains resulting from the redemptions caused by all of the checks you wrote.

Dividend Reinvestment

All funds offer you the option to automatically reinvest your dividend and capital gains distributions in the same fund or in another fund in the same family. (You can also elect to have either or both of them paid out to you as cash.) Most permit investors to reinvest this money at the fund's net asset value (NAV). However, there are some front-end load funds that permit reinvestment of dividends at the NAV, but capital gains are reinvested only at the fund's POP. (This variation is not popular with shareholders.)

If these dividends and capital gains are reinvested in the same fund, it enables shareholders to take advantage of compounding—earning interest on interest. Over the long term, this helps you to accomplish your investment goals faster because you have more shares working for you. If the money can be invested in another fund in the same family, this provides a way for a shareholder to diversify his or her investment holdings.

Exchange Privileges

Many companies group their individual mutual funds into a family of funds—different funds with different investment objectives sometimes managed by the same investment advisory service. Investors in a given fund within a family can usually exchange their shares for an equal dollar amount of another fund within the same family. If a fund has different classes of shares (A shares, B shares,

C shares), an investor can only exchange his or her existing shares for the same classes of shares of another fund within the same family. If you exchange A shares, then no front-end sales charge applies to the new fund shares. You purchase them at their NAV. If you exchange B shares, then the existing holding period applicable to the back-end load of the old shares transfers to the new shares.

This feature gives investors the flexibility to switch their holdings to different funds should their investment objectives or their expectations of the returns from an industry sector or type of investment change. Usually you can switch from one fund to another fund in the same family at the new fund's net asset value with no additional charges. However, some funds do charge a modest transfer fee, sometimes called an exchange fee. The specific terms of an exchange are set by the mutual fund and explained in its prospectus.

Virtually all funds reserve the right to restrict customers' exchange privileges. This is especially true if the fund perceives that a person or a group of people is trading excessively—that is, buying and selling a fund to make short-term gains. In short, they are trying to use a fund to time the market. This type of activity can hurt a fund's performance and is contrary to the long-term investment time horizon of this type of security. Therefore, a fund may charge a stiff fee for an exchange or may refuse to execute the order if (1) the number of exchanges within a period of time exceeds a number set by the fund, or (2) the total dollar value of the transaction is less than the amount set by the fund. In these situations, the fund sets it own restrictions.

It is also important to keep in mind that each exchange is a taxable event. You are literally selling the old fund shares and buying those of the new fund. As a result, exchanges can generate taxable capital gains and losses for the year in which the sale and subsequent purchase occur.

Information Online

Today, you can go online to check the value of your holdings 24 hours a day. [Note: Remember there is no intraday pricing of mutual funds. The value you receive during the trading day is the previous day's NAV.] You can ask a customer service representative or a broker questions, and place an order to buy or sell (i.e., redeem) mutual fund shares. (The order will be executed at the end of that business day when the fund computes its NAV.) You can research the performance history and other details of a mutual fund you are interested in buying. And you can easily compare its history with that of other funds in the same or a different category.

The more information funds have made available to the public, the more questions it has generated. Virtually all web sites include an FAQ (Frequently

Asked Questions) section. Many funds also offer access to a real customer service representative. One of the largest fund companies in America has been actively discouraging certain investors from calling the fund. If you are a small shareholder, you must now send questions over the Internet. Only customers with high account balances (set by the firm) can speak with an actual person over the telephone.

Investment Guidance and Asset Allocation Models

The proliferation of mutual funds has resulted in investors facing a dizzying number of choices. Investors need help differentiating products, investment strategies, and their relative advantages and disadvantages. Help can come from third-party publications such as Morningstar, Value Line, or Standard & Poor's, or directly from the mutual fund companies. While many fund companies provide analyses of only their own funds, some firms furnish both their own analysis and third-party analyses of any funds available through their fund families and fund supermarket.

Further recognizing these investors' need for more in-depth help, funds also offer asset allocation models for investors at different ages, with varying risk tolerances and different objectives. Remember that you do not have to follow these recommended allocations exactly. However, they can be a useful way for you to begin learning about mutual funds and deciding how to best invest and diversify your assets.

Low Initial Investment Amounts

It is relatively easy for small investors to buy shares of mutual funds because many have low initial investment amounts. While a large percentage of funds still require investors to make an initial contribution of $1,000 or more, quite a few have initial deposits of $250 or less. Some are even as low as $25. The specific amount is contained in each fund's prospectus and is disclosed in the mutual fund surveys published by Morningstar, Value Line, and Standard & Poor's. This lower amount, however, comes with some caveats. First, most funds require that the customer sign an agreement giving it the right to withdraw the money to be invested directly from a customer's bank account. Low investment minimums are an important benefit for people who do not have a large amount to invest, but still want to begin investing for their future.

Reinstatement Privileges

If you redeem shares of a fund and shortly thereafter decide you want to reinvest in the same fund, many mutual funds permit you to do so with no additional fees. This is known as the reinstatement privilege. It applies to all or part of the proceeds of the redemption as long as the reinstatement occurs within a period of time set by the fund, usually up to 120 calendar days.

You can repurchase only the same class of shares you originally redeemed. If you reinstate shares that have a front-end load, then you pay no sales charge on the repurchased shares. If you reinstate shares that had a back-end load, then you receive a credit for the amount of the sales charge assessed at the time you redeemed the prior shares.

A reinstatement does not mean that you avoid paying taxes on the sales proceeds from the redemption. The original redemption (that preceded the reinstatement) is a taxable event. Any capital gains made will be subject to taxation. However, if the shares are sold at a loss, the amount of a capital loss that may be deductible will vary. You should consult your broker or accountant for an explanation of current applicable tax laws.

Shareholder Reports and Other Documents

When you buy or sell a mutual fund, the company must send a confirmation to you no later than the next business day. (You will receive it in the mail several days later.) During a month in which there has been activity in the account, the fund must mail a monthly statement to the customer. If there is no activity in the account, the fund is required to send account statements quarterly.

All mutual fund shareholders have the right to vote. Funds are required to send proxies to their customers. Today, a customer can vote in one of three ways:

1. Send in the written proxy with your choices checked off.

2. Vote via the telephone (a toll-free number).

3. Vote via a web site specified on the proxy document.

The second and third choices save mailing expenses for the fund.

Each mutual fund must send semiannual (unaudited) reports to its shareholders. All annual reports must be audited. It is in these reports that the mutual fund discloses the specific securities in its portfolio, information about its board of directors, and detailed financial documents. A Statement of Additional Information—which lists the details about the board and other information—is made available to shareholders online or on request.

Simplified Record Keeping

For record-keeping purposes, a mutual fund investment is treated as an investment in a single security. At year-end, the fund provides a detailed statement of purchases, redemptions, dividends, and capital gains distributions (distinguishing short-term from long-term), as well as all reinvestments. The fund provides a single tax statement (Form 1099-DIV) early in the calendar year so that you can file your tax return accurately and timely. Thus, you are spared the bookkeeping problems that often face investors in individual stocks and bonds—tracking down the dividend or interest distributions and realized capital gains on each different security.

Systematic Withdrawal

Once you have accumulated a certain amount of money in a mutual fund, you can begin making regular withdrawals. This usually happens when you retire. The terms of the withdrawal, including how dividend payments and capital gains distribution will be handled during this period, are detailed in the fund's prospectus. There are four withdrawal plans that a fund can offer investors:

1. *Fixed Dollar.* You specify a fixed-dollar amount you want to receive at each payment period, and the fund regularly liquidates as many shares as necessary to pay the stated amount.

2. *Fixed Shares.* You specify a fixed number of mutual fund shares you want the fund to liquidate at each regular payment period. The proceeds, which will vary with the net asset value at which the shares are redeemed, are paid to you.

3. *Fixed Percentage.* You specify a fixed percentage of your total mutual fund holdings to be liquidated at each payment period. The amount of each payment will vary with the net asset value of the shares at the time they are redeemed.

4. *Fixed Time.* You specify the number of years over which your total holdings in the fund will be liquidated. This withdrawal method may be chosen for a fund set aside to pay for education, under a 529 plan, for example.

If you choose one of the first three withdrawal plans, it is generally recommended that you withdraw no more than 6 percent of your entire holdings in the fund each year. Large withdrawals can reduce your holdings more rapidly than anticipated and result in the total depletion of your investment.

Once you have chosen a particular withdrawal plan, you are not locked into it for life. You can (1) change the time (monthly, quarterly, annually) at which the payments are made; (2) switch from one withdrawal plan to another; (3) increase or decrease the number of shares, dollar amount, percentage, or time period that applies to the plan; or (4) discontinue the withdrawal plan at any time.

Tax-Deferred Retirement Accounts

Virtually all mutual funds allow investors or institutions to establish tax-deferred retirement accounts: Individual Retirement Accounts (IRAs), Simplified Employee Pension Plans (SEPs), Keogh Plans (for self-employed individuals), corporate plans, 401(k) plans, nonprofit plans (403(b) plans), or college savings plans (529 plans). The specific plans that a fund permits are detailed in its prospectus. As a general rule, large fund companies are making more types of tax-deferred accounts available to investors because of the amounts of money they bring in. The minimums for these accounts are usually lower than those for a regular non-tax-deferred account; hence, mutual funds are available to more people as an investment tool for retirement and for paying for their children's education.

Many funds charge an annual service or custodial fee for maintaining your tax-deferred account. Increasingly, you can find funds that wave this charge or have eliminated it completely. Over the years this can add up to a substantial savings in your tax-deferred retirement account. However, the elimination of this fee frequently results in a restriction of certain services. Each fund sets its own restrictions, if any.

Web Sites

Mutual fund investors are continually demanding expanded service from their fund providers. While once satisfied with accessing account information by telephone, investors' expectations have now been raised by the ease and speed of processing transactions and accessing information online. Almost all funds offer round-the-clock access to real-time market updates, account status, electronic transfers, research data, and news.

In an industry as competitive as that of mutual funds, no fund company can afford to offer anything less than state-of-the-art shareholder services. Virtually every mutual fund company and mutual fund supermarket maintains a web site at which shareholders and interested persons can obtain information about the various funds the company offers and learn about mutual funds.

Many sites now contain features that help you sort through a group of funds according to your specific parameters, such as investment objective, performance, and cost.

Sites where mutual fund investors can find compact summaries of a fund's performance, investment style, fees and expenses, shareholder services, and an assessment of the portfolio manager are also maintained by information service companies like Morningstar (www.morningstar.com), Value Line (www.valueline.com), and Standard & Poor's (www.standardandpoors.com/onfunds), as well as by newspapers and magazines that report on and track mutual fund performance. The Investment Company Institute (ICI), a mutual fund industry trade association, maintains a web site (www.ici.org) with general information, statistics about mutual funds, and other investment companies (including ETFs) as well as basic education brochures and resources.

Wire Transfers

When your liquidate your mutual fund holdings, you can have the sales proceeds wired into your checking or savings account for a small service fee, instead of having the fund issue a check. Conversely, you can arrange to have funds wired from your bank account into your mutual fund account.

Seven Wisdoms of Mutual Fund Investing

"Isn't there a simple way to choose a mutual fund? What are the few important guidelines I must keep in mind when making my decision?" These are perhaps the two questions that most frequently emerge from the uncertainty and frustration of selecting a suitable mutual fund in which to invest your money. Given the many investment objectives, investment styles, expenses, fee structures, performance measures, and historical information that should be evaluated before you invest in a fund, the desire for some quick and easy guidelines to making the best choice for you is understandable.

While there are few hard-and-fast rules for making any investment, there are some commonsense *wisdoms* you should always keep in mind. The seven wisdoms or rules of thumb that follow are distilled from questions and concerns that are likely to be expressed by people before and after investing in mutual funds. By applying these rules thoughtfully and with an understanding of their limitations as well as their strengths, you will be able to simplify the process of selecting a mutual fund without oversimplifying it. As Einstein said, "Everything should be made as simple as possible, but no simpler."

1. *Keep your ongoing mutual fund expenses as low as possible.*

Always pay attention to the sales charges and expenses of your mutual funds. This is especially important for beginning investors. Because you probably start by investing small amounts of money, you want as much of it as possible to begin working for you immediately. No-load funds are certainly preferable to load funds. But if you do invest in a load fund, it is wise to select a low-load fund.

While sales charges are taken off the top of your money, it is a fund's ongoing expenses and fees (especially management fees and 12b-1 fees) that must be watched carefully. The same attention should be paid whether you are investing in funds with typically low expenses—such as an index fund—or those with high expenses—such as sector funds, international funds, and foreign funds.

In a bull market, everyone tends to ignore the ongoing expenses because they are such a small percentage of the annual return the fund is producing. If your fund has an expense ratio of 1.5 percent and its gross return for a year is 18 percent, then the expenses represent 8.33 percent [1.5% ÷ 18%] of the fund's return. If, however, the fund's return is only 4 percent, then the 1.5 percent expense ratio is 37.50 percent [1.5% ÷ 4%] of the fund's return.

A mutual fund's ongoing costs are seldom reduced as its NAV declines. They usually stay the same. During a bear market, these costs eat up an even larger percentage of your annual return, and as performance declines further, they erode it at an even faster rate. As the two examples show, if your fund is not delivering double-digit returns, the effect of its expenses becomes more pronounced. Don't let the euphoria of a bull market blind you to a high-maintenance relationship with your mutual fund. You pay these fees for as long as you are with the fund, even though you don't actually write the check. If investors had to pay the fund's annual expenses directly by writing a check, the costs would be more real. Because they are deducted automatically, they are out of sight and, largely, out or mind.

A no-load fund may not assess a front-end sales charge or a contingent deferred sales change, but it does charge ongoing fees to cover the cost of running the fund. The phrases *no-load* and *pure no-load* do not mean completely free of fees. (Surprisingly, the idea that they do is widely held among many investors.) You just may find that the fund's ongoing expenses are sometimes equal to or higher than those of load funds.

The same may be true for funds without a portfolio manager. Just because a mutual fund does not have an active adviser does not mean that the advisory company waives its management fee and administrative fee. It just lowers them.

High ongoing expenses can be particularly detrimental to the returns of bond funds. These funds produce lower returns (usually single-digit) than stock funds. The primary source of the return is the interest payments on the debt held in the fund's portfolio. There is little opportunity for significant capital gains. Choosing a bond fund with low expenses is one of the keys to maximizing the percentage of the total return that ends up in your pocket.

Do not ignore the expense ratio of any fund, especially a sector fund, no-load fund, unmanaged fund (such as an index fund), or bond fund. Just because you are not paying the fees up front does not mean you are not paying them in other ways and for a longer period of time. Sometimes, what appears to be cheap in the beginning is expensive in the long term.

2. *Don't chase short-term performance.*

"Money always seeks the highest return." With this adage echoing somewhere in your mind, you begin to peruse lists of mutual funds and their performance results. Of course, you want to find the fund or funds with the best return. This may lead you—like many investors—to focus on total return over all other considerations. "Where can I earn the most on the money I'm investing?" As you scan through the listings or peruse the results of a fund company's sorting features, your eyes focus on those funds that have produced spectacular one-year returns. As tempting as such returns make the fund appear, you should not base your investment decision on these short-term results.

Mutual funds are long-term investment vehicles. Long term is generally thought of as a period of five years or more. In order to assess whether a mutual fund is a worthy long-term investment, you must look at its past performance over the long term—3 years, 5 years, 10 years. You are looking not only at the fund's total return over this period of time, but also at:

- The consistency of the return.
- How the fund performed relative to its peers.
- How it performed relative to its benchmark index as well as the overall market as measured by the S&P 500 Index or another appropriate index.

You must also examine the annualized returns to see if a few years of spectacular performance mask even more years of mediocre performance. If this later situation is the case, don't buy the fund.

One year's top performance results may be just a flash in the pan, like the brilliant performance of a first-time actor in a play or movie. Of course, occasionally a fund manager starts off hot and continues to do well for years. Such individuals and teams are, however, rare. A proven track record over a number of years, preferably with the same portfolio manager or team in charge, is what you should be looking for. Invest with the long term in mind.

3. *Know the track record of the fund manager.*

Would you put your hard-earned investment dollars in the hands of someone you do not know? That's what tens of thousands of Americans do every year when they invest money for their retirement, a child's education, and other purposes in mutual funds. Few people think to look at the track record of the fund's manager—whether it is an individual or a team. Instead, as the second wisdom points out, almost everyone focuses primarily on total return.

When you buy a managed fund, you are buying that manager's or team's expertise in picking stocks, bonds, and other securities. It is a given that they are all investment professionals, usually with MBAs and other professional affiliations and designations. But how good is he or she at picking securities? What style or type of analysis does he or she employ in evaluating and making the selections?

Always check how long an adviser has managed or been in charge of a particular fund. Look for an investment adviser who has not only managed the fund for a long period of time (e.g., five years or more), but who has been in charge of the fund when it produced its best results. Importantly, you also want to see what return the manager produced during a bear market and compare this return to the overall negative return in the market. Did the manager do better or worse?

Look for a manager who follows a consistent strategy (with some flexibility) and who delivers consistent (and hopefully increasing) returns over a relatively long period of time. It is probably wise to avoid managers whose year-to-year performance records look like a cardiogram of a person developing a heart attack. Unless you can handle this volatility well, what eventually happens with the money you've invested may cause *you* to have a metaphorical heart attack.

You can find the details of the manager's experience disclosed in the prospectus. A more objective, dispassionate assessment of the manager's skills can be found in the mutual fund summary sheets published by Morningstar, Value Line, Standard & Poor's, and other information services. Remember that when you invest in a managed fund, your returns depend on the manager's skill at selecting the right securities. If you are entrusting your money to someone else's skill, it is good common sense to know something about the person.

4. *Make investing as easy as possible and make it a habit.*

Writing that first check to the brokerage firm, bank, or mutual fund company is a difficult step for any person new to (and skeptical about) the investment markets. Deciding to participate in a company's 401(k) program stymies some people because they do not understand the basic product or the differences among the choices presented to them and, perhaps more pervasively, they do not know what questions to ask. Like Miss Scarlett O'Hara, many people end up deciding to "think about it tomorrow." Or they start by investing a token amount and then fail to increase it as their financial situations improve.

The easiest way to invest in a mutual fund is to set up an automatic investment plan with your employer or your mutual fund company. Participate in your employer's 401(k) plan, having the money automatically deducted from your paycheck before taxes. Not only are you painlessly building up money for your retirement, but you also get the additional benefit of lowering the taxes on your wages.

Many people don't invest because they erroneously believe they need to be rich to invest. This is simply not true. Many mutual funds have very low minimum initial investment amounts. A nonretirement account at a mutual fund company can have minimums as low as $100 to open the account. Minimums this low usually require you to sign up to have they money automatically debited from your checking or savings account each month. For retirement accounts, initial minimums can be as low as $25. Again, funds prefer all additional purchases to be made by an automatic debit from your bank account.

Recall the truth in the observation that you can't spend the money if it's taken out of your paycheck or account before you get your hands on it. By setting up an automatic investment plan, you make buying shares of a mutual fund easy, consistent, and painless.

5. *Periodically monitor your mutual fund's performance.*

You don't need to obsessively check your mutual fund holdings every day. But you do need to be responsible. Even when an airplane is on autopilot, the pilot must be in the cockpit. As an investor, you should not ignore your investments as if they too are on autopilot. You need to monitor their performance monthly or quarterly. This will help you:

- Keep track of how your fund is performing.
- Determine whether you should increase or decrease your investment in the fund.
- Decide if it is time to redeem (sell) the fund.

During your periodic reviews, keep the following two questions in mind:

1. What return is your fund providing relative to that of the overall market or other funds with the same investment objectives?
2. And if it is doing worse, what is the reason?

This second question is critical. The reason for the fund's disappointing performance may have nothing to do with the manager's inherent stock picking expertise. The investment style he or she uses—growth, value, momentum core, or a blend—may not be working in current market conditions. The stocks or bonds that are the manager's primary focus—large-cap, mid-cap, small-cap—may not be the securities that are producing the best returns and attracting retail and institutional investors' money. Or, in the case of an international fund, the country or area in which the fund invests may be in the midst of economic or political turmoil and all securities in the area are performing poorly.

The information you ascertain will cause you to examine your options.

- You may decide to suspend all further investments in the fund and let the money that is already invested remain in the fund. The reasons for making this choice can be numerous. However, the usual reason is that the losses are so substantial that selling the remaining shares is simply not worth it or realizing the losses is too painful.

> **averaging down**
>
> purchasing additional shares of a fund as the price declines thereby lowering the average cost of all shares held.

- You may decide to take advantage of the price decline and invest more money in the fund. This is known as *averaging down.* By investing more money you are lowering the average cost of all of the shares you've purchased. If the market subsequently recovers, you own more shares on which to make gains.

- You may decide it's time to sell the shares and realize your losses. You believe that your fund's recovery is either unlikely or so far in the future that you can get a better return sooner in another fund.

Many investors find it hard to sell a fund. Unfortunately, there are no hard-and-fast rules about when to sell. However, consider the following scenario. If "long-term" in the mutual fund world is a period of more than five years, and your fund has had two or three years of disappointing performance, the number of bad years is becoming a significant percentage of the total years considered to be long-term. Perhaps it *is* time. The ultimate choice is, however, yours.

The old idea that you could just invest your money in a fund, do a Sleeping Beauty imitation, and then wake up wonderfully rich is more myth than reality. You must take responsibility not only for your economic well-being, but also for making sure that your investments continue to provide returns that satisfy your needs and objectives. And when a change needs to be made, do it decisively. And don't look back with regret.

6. *Always diversify using asset allocation.*

"Don't put all of your eggs in one basket" and "diversify your investment assets" should probably appear in *The Guinness Book of World Records* as the most frequently repeated phrases of investment advice. It is true that the majority of mutual funds are diversified. It is one of this investment vehicle's primary benefits that make it attractive. You are investing in a large portfolio of stocks, bonds, and other securities from various industries. This breadth should decrease your exposure to financial loss due to a severe price decline of any one stock or business sector.

Mutual funds are usually diversified within a certain group of securities (e.g., large-cap stocks, small-cap, value stocks, growth stocks, municipal bonds, international bonds). You also want to be diversified across various asset classes (stocks, bonds, and cash equivalents), and among the various types of stocks and bonds.

The traditional fixed or robot asset allocation model (using mutual funds) suggests the following combination of funds: 55 percent stock funds, 35 percent bonds funds, and 10 percent money market fund. You then have to decide how much of the money you are putting in stock funds will be allocated to those that focus on large-capitalization stocks (as represented by the S&P 500 index), mid- or small-capitalization stocks, international stocks, or stocks in a particular sector.

The rationale behind this further allocation of money is based on historical performance data. Different groups of stocks and different national economies provide better returns at different times. The economies and stock markets around the world do not move together. In the late 1990s, large-capitalization stocks outpaced all others. In the early 1990s, many of the Asian markets produced double-digit returns. For example, as the economy began gradually coming out of the recession in 2009, the stocks of technology material companies and producers of consumer discretionary goods led the way. Also, stocks in the emerging markets outperformed those in developed markets. To paraphrase the legendary Yankee pitcher Catfish Hunter after a less-than-stellar performance in a World Series game: *The sun don't shine on the same dog all the time.* As the sun—that is, the markets' performance—moves from one group of securities to another, you need to be in a position to reap the profits. Diversification makes this possible.

How much should you allocate to each group of stocks and bonds? Mutual fund companies—such as Vanguard, Fidelity, and Charles Schwab—publish and make available online recommended asset allocation models that you can use as a guideline given your risk tolerance, your time horizon, and your desired returns. Keep in mind that these models are well-researched suggestions only. You can implement them exactly as shown or you can adapt the allocation percentages to suit your specific objectives and needs.

If you are just getting started and do not have enough money to implement an asset allocation model and, perhaps most importantly, have not experienced the volatility of the investment markets, it is best to be a bit conservative when choosing your fund. If you are a bit nervous about the volatility associated with growth and are not old enough to need the income for retirement, then a fund that combines both income and growth objectives might be an appropriate middle-of-the road choice.

A final note of caution: Many investors interpret diversification to mean covering *all* the bases. In trying to construct a diversified portfolio, they invest a little money in far too many funds, holding 10, 12, or more funds covering different groups of securities. This is far too much diversification. By spreading your money so thinly, you diminish your chances of beating the overall stock market. You have, in essence, over-diversified. In fact, investors who do this tend to end up with a combined total return significantly below that represented by the industry's standard benchmark index.

Keep the number of funds in which you invest focused in the areas most appropriate to your long-term investment objectives. Do not try to be an investor in all markets and securities—especially when you don't fully understand them. Owning three broad-based index funds should provide sufficient diversification for most investors, there by avoiding the dublication the comes with over-diversification.

7. *Don't try to time the market.*

Market *timing* is the holy grail of stock market analysts and short-term investors. Too many investors spend lots of time developing theories and formulas they hope will tell them the best time to sell their mutual fund holdings before a substantial market decline, and the optimum time to buy as the market reaches a low point. Studies have repeatedly shown that market timing does not work, especially using mutual funds. Your money is, after all, invested in a portfolio of diversified securities with a long-term investment objective.

timing
attempting to buy or sell a security at the optimum moment in its price movement.

The fund's portfolio manager may use *technical analysis* to attempt to buy or sell individual shares in the portfolio at relatively optimum times. However, it is worthless for you, a mutual fund shareholder, to attempt to use the same analysis to buy and redeem shares of a mutual fund. Not only does the fact that mutual funds' purchase and sales prices are calculated at the close of the trading day undermine your effort, but you are also one step removed from the stock selection process.

technical analysis
research that uses charts of a stock's past price and volume movements to predict its future price movements.

Returning to the second wisdom discussed near the beginning of this chapter, mutual funds are most effectively used to accomplish long-term investment objectives. Rather than attempting to time the market, simply invest regularly and let the effects of dollar-cost averaging (discussed in Chapter 4) work to your advantage.

Several independent publications and services, such as Value Line Mutual Fund Survey (Figure 5.3), Morningstar (Figures 5.2 and 5.4), and Standard & Poor's provide useful and easy-to-understand summary sheets about individual mutual funds. Also, there are a number of useful web sites that provide more detailed analysis and evaluation of specific funds. This makes it easy to implement the commonsense practices inherent in the seven wisdoms discussed in this chapter. Each mutual fund summary sheet discloses the fund's investment objective; reveals the composition and specific contents of the investment portfolio; ranks the fund's performance and risk; lists shareholder services provided by the fund (such as the minimum initial investment amount, automatic investment, systematic withdrawal, telephone exchanges, and so on); gives the name (and sometimes an assessment) of each investment adviser; and provides other important data.

By using this information and keeping in mind the seven wisdoms discussed in this chapter, an interested or beginning investor can more carefully and knowingly select a fund appropriate for his or her investment objectives and risk tolerance, and understand the potential financial rewards of staying the course for the long term.

account executive also known as a broker or registered representative, an individual who is employed by a broker/dealer to handle customer accounts and to advise individuals about investing in securities. This person must be registered with and licensed (Series 7) by the National Association of Securities Dealers or an exchange. If this person is selling mutual funds only, then he or she must have a Series 6 license. Additionally each broker must be licensed in the state in which he or she does business.

actively managed fund a mutual fund that has a portfolio manager who decides which securities should be bought into and sold out of the fund's portfolio. The returns on this fund are strongly affected by the manager's investment style, stock selection method, management fees, and portfolio turnover—i.e., how frequently the manager trades in the portfolio. (*Compare* passively managed fund.)

adjustable rate debt also called a floater, a debt security whose interest rate is periodically—semiannually or annually—to reflect current interest rates, as determined by a formula specified in the bond's or note's covenants.

adjustable rate preferred (ARP) a preferred stock whose dividend amount or percentage is adjusted periodically to reflect interest rate changes. The rate may change monthly, quarterly, or annually. Usually the rate is set to the highest of either a selected T-Bill or T-Bond rate.

ADR commonly used abbreviation for American Depositary Receipt. (*See* American Depositary Receipt.)

ADS commonly used abbreviation of American Depositary Share. (*See* American Depositary Receipt.)

advisory fee synonym for management fee. (*See* management fee.)

aftermarket *See* secondary market.

agency securities also called Federal agency securities, these are debt securities issued securities by government-sponsored enterprises and government-owned enterprises. These enterprises include the Federal National Mortgage Association (FNMA), the Federal Home Loan Mortgage Corporation (FHLMC), Federal

Farm Credit Bank, and Student Loan Marketing Administration (SLMA). Except for Government National Mortgage Association (GNMA) securities, these securities are not direct obligations of the U.S. government.

agent   a registered person or business organization that acts as the intermediary in the purchase or sale of a security and charges a commission for the service. A broker, registered representative, or account executive is an agent. A brokerage firm may be an agent in certain transactions. (*See* account executive.)

American Depositary Receipts (ADRs)   commonly known as ADRs, these are negotiable securities representing ownership of the common or preferred stock of a foreign company that is being held in trust. The company's securities are deposited in a foreign branch of an American bank. Receipts (ADRs) issued in the United States are backed by this deposit. An ADR holder receives all the dividends and participates in the capital appreciation of the foreign company's securities. The number of ADRs issued relative to the number of the company's shares on deposit is usually not on a one-for-one basis. ADRs are perhaps the easiest and most popular way for Americans to invest directly in the securities of foreign companies. Another name for these securities is American Depositary Shares (ADSs).

American Depositary Shares   *See* American Depositary Receipts.

annual report   an abbreviated version of Form 10K which all public companies, including mutual funds, are required by the SEC to print and distribute to their shareholders annually. Contains audited financial statements as well as other information about the funds performance, actual expenses, and the composition of the portfolio. The information contained in the reports is made public so that shareholders and potential investors can use it to evaluate the mutual fund.

annuity   an investment contract, typically issued by an insurance company, into which the purchaser (known as the annuitant) makes a lump-sum payment or scheduled payments for a period of time. At a fixed date in the future, the annuitant begins receiving regular distributions. These payments typically begin at retirement and the annuitant chooses the payout period (e.g., for life or for a fixed period). If the return on the money invested in the annuity is guaranteed by the insurance company at a specific rate, then the contract is known as a fixed annuity. If the return on the money invested varies with the market value of the securities underlying the contract, then it is called a variable annuity. (*See* fixed annuity, variable annuity.)

asked price   also known as the offer price, the price at which an investor can buy shares of stock or a mutual fund. (*Compare* bid price, net asset value (NAV).)

asset   on a balance sheet, any item owned by a company that can be exchanged for cash or has value.

asset allocation   the systematic and thoughtful placement of investment dollars into various classes of investments such as stock funds, bond funds, and money market funds.

asset allocation fund   a mutual fund that (1) allows the manager to shift among the various classes of assets depending on where he or she believes the best investment opportunities are, or (2) maintains a fixed percentage of the mutual funds assets in stocks, bonds, and cash-equivalents.

asset management firm   an investment management firm that is hired by the fund's sponsor to manage a particular mutual fund or group of mutual funds. This firm is not part of the mutual fund group, but is an outside company that has expertise in types of securities or investment analysis the mutual fund company may not. An asset management firm may be the fund's principal invest advisor of subadvisor. An asset management firm may work for more than one mutual fund company.

automatic investment plan   a method of investing in a mutual fund where you arrange with the fund to have money automatically debited from your bank account at regular intervals (e.g., every two weeks, monthly, quarterly) and immediately used to buy shares of a specific fund.

average   a composite measure of the movement of the overall market or of a particular industry. Typically, it consists of a small number of stocks and is usually not weighted. (*Compare* index)

averaging down   a strategy by which an investor lowers the average price paid for each share he or she already owns by purchasing more shares of the mutual fund or individual stock as the price declines.

back-end load   also called a contingent deferred sales charge (CDSC), a fee that is charged when an investor redeems mutual fund shares. Back-end loads can sometime apply to a mutual fund for up to five years, although shorter time period are becoming more common. Typically a back-end load declines over a number of years (usually 1 percent per year), as explained in the prospectus, until it is zero. (*Compare* redemption fee.)

balance sheet   a snapshot of a company's financial position that shows all of its assets, liabilities, and net worth (stockholder's equity). On a balance sheet, the total assets (current, fixed, and intangibles) must equal the total liabilities (current and long-term) plus the net worth.

banker's acceptance   a short-term letter of credit issued by a bank and used to fund international trade.

basis   the yield to maturity on a bond. (*See* yield to maturity.)

basis point   0.01 percent or 1/100th of 1 percent. 1 basis point equals 0.0001. In the mutual fund industry, certain expenses are stated in terms of basis points. For example, some brochures may describe a mutual fund's annual 12b-1 fees as being equal to 25 basis points (0.25 percent) of a fund's total net asset value. If an investor's mutual fund shares have a net asset value of $10,000, then the annual 12b-1 expense would be $25 ($10,000 × 0.0025).

bear market   a period during which the overall prices of securities are declining.

bellweather security   a security that is a leading indicator of the overall movement of the market, a particular classes of assets (such as bonds), or of a specific sector of the market.

beneficial owner   industry term for the investor who actually owns securities held in street name. (*See* street name.)

best ideas fund   a type of focused fund in which the portfolio manager or managers invest in the companies that constitute their best investment ideas. The portfolio's holdings are reviewed periodically and changes are made when the manager comes up with his or her next best idea.

Beta   also called the Beta coefficient, the relative volatility of a particular stock relative to the overall market as measured by the S&P 500 index. If a stock's Beta coefficient is 1, it means that its price rises and falls in direct relationship to the movement of the S&P index. A Beta that is less than 1 indicates that a stock is less volatile than the overall market, while a Beta of greater than 1 indicates that a stock is more volatile. Each mutual fund is given a Beta based on the overall volatility of the securities in the portfolio. The beta changes as the fund manager trades securities in the portfolio. (*See* R-squared.)

bid price   (1) for mutual funds, the Net Asset Value (NAV). This is the price at which an investor can redeem his or her mutual fund shares; (2) for stocks and bonds, the price at which a customer's sell order is executed. (*Compare* asked price.)

Big Board stocks   a popular name for stocks that trade on the NYSE-Euronext.

blue chip stock   a term used to describe securities issued by the well-established, senior, and most consistently profitable American companies. These companies have a history of steady growth and dividend payments. These companies are considered to be relatively safe and conservative, especially when compared to other types of securities. The term *blue chip* was adopted from poker, where a blue chip has the highest value.

Blue-Sky laws   commonly used name for the state laws that govern the securities industry under the Uniform Securities Agent State Law Act. An account executive or registered representative must take the NASD Series 63 examination to be properly registered in the 39 states that have adopted the Act. Additionally any security, including mutual funds, offered for sale in a state must be registered with the appropriate securities agency of that state.

board of directors　(1) for mutual funds, individuals elected by the mutual fund's shareholders who are responsible for overseeing the activities of the mutual fund and the portfolio managers. Its primary responsibility is to make sure the fund is run for the benefit of the shareholders; (2) for corporations, the individuals, elected by the company's common shareholders, responsible for setting the company's management policies, including determining the amount (if any) of the dividend that common shareholders will receive and approving stock splits.

bond　a long-term debt security or IOU issued by a corporation, municipality, or government. The purchaser of a debt security, in effect, loans the issuer money. In return, the issuer agrees to pay interest on the loan, either at a fixed or variable rate, and to repay the bond's principal or face value at maturity. Traditionally in the US, most bonds pay interest semiannually. A zero-coupon bond, however, does not make any periodic interest payments over the life of the security. (*See* zero-coupon bond.)

book entry　term describing securities for which no certificates are issued, such as mutual funds. The names, addresses, and holdings of investors are listed only in the computerized records of the issuer, its registrar, or its transfer agent. (*See* beneficial owner.)

book value　the theoretical value of a company that would remain if all the assets of the company were liquidated at the values carried on the balance sheet and then all liabilities paid off. Intangible assets such as goodwill, patents, and copyrights are excluded from the total assets.

bottom-up security selection strategy　using a method for analyzing individual companies (e.g., quantitative analysis, financial statements analysis, technical analysis), a financial advisor selects those companies whose fundamental indicators show good investment prospects. Then, from among those companies, he or she evaluates and selects those that are expected to perform relatively well during current economic conditions. (*Compare* top-down security selection strategy.)

breadth of the market　the total number of individual stocks listed in a particular market whose price movements are in the same direction as an advance or decline of the overall market.

breakpoint　a reduction of the front-end sales charge for large amounts of money invested in a mutual fund. It is often referred to as a quantity discount on the sales charge. Breakpoints are designed to encourage people to invest more money in the fund and thereby lower the cost of making the investment. (*See* breakpoint schedule.)

breakpoint schedule   a table, published in a fund's prospectus, showing the reduction of the front-end sales charge when stated amounts are invested in the fund. Each front-end load fund creates and publishes its own breakpoint schedule. In many cases, the sales charge declines to 0 percent when an individual invests $1 million or more in the fund.

broker   (1) an account executive; (2) a FINRA-registered financial services firm that acts as an intermediary in a securities transaction. A broker also advises investors about the purchase and sale of securities. The terms broker and agent are synonyms. *Compare* dealer.

bull market   a period during which the overall prices of securities are rising. (*Compare* bear market.)

call protection   a period of time (usually 5 or 10 years) after the issuance of a bond or preferred stock when the issuer cannot call (i.e., retire or buy back) the outstanding security.

callable bond   a bond with a feature (a call covenant) that permits the issuer, at its option, to redeem all or part of the issue before its maturity date. Usually, the bond is called at a price that is a slight premium above its par value.

callable preferred stock   a preferred stock with a feature (a call covenant) that allows the issuer, at its option, to repurchase all or part of the issue at a specified price from the stockholder. Usually, the preferred stock is called at a slight premium over its par value.

capital appreciation   an increase in the market value of a security or the overall market.

capital appreciation fund   a highly speculative mutual fund that seeks to earn money by investing in common shares whose prices are expected to rise. The time horizon of the price rise may be short-term or long-term. The manager trades frequently; hence the portfolio has a high turnover and high transaction costs. The manager may trade on margin, buy options, and may, under certain market conditions, maintain a large percentage of the fund's assets in cash. (*See* turnover.)

capital gain   the profit that results when the proceeds from the sale of a security are higher than price at which the security was purchased. For tax purposes, a capital gain is short term if the security has been held for one year or less, and long term if the security has been held for more than one year. A mutual fund can distribute capital gains only once a year. (*See* realized gain, unrealized gain.)

capital loss   the loss that results when the proceeds from the sale of a security are lower than price at which the security was purchased. For tax purposes, a capital loss is short term if the security has been held for one year or less, and long term if the security has been held for more than one year. (*See* realized capital loss, unrealized capital loss.)

capital market security   a debt obligation with a maturity longer than one year. (*Compare* money market security.)

capitalization   (1) also called market capitalization, the total market value of a company's issued-and-outstanding common shares (*See* market capitalization); (2) for accounting purposes, the value of all sources of long-term capital for a company including common shares, preferred shares, bonds, and other securities.

cash account   a brokerage account in which an investor buys securities and pays for them in full.

cash dividends   part of a company's after-tax earnings, which its Board of Directors decides, usually quarterly, to distribute to the shareholders. Preferred shareholders received their cash dividend payments before common shareholders. (*See* stock dividends.)

cash-equivalents   short-term debt securities that are virtually like cash because of their high liquidity and safety.

CDSC   *See* contingent deferred sales charge.

certificate of deposit (CD)   a short-term debt instrument issued by a bank at par that pays principal and interest at maturity.

cheap stock   *See* penny stock.

closed-end fund   also called a publicly traded fund, a type of management company that creates a portfolio of securities and then issues a fixed or limited number of common shares to the public backed by the portfolio. These shares are not redeemable by the fund. They trade in the secondary markets—exchange and OTC—like stocks, and are purchased through a broker/dealer. The shares' market price may be at, above, or below the shares' net asset value in the underlying portfolio.

closed-end management company   legal name for a closed-end fund. (*See* closed-end fund.)

closed-end mutual fund   a widely misused phrase used in the investment media to describe a closed-end fund whose portfolio is actively managed. However, a closed-end fund and a mutual fund are completely different products and cannot legally exist as the same entity. The phrase is, therefore, an oxymoron.

closed mutual fund   a mutual fund that no longer permits new investors to buy its shares. Investors who already own shares in the fund can continue to buy and redeem shares; however, once they have sold all of their holdings in the fund, they cannot buy more shares. While new retail investors cannot buy the fund, people who are new hires at a company or organization that offers the fund through its pension plan (e.g., a 401(k) plan) can buy shares in a closed fund. Also, closed mutual fund may temporarily reopen, permitting new investors to buy the shares for a short period of time. Some reopen permanently.

commercial paper   unsecured short-term debt issued by a corporation with a maximum maturity of 270 days, although most commercial paper is issued with shorter maturities. Commercial paper is issued at a discount and matures at face value.

commission   the fee charged by a broker or agent for executing an order for a customer. Commissions are added to a security's purchase price or subtracted from a security's sale price. All commissions must be disclosed on a customer's confirmation. (*Compare* sales load.)

common stock   an equity security that gives the owner the right to receive dividends, vote on company issues, and vote for the board of directors of a company. If a company goes bankrupt, common shares are last in line for claims on the company's asset. (*Compare* preferred stock.)

common stock equivalent   a security that can be converted into common stock. Convertible bonds and preferred stocks as well as right and warrants are considered common stock equivalents.

conduit tax treatment   a provision in subchapter M of the IRS code that permits a mutual fund to pay no taxes on the net investment income that it distributes to its shareholders. The income, therefore, flows untaxed through the fund to the shareholders, who are then responsible for reporting the income on their personal tax returns. To qualify for conduit tax treatment, a mutual fund must distribute 90 percent or more of its net investment income to its shareholders. If it complies with this regulation, a mutual fund is described as a regulated mutual fund. (*See* regulated mutual fund.)

confirmation   a notice sent from the broker-dealer to the customer no later than the day after the trade date that discloses the details of the execution of an order, including price, number of shares, settlement date, and commission (if any).

constant-dollar plan   a investment method in which a person maintains a fixed-dollar amount of a portfolio in stocks or stock mutual funds, buying and selling shares at regular intervals to re-establish the fixed dollar amount.

constant-ratio plan   an investment method in which a person establishes a fixed ratio and then invests the appropriate dollar amounts in stocks, bonds, mutual funds, or cash. At regular intervals, securities are bought and sold compensate for price changes over time. The money is then reinvested in the appropriate asset class to restore the ratio.

contingent-deferred sales charge (CDSC)   also called a back-end load, a fee that is charged when an investor redeems mutual fund shares within a relatively short period of time (usually three or five years) after purchasing them. The fee declines the longer the securities are held. The required holding period and the declining CDSC percentages are disclosed in the fund's prospectus. (*Compare* redemption fee.)

contractual plan   a method of purchasing an annuity contract in which the investor agrees to make regular, periodic payments over a contracted period of time, usually 10 to 20 years.

contrarian fund   a mutual fund that seeks to make money by implementing strategies that are the opposite to what most investors believe will happen in the market. If, for example, everyone believes that the market will continue to rise, a contrarian will see this as an indicator that the market is overbought and therefore ready for a price decline.

contrarian indicator   information used to establish the bullish or bearish sentiment of the market to which an investor or strategist responds by taking the opposite position—e.g., if a contrary indicator is bullish, then this is a sign for an investor to sell.

convertible debenture   a bond that the holder can convert into a fixed number of common shares. The conversion ratio and conversion price are set when the bond is issued.

convertible preferred   a preferred stock that the shareholder can convert into a fixed number of common shares. The conversion ratio and conversion price are set when the preferred stock is issued.

core and explore   an asset allocation strategy for investing in a combination of index funds and actively managed funds. Index funds form the core of an investment, thereby providing diversification and performance returns that will track the increase (or decrease) of the overall markets. Actively managed funds in particular sectors or regions constitute the "explore" part of the strategy. You select a fund whose performance is expected to exceed that of the overall markets, providing your portfolio with additional returns that will hopefully exceed that of the overall market.

core investment strategy   a strategy in which the fund manager invests the majority of a fund's money in the securities that make up a specific index, such as the Russell 2000 or the S&P 500, and then uses the remainder of the money to achieve a return above the index by investing in carefully chosen securities that are expected to rise in value.

corporate bond   long-term, secured and unsecured debt security issues by a corporation. Most corporate debt has a maturity of 10 to 30 years. A few companies issued bonds with 100 years to maturity. These corporate bonds are referred to as century bonds.

cost basis   for tax purposes, the original price paid for a security including all sales loads, commissions, and markups. (*Compare* sales proceeds.)

country fund   usually a closed-end fund that invests in the securities of companies located in one country, whose name the fund bears. A mutual fund can also be country fund.

coupon rate   stated as a percentage of the note's or bond's face value, the annual fixed interest rate paid on a bond to the bond holder. Also known as the nominal yield or stated yield, the rate is a fixed percentage of the bond's par value ($1,000).

credit risk   the risk that the issuer of a bond (or preferred stock) may default on interest and principal payments. (*See* investment grade bond.)

current yield   the return that the dividend on a stock or the interest on a bond provides relative to the security's current market price. The formula computing the current yield for a bond, it is the annual interest amount divided by the bond's current market price. For a stock the formula is the annual dividend amount divided by the stock's current market price. The current yield on a stock is more often referred to as the dividend yield.

custodian   (1) for mutual funds, the entity, usually a commercial bank or trust company, whose primary responsibility is safeguarding the fund's assets. A custodian can also act as a paying agent and transfer agent. A custodian can be an outside entity (usually a bank or trust company) or the mutual fund may establish its own custodian, which must be maintained as a independent division. The custodian earns custodial fees; (2) an adult who opens a securities or mutual fund account for the benefit of a minor.

custodian account   opened by only one adult (the custodian) for the benefit of one minor, a fiduciary account in which the named adult makes all of the investment decisions on behalf of the minor. This account is regulated by the Uniform Gifts to Minors Act.

dealer   also called a principal or a market maker, a dealer is a brokerage firm that makes a market in a security by buying shares into and selling them out of its own inventory. A firm acting as a dealer in a transaction is prohibited from earning a commission. It can charge a customer a mark up on a purchase or a mark down on a sale.

debenture   a long-term, unsecured corporate bond backed by the full faith and credit of the issuer.

debt security a bond, note, and other type of security on which the issuer must pay interest security and repay the principal at maturity. (*Compare* equity securities.)

defensive stock the stock of a company that tends to be more stable during periods when the overall stock market or shares in a specific sector declines; yet, investors can still earn a good return when the market is rising.

defined benefit plan a tax-qualified pension plan in which the employer promises to provide each covered person with a pre-set benefit amount upon retirement. The employer works with an actuary to determine the annual contribution that must be made to the plan in order to provide this benefit. The employer must contribute to this plan regardless of the profitability of the company. (*Compare* defined contribution plan)

defined contribution plan A tax-qualified retirement plan in which the employee sets a fixed percentage his or her annual salary that will be deducted each pay period throughout the year and invested in securities, typically stock and/or bond mutual funds, offered by the plan. The employer may or may not match all or part of the employee's contributions. The amount of money the individual will have at retirement depends on the performance of the specific investment selected by the employee. There is no guaranteed rate of return and the money contributed to the plan is at risk. 401(k) and 403(b) plans are types of defined contribution plans. (*Compare* defined benefit plan.)

derivatives a security (e.g., an option, a future, a right, a warrant) whose price is determined by two factors: the market price of the underlying security, as well as the supply of and demand for the derivative security. Derivative securities typically enable an investor to profit from the capital appreciation of the underlying security without ever owning the underlying instrument, and usually at a lower cost per unit.

disciplined fund *See* enhanced index fund.

discount (1) for closed-end funds, the percentage by which the market value of a fund's shares are trading below the shares' net asset value; (2) for fixed income securities, the amount by which the market value of a bond or preferred stock is below the security's par value.

discount rate the interest rate that the Federal Reserve charges member banks for loans. Increases and decreases in the discount rate are tools of monetary policy employed by the Federal Reserve to tighten or loosen the money supply, and therefore raise or lower interest rates respectively.

distribution fee *See* 12b-1 fee.

distributor the entity through which a mutual fund sells its shares to the public. Some funds act as their own distributors. Other funds hire selling groups (i.e., brokerage firms, banks, insurance companies, and other financial service companies) through which they distribute their funds. Mutual fund supermarkets are used by mutual funds to reach the widest possible number of investors.

diversification investing in securities of companies in different industries in order to diminish stock-specific risk—i.e., the risk associated with investing too much money in too few securities. Diversification is an inherent feature of most, but not all mutual funds. (*Compare* stock-specific risk.)

diversified fund a mutual fund that invests 75 percent or more of its assets in a diverse group of securities, with no more than 5 percent of its assets in any one company's securities, and with the fund holding no more than 10 percent of the voting stock of any one company. (*Compare* non-diversified fund.)

dividend (1) also called investment income, the commonly used name for the distribution that a mutual fund makes from monies earned from common stock (dividends) and/or bonds (interest) held in its portfolio. The fund can schedule dividend distributions as frequently as it wishes, although many payout once a year. (*Compare* capital gain) (2) that portion of the company's earnings per share which its Board of Directors (BOD) decides to distribute to the shareholders. Cash dividends are usually declared and paid quarterly. (*See* stock dividend.)

dividend payout ratio the percentage of a company's total earnings per share that are distributed as dividends to shareholders.

dividend reinvestment plan a plan whereby the existing shareholders of a mutual fund or a company's common stock can choose to have their cash dividend payments automatically reinvested in additional shares of the fund's or company's stock. In the mutual fund industry, capital gains distribution can also be invested.

dollar-cost averaging a strategy whereby a person invests the same amount of money at regular intervals in a stock or a mutual fund without regard for the price fluctuations of the security. Over time, this investment strategy usually results in an investor's average cost per share for a security being lower than the stock's average price per share.

Dow Jones Average the oldest measure of the activity and movement of the overall market, which consists of 30 industrial stocks, 20 transportation stocks, and 15 utility stocks. The average for the 30 industrial stocks, called the Dow Jones Industrial Average (DJIA) is the most widely quoted, and narrowest measure, of stock market movement.

downtrend   the downward movement of a stock's price or of the market as measured by an average or index over a period of time.

earnings per share (EPS)   that portion of a company's profit that is allocated to each outstanding common share after interest on debt securities, taxes, and preferred dividends have been paid. A company's Board of Directors (BOD) decides what portion of the EPS is distributed as a dividend.

economy of scale   spreading the cost of creating and making an item over more and more units. The result is a lower cost for each item produced. As a mutual fund grows and the number of shareholders increases, the costs associated with operating the fund are spread over more shareholders, and therefore, the cost of investing for each person should, theoretically, be lower.

Efficient Market Theory   the theory that all information about stocks is available to all participants in the market at the same time and that the expectations created by this information are immediately reflected or incorporated into the stocks' market prices. Therefore, attempting to profit by buying undervalued stocks or selling short overvalued stocks is futile because all stocks afford an equal opportunity of gain or loss. Prudent stock selection should therefore focus on those shares that provide the highest yield and lowest risk.

embedded capital gain   a mutual fund that has already sold securities out of its portfolio to realize a gain but has not made its annual distribution of those capital gains to shareholders. If an investor buys a mutual fund just before the capital gains distribution date, he or she could receive a large distribution after holding the shares for only a brief period of time and have to pay the capital gain taxes on that distribution.

enhanced index fund   an index fund in which the fund manager tries to beat the performance of the benchmark index by at least 0.1 percent but no more than 2 percent. The fund's portfolio of securities will consist of those that constitute the index as well as others, not in the index, but with similar capitalization and investment profiles. The additional securities provide the extra return above the index. This fund is also known as an index-plus fund or a disciplined fund.

EPS   *See* earnings per share.

equity fund   a mutual fund that invests only in common and/or preferred stocks.

equity REIT   a real estate investment trust (REIT) that buys or leases real estate. Shareholders' dividends are paid from the lease or rental income from the properties in the portfolio. They also receive capital gains when a property the REIT owns is sold. (*Compare* mortgage REIT.)

equity security commonly called a stock or a share, a security representing a proportionate ownership of a business and the right to receive dividends. Common and preferred stock are equity securities.

ERISA acronym for Employee's Retirement Income Security Act, the 1974 act that regulates employer-sponsored pension plans. A plan that meets ERISA's guidelines for vesting, non-discrimination, and fiduciary responsibility is consider a tax-qualified plan. (*See* tax-qualified plan).

Eurobond a bond underwritten by an international syndicate and issued outside the country in whose currency the security is denominated. The bond, however, is sold internationally, even within the country of the currency. An example would be Disney, a U.S. corporation, issuing bonds in France denominated in dollars.

Eurodollar U.S. dollars held in banks in European countries. Originally, these dollars were used to facilitate international trade payments. Many European countries issue Eurodollar securities. The dividend or interest payment on these securities will be made using the U.S. dollars on deposit in the European banks.

eurodollar bonds bonds whose principal and interest will be paid in dollars. The bonds can be issued by an American or European corporation. (*See* Eurodollar.)

Euroland fund a mutual fund that invest in countries that have adopted the Euro currency.

ex-dividend date the day on which the net asset value of a mutual fund or the market price of a stock is reduced by the dividend amount. Anyone purchasing the fund or stock on or after this date will not be eligible to receive the dividend. For mutual funds, the ex-dividend date is set by the fund's board of directors. For stocks, FINRA sets the ex-dividend date. (*See* record date.)

ex-SIPC insurance literally excess SIPC insurance, this is insurance coverage beyond that provided by Securities Investor Protection Corporation (SIPC), the non-profit, membership corporation that is funded by member broker-dealers. SIPC insures customer accounts for up to $500,000 (of which no more than $250,000 can be cash) if a brokerage firm goes bankrupt. Any claims beyond the limit are paid using recovered funds. Brokerage firms who wish to provide extra coverage for customer accounts whose assets exceed SIPC limit must do so through private companies, like Lloyds. (*See* SIPC.)

exchange redeeming mutual fund shares and using the proceeds to purchase shares of another fund in the same family.

exchange rate also called the foreign exchange rate, the price at which one country's currency can be converted into another country's currency. Some exchange rates are described as "floating" because they change daily in response to supply and demand forces in the market place. Other exchange rates are "fixed," set by a country's government or central bank.

exchange-traded fund   Commonly referred to as an ETF, a registered investment company product that is similar to (but not exactly the same as) a mutual fund but trades on a stock exchange like common stock. Therefore ETFs can be bought and sold at anytime during the trading day. In contracts, mutual funds, which are not tradable securities, can be purchased or redeemed only at a price determined after the close of the stock exchanges. Many ETFs are index funds and are organized and registered as unit investment trusts (UITs), which is not the same as a mutual fund which is a management company under the Investment Company Act of 1940.

exchange traded products   a category term that includes the various exchange-traded investment company products including exchange-traded funds (ETFs), exchange-traded notes (ETNs), exchange-traded commodity based products (like Gold ETFs), and others.

exempt securities   securities, such as municipal bonds, U.S. government securities, and agency securities that are exempt from certain SEC requirements, such as registration and reporting.

expense guarantee   a guarantee that the costs of servicing and maintaining an annuity will not rise above a certain level. If they do, then the company that issued the annuity (usually an insurance company) agrees to pay the excess.

expense ratio   stated as a percentage of the fund's net assets, the expense ratio is calculated by dividing the fund's total expenses (the costs associated with operating the fund including management fees, custodial fees, and 12b-1 fees) by the funds total net assets. This calculation does not include sales charges, redemption fees, or trading costs. Expense ratios vary according to the type of mutual fund and are generally used to judge how efficiently a mutual fund operates. In theory, as a fund's assets grow, the overall expense ratio should decrease because the costs are being spread over more customers.

Face Amount Certificate   one of the three types of investment companies defined in the Investment Company Act of 1940. The purchaser of this debt instrument agrees to pay a fixed amount either periodically or in a lump sum. In return, the issuer agrees to pay the purchaser the face amount of the certificate at some future date. The face amount is always greater than the investor's total periodic payments. The difference between the amount that the purchaser pays and the face amount of the certificate is the investor's return. Virtually none of these certificates are issued today.

face value A synonym for a bond's principal amount or par value. (*See* par value.)

family of funds a group of mutual funds with different investment objectives or with portfolios made of different securities all created by the same sponsor. Investors can usually buy and sell funds within the same family with little or no additional costs.

Fannie Mae *See* Federal National Mortgage Association.

Federal Home Loan Bank (FHLB) this government-sponsored enterprise issues non-callable, book-entry bonds, and short-term discount notes whose proceeds are used to buy mortgages from savings and loans, and other companies that make mortgage loans.

Federal Home Loan Mortgage Corporation (FHLMC) commonly called "Freddie Mac," a government-sponsored enterprise that issues bonds backed by a pool of single-family residential mortgages that the FHLMC has purchased from lenders. In effect, the FHLMC repackages the mortgages it buys into a mortgage-backed security. This enables it to raise additional money to buy more mortgage loans. Payments from Freddie Mac bonds consist of both interest and principal, the interest portion of which is fully taxable. FHLMC bonds are referred to as participation certificates.

Federal National Mortgage Association (FNMA) the full name for the government-sponsored enterprise that issues bonds and pass-through certificates most commonly referred to as Fannie Maes. FNMA buys federally insured and conventional mortgages from lenders, thereby providing the lenders with more money to make mortgage loans. FNMA then repackages the mortgages it buys into the pools and issues bonds (called pass-through certificates) backed by the pool of mortgages. Payments from FNMA bonds are "pass throughs" of mortgage payments, and therefore include both interest and principal, of which the interest portion is fully taxable.

Federal Reserve Board (FRB) often called the Fed, the governing board of the Federal Reserve system, which sets the policies that affect the money supply and interest rates. Tools of the FRB include changing reserve requirements, changing the discount rate, open market operations (the daily buying and selling of U.S. Government Securities), and changing margin requirements on non-exempt securities under Regulation T.

fiduciary a company, trust or person who holds or invests funds for the best interest of the account owner. Trust, guardian, and custodian accounts are all fiduciary accounts.

FIFO abbreviation for First In, First Out. An accounting method in which inventory is sold in the order in which it was received. (*Compare* LIFO.)

financial adviser   (1) a synonym for portfolio manager, the person who manages the mutual fund portfolio, deciding which securities to buy and sell in the portfolio; (2) an individual or company who, for a fee, provides advice to investors about the advantages or disadvantages of buying and selling specific securities or types of securities.

financial profile   an assessment of an investor's assets, liabilities, investment objectives, and willingness to bear risk.

financial statement   the generic name for the balance sheet, income statement, statement of changes to retained earnings, and flow of funds statement that a public company must file with the SEC and send to investors regularly. (*See* balance sheet, income statement.)

FINRA   Abbreviation for the Financial Industry Regulatory Authority. Formed from the merger to the NYSE-Euronext and NASD regulatory divisions, this organization makes and enforces rules and regulations to govern the participants in the securities industry, monitors the markets for violations, and offers educational materials to the public about investing.

Fitch's rating   *See* rating services.

fixed annuity   an annuity that provides the annuitant with a fixed rate of return over the accumulation period of the contract. Because the insurance company issuing the contract bears all of the investment risk by guaranteeing the rate of return, in most states a fixed annuity is an insurance product, not a security. Upon retirement a fixed annuity pays the annuitant a fixed amount for life or for a fixed period of time. (*See* annuity.)

fixed asset allocation fund   a fund whose manager must maintain a fixed percentage of the portfolio's assets in stocks, bonds, and cash. (*Compare* flexible asset allocation fund.)

fixed UIT   a type of unit investment trust in which a portfolio, usually containing one type of security (bonds), is set up and does not change. Units of the portfolio are sold to the public. There is no management of the portfolio. As the securities mature or are called, the portfolio self-liquidates. The principal and any gains are distributed to the investors, who may choose to invest in another fixed portfolio.

529 Plan   also a called college savings plan or a prepaid college plan, it is a tax-advantaged savings plan that lets parents save or invest money, usually in mutual funds, to help pay for a child's college education. The plan is named after the IRS regulation that created it and is sponsored by states, state agencies, and educational institutions. Account holders pay no taxes on the money withdrawn (including all gains) as long as it is used to pay expenses for college education only.

flex cap fund   a mutual fund in which 75 percent of the fund's assets are not invested in companies whose capitalization do not fit in to a specific classification—i.e., large cap, midcap, small cap, and micro cap.

flexible asset allocation fund   a fund whose manager can change the amounts of the fund's assets invested in stocks, bonds, and cash depending on what he or she believes will be the future movement of the market or a particular group of securities. (*Compare* fixed asset allocation fund.)

flow of funds indicators   statistics that enable an analyst to determine in which markets—money markets, stock, bonds, savings accounts, etc.—individuals and institutions will most likely invest their money during given economic conditions or periods of time.

focused fund   also called a select fund, a focused fund is a mutual fund that invests in small number of stocks, usually 25 stocks or less, although some contain as many as 40 different stocks. It can also invest more than 10 percent of its net assets in any one company. Because of the concentration in a few companies' stocks and the high percentage of its assets it can invest in a single company, select funds are not diversified.

foreign bond   a bond issued in a country that is not the primary domicile of the issuer. The bond is denominated in the countrys currency where it is issued and is sold to that country's citizens.

Form 10K   *See* annual report.

Form 10Q   the form on which a publicly held company must file its quarterly report with the SEC. The financial statements included in a 10Q do not have to be audited.

forward pricing   in the mutual fund industry, the convention by which the net asset value (NAV) of a mutual fund is calculated at the end of each business day after the securities markets close. All purchases and redemptions of a fund take place at that time. The NAV must be reported to the FINRA by 5:30 P.M., after which time it is distributed to the public via various information sources.

401(k) plan   *See* payroll deduction savings plan.

403(b) plan   *See* tax-deferred annuity.

Freddie Mac   *See* Federal Home Loan Mortgage Corporation.

front-end load   a sales charge that is applied when an investor buys a mutual fund share. A front-end load is incorporated into a mutual fund's public offering price.

fund manager   *See* portfolio manager.

fund of funds a mutual fund that invests in the shares of other mutual fund companies. This type of fund usually buys the shares of the best-performing mutual funds. These funds may be in different industries, different countries, or different asset classes. The combination can enable an investor to create a diversified portfolio by purchasing only one fund.

fund of top fund managers similar to the best ideas funds, a mutual fund company creates a mutual fund whose portfolio consists of the securities picks of its top fund managers. (*See* best ideas fund.)

fundamental analysis evaluating a company's balance sheet, income statement, management, marketing strategies, and research and development as a means of predicting the future, long-term price movement of its stock. (*Compare* technical analysis)

GARP acronym for *growth at a reasonable price*, a conservative investment style that looks for reasonably priced stocks with significantly above-average earnings growth, compared to others in the same sector or the overall market.

General Obligation (GO) bond commonly referred to as a GO bond, a municipal debt security that is backed by the full faith, credit, and taxing power of the municipality. For bond issues by cities and towns, the interest and principal on the bond is usually paid out of ad valorem (property) taxes. For GO bonds issued by states, income and sales taxes are usually used to pay off the bonds.

Ginnie Mae *See* Government National Mortgage Association.

global fund also called a world fund a mutual fund or closed-end fund that invests in the securities of corporations located in the United States and abroad.

Government National Mortgage Association (GNMA) an agency of the U.S. government that buys VA- and FHA-insured mortgages from lenders thereby providing them with more money to make loans. GNMA then places the mortgages it has purchased into pools and issues certificates representing an undivided participation in this pool of mortgages. Monthly payments from Ginnie Maes consist of both interest and principal, the interest portion of which is fully taxable. Ginnie Maes are the only agency securities that are a direct obligation of the U.S. Government.

government-sponsored enterprise (GSE) a government-created financial services corporation, like Fannie Mac, Ginnie Mae, and Freddic Mac that makes more credit available to banks and other lenders by buying and packaging their loans.

govies the commonly used name for U.S. Treasury securities.

green fund the commonly used name for a socially responsible fund that focuses on environmental issues, investing in companies whose policies do not damage or pollute the Earth or companies that are proactive in protecting and caring about the environment. (*See* socially responsible fund.)

growth fund a mutual fund whose primary objective is to invest in stocks whose prices are expected to rise. Dividend income is not a consideration. (*Compare* income fund)

growth investing selecting a company in which to invest based on expectations of strong growth in earnings and/or sales.

growth stocks stocks of new, expanding companies whose market values are expected to appreciate rapidly. A company whose equity security is described as a growth stock pays little or no dividends.

hedge establishing a securities position that eliminates or decreases the risk associated with a securities position that an investor already owns.

hedge fund private investment partnerships or limited liability corporations that not only invest in shares and bonds, but can also invest in foreign currencies, precious metals, futures, and derivative securities (e.g., options, swaps). Using leverage, hedge funds also engage in more sophisticated and risky strategies, such as short selling, and risk arbitrage. Investing in hedge funds is appropriate for only high net worth investors, including institutions that can understand and financially withstand the risk.

hedging protecting against or limiting losses on an existing stock position by establishing an opposite position in the same or an equivalent security.

high-yield bond The marketing friendly name for a low quality bond. (*See* junk bond.)

holder of record the person whose name appears as the owner of the security in the company's records as of the record date. (*See* record date.)

HR-10 plan *See* KEOGH plan.

hub-and-spoke a mutual fund which is marketed and sold through different organizations (retail brokerage firm, banks, pension plans) with each having a different arrangement of expenses. The mutual fund serves as the "hub" and each of the various organizations through which it is sold acts as a "spoke."

income fund a stock or bond mutual fund that creates a portfolio made up of securities that pay high, steady dividends or interest. (*Compare* growth fund)

income return the amount of a mutual fund's total return that is being generated by dividends and interest payments. This is an important measure when evaluating equity income funds and bond funds, which offer little opportunity for capital gains. (*See* total return.)

income statement a profit-and-loss statement showing all of the income and expenses of a business for a period of time.

income stocks equity securities that make regular and substantial dividend payments to shareholders, thus providing the investors with current cash. The securities may or may not offer substantial opportunity for long-term capital appreciation, but will rise with the overall market or when income stocks are strongly favored by investors. (*Compare* growth stocks.)

index a composite measure of the movement of the overall market or of a particular industry. Typically, an index consists of a large number of stocks and is usually weighted by other factors, such as capitalization, price, number of shares outstanding, etc.

index fund an unmanaged mutual fund that invests in a group of securities whose performance reflects the performance of a particular stock market index, such as the S&P 500, Russell 2000, or Wilshire 5000. There are stock index funds and bond index funds. An index fund usually has a low expense ratio, especially trading fees. The portfolio only changes when the composition of the index changes.

index-plus fund *See* enhanced index fund.

Individual Retirement Account (IRA) a personal retirement plan that allows individuals with earned income to deposit a specified amount annually based on age. The earnings from investments in an IRA accrue on a tax-deferred basis. As a result of the Tax Reform Act of 1986, the deductibility of the deposit varies with the individual's income. There are substantial penalties for early withdrawal. (*See* Roth IRA)

inflation a rise in the price of goods and services that results when consumer demand increases relative to the supply of goods or services available. In short, there is too much money chasing too few goods; hence, prices rise.

inflation-adjusted total return the total return for a mutual fund that has been lowered to reflect the effects of inflation on the dividends, capital gains, and rise of the NAV.

inflationary risk also called purchasing power risk, the risk that inflation will, over time, erode the value of the money that an investor holds today or will receive in the future.

initial public offering (IPO) commonly referred to as an IPO, the first time that a company issues or sells its stock to the public. (*See* IPO fund.)

insider any officer, director, or partner of a company or any person with material, non-public information that may affect the market price of the security.

interest rate   expressed as a percentage of the principal, the annual rate that is paid over the time that money is borrowed.

interest rate risk   the risk that an increase in interest rates will result in lower bond prices.

international fund   a mutual fund or closed-end fund that only invests in the negotiable securities of companies located outside the United States. (*Compare* global fund.)

investment adviser   *See* portfolio manager.

investment advisory service   SEC-registered company or individual who, for a fee, provides investment advice or money management, usually in specific types of investments.

investment banker   also called an underwriter, a securities firm that assists businesses in raising capital through issuing securities; the term is also used to describe a person who works in investment banking who is involved in advising the company issuing the securities.

investment company   generic name for one of the many companies whose primary business is investing and reinvesting in securities using monies from individuals with the same investment objectives. These companies include mutual funds, closed-end funds, variable annuities, unit trusts, etc.

Investment Company Act of 1940   The federal legislation that defines the types of organizations that qualify as investment companies, requires that investment companies and their securities registered with the SEC, delineates the reporting requirements to shareholders and the SEC, and denotes how certain prices and returns must be calculated and reported to the public and the SEC.

investment dollars   the money in excess of living expenses, savings, insurance, and other essentials that can be invested in securities and can be at risk.

investment grade   the highest quality of fixed income security with the least likelihood of default. It is the first four ratings for long-term debt securities issued by both Moody's, Standard & Poor's, and Fitch.

investment grade bond   any bond rated from AAA to BBB by Standard & Poor's and Fitch, or rated Aaa to Baa by Moody's. These ratings indicate bonds of the highest quality and least risk of default. (*See* default risk.)

investment income   in mutual funds, the distribution of dividend and interest income by the fund. The fund can distribute investment income as frequently as it wishes. For tax purposes, investment income and capital gains must be reported separately. (*Compare* capital gains.)

investment manager   *See* portfolio manager.

investment objective   (1) stated in each fund's prospectus, the method by which a mutual fund hopes to provide a return to its investors; (2) an individual investor's goal or reason for investing in securities.

investment planning   defining an investment objective and establishing the systematic approach and asset allocation plan to achieve it.

investment risk   the risk that a person may make no profit, or lose some or all of the money invested in a security or securities due to an adverse movement of the securities' market value.

IPO   *See* initial public offering.

IRA   *See* Individual Retirement Account.

IRA rollover   a provision in the rules of Individual Retirement Accounts that allows an individual to rollover a distribution from any tax-qualified pension plan into an IRA within 60 days in order to avoid taxation. While an IRA can only be rolled over once a year, there is no limit on the dollar amount that can be rolled over. (*See* Individual Retirement Account.)

joint account with right of survivorship   an account in which each individual owns an undivided interest. (Each person is, technically speaking, a 100 percent owner.) When one party dies, the account is the sole property of the survivor. (*Compare* joint account with tenants in common.)

joint account with tenants in common   an account in which each individual owns a divided interest. When one party dies, his or her interest or percentage of the account becomes part of the person's estate and can be willed to anyone. This portion may also subject to estate taxes. (*Compare* joint account with rights of survivorship.)

junk bond   a low-quality, long-term bond rated BB (by Standard & Poor's and Fitch), Ba (by Moody's), or lower. These bonds are quite speculative, and therefore must pay the investor higher interest rates. Junk bonds are also called high-yield bonds. (*Compare* investment grade bond.)

KEOGH plan   also called an HR-10 plan, a retirement plan for self-employed individuals as well as their employees. Contributions to a KEOGH are fully deductible from a person's gross income. Income from a KEOGH accrues on a tax-deferred basis. There are substantial penalties for early withdrawal.

large cap   a company whose total market capitalization is $5 billion or more. In reality, there is not a hard and fast number to define large cap. For example, Lipper Inc. defines large cap as a company whose capitalization is more than $7.6 billion. (*See* market capitalization.)

legal list securities   a state-approved list of securities that can be purchased by commercial banks, savings and loans, pension plans, and for fiduciary accounts. This list typically consists of conservative, high-grade bonds and preferred stocks.

legislative risk   the risk that new laws, in particular tax laws, will result in the decline in the value of a security. It is virtually impossible to protect municipal bonds against legislative risk.

Letter of Intent (LOI)   in mutual funds, an agreement that permits a mutual fund purchaser, whose investment amount is approaching a breakpoint, to take advantage of the reduced sales charge by agreeing to invest a fixed amount of additional money in a front-end load fund within a fixed amount of time. A letter of intent for a mutual fund can be forward dated for up to 13 months or back dated for up to 90 days. (*See* breakpoint.)

leverage   the purchase (or sale) of a large amount of a security using a large percentage of borrowed money (i.e., credit). Buying stock on margin is an example of a leveraged transaction.

leveraged mutual fund   a mutual fund that resembles an index fund, but can buy options, futures, and other investments that require a low initial deposit. In buying these leveraged instruments, the fund hopes to provide a total return that is far better, usually 1 to 2 times better, than a benchmark index (e.g., S&P 500 index) against which its performance is measured. In a bear market, the funds tend perform worse than the benchmark index because the leverage investments exaggerate the loss.

leveraged short fund   a mutual fund that sells short stocks and uses options and futures to profit from a market decline.

life annuity   an annuity that makes payments to the annuitant for his or her entire life.

LIFO   acronym for Last In, First Out, an accounting practice whereby the most recently acquired inventory is the first to be sold. (*Compare* FIFO.)

limited partnership   more commonly known as a tax shelter, this is a partnership that permits the gains and losses of the business to flow through from the partnership to the investors (known as limited partners) untaxed. The partners include the income and loss on their individual tax returns, and thus, directly participate in the results of the enterprise.

liquidity   the ease with which a security can be bought or sold.

liquidity risk   *See* marketability risk.

listed stock   a company whose stock meets the listing requirements of one of the exchanges and therefore, when the company goes public, begins trading on that market's trading platform. A company must choose an exchange on which its securities will "list" when it issues shares or bonds.

load *See* sales charge.

load fund a mutual fund that charges its purchasers a sales charge when they buy or sell shares of the fund. The load may be a front-end sales charge or a back-end sales charge. (*See* sales charge.)

load-adjusted total return the total return adjusted for any sales charges or redemption fees that the fund would assess a shareholder who bought or sold the fund during the time period for which the return is being calculated. For a fund with front-end sales charges, contingent deferred sales charges, or redemption fees, the load-adjusted total return is a more accurate performance measure than total return. (*See* total return.)

long industry jargon denoting ownership of a security, that includes the right to transfer ownership and to participate in the rise and fall of its market value.

low-load fund a mutual fund whose front-end sales charge is 3 percent or less. (*See* front-end load, sales charge.)

lump-sum purchase investing a large amount of money at one time in a front-end load mutual fund in order to take advantage of a lower sales charge specified in the fund's breakpoint schedule. (*See* breakpoint, breakpoint schedule.)

management company one of the three types of investment companies defined under the Investment Company Act of 1940. This investment company is organized like a corporation or trust and may employ an investment advisor to manage a portfolio of securities against which it issues shares to the public. Depending on how it issues securities to the public, a management is described as either an open-end management company (i.e., a mutual fund) or a closed-end management company (i.e., a publicly traded fund).

management fee for investment companies, a percentage of a fund's total assets that the fund's portfolio manager or investment advisor charges annually for making investment decisions. A small amount of the total annual amount is deducted each day when the fund computes its net asset value. It is typically the largest expense of a mutual fund.

margin account an account in which a customer buys or sells short securities by depositing cash equal to part of the securities' market value. Only "marginable securities," as defined under the Federal Reserve Board's Regulation T, can be purchased or sold short in a margin account.

mark to market industry phrase for the process by which a brokerage firm, custodian bank, or other entity computes the value of the securities in an investor's account or in a portfolio based on the daily closing price.

markdown   the charge that a market maker, principal, or over-the-counter dealer deducts from the bid price when it buys securities into its own inventory from a customer. Markdowns on securities transactions may or may not be revealed to the customer. This depends on the type of security and the market in which it trades. (*Compare* commission.)

market capitalization   the total value of a company's outstanding common stock. This value is computed by multiplying the market value of a company's common stock by the total number of common shares outstanding. (*See* large cap, mid cap, small cap, micro cap.)

market risk   *See* systematic risk.

market value   the price of a security determined by the forces of supply and demand in the market place. The market value of common stock is strongly influenced by the expectations of a company's earnings, revenue, or market share growth; the market value of preferred stocks and bonds are influenced by changes in interest rates.

marketability risk   also known as liquidity risk, the risk that a securities position will be difficult to liquidate.

marketing fee   *See* 12b-1 fee.

markup   the charge that a market maker, principal, or over-the-counter dealer adds to the asked price when it sells a customer a security from it own inventory. Markups on securities transactions may or may not be revealed to the customer. This depends on the type of security and the market in which it trades. (*Compare* commission.)

maturity date   the date on which the borrower must repay the principal or face value on an outstanding debt security.

medium-term bond   a bond maturing in two to five years.

merger   the joining of two companies either under friendly or hostile terms.

micro cap   a company whose market capitalization is less than $500 million. Lipper Inc. defines micro cap as a company whose capitalization is less than $300 million. (*See* market capitalization.)

mid cap   a company whose market capitalization is between $1 and $5 billion. These valuations vary. For example, Lipper Inc. defines mid cap as a company whose capitalization is between $1.5 billion and $7.6 billion. (*See* market capitalization.)

momentum investing   investing in the common stock of a company whose market price is expected to increase rapidly over time. The fund manager ignores value when selecting a stock for the fund's portfolio. Hence, some of the stocks may be overpriced and others may be underpriced; however, the manager believes that as long as interest in the company remains strong and the company's profits, sales, or market shares increase strongly and on target with expectations, then the market price of the share will continue to rise.

money manager *See* portfolio manager.

money market mutual fund an open-end management company that invests in short-term, low-risk debt securities. This fund seeks to maintain a net asset value of $1.00. It buys very liquid, short-term securities that are trading at a slight discount and will mature at face value any time between one and 90 days. There is no sales charge for investing in a money market mutual fund.

money market securities short-term, highly liquid debt securities that mature in one year or less, such as U.S government T-bills, commercial paper, banker's acceptances, and certificates of deposit. (*Compare* capital market securities.)

money purchase plan a retirement savings plan in which an employee of a company deposits money on a pre-tax basis from his or her pay check. The employer may choose to match all, part, or none of the contribution. The money accumulated in the plan is used by the employee to fund his or her retirement. (*Compare* defined contribution plan.)

Moody's Investors Service *See* rating agencies.

mortality guarantee a guarantee that a life annuity will pay the annuitant throughout his or her entire life no matter how long he or she lives.

mortgage bond a corporate bond that is backed by specific real estate the company owns. The bondholder, in effect, has a lien on the company's real estate. (*Compare* mortgage-backed security.)

mortgage REIT a highly leveraged real estate investment trust that makes construction loans to builders and an mortgage loans to buyers of real estate. The REIT profits from the difference between the rate at which it borrows money and the rate it charges on construction and mortgage loans. (*Compare* equity REIT.)

mortgage-backed securities (MBS) the group name for the debt securities issued by the Government National Mortgage Association (GNMA), Federal National Mortgage Association (FNMA), Federal Home Loan Mortgage Corporation (FHLMC), and many financial services companies, like brokerage firms. These securities are backed by the pool of residential or commercial mortgages. (*Compare* mortgage bond.)

multi-class fund   a mutual fund that offers several different classes of mutual fund shares, each with a different fee structure, all backed by the same portfolio of securities.

municipal bond   a debt security issued by a municipality, state, political subdivision, or territory of the United States. Also called a muni, these debt securities can be backed by property taxes, sales, taxes, income taxes, or revenues generated by a specific facility or project. Interest income from most municipal securities is exempt from Federal taxes.

municipal bond insurance companies   companies that insure the timely payment of interest and principal on a municipal bond issue should the issuer default. This "insurance," for which the municipality pays a fee, results in a better credit rating and therefore lower interest costs for the issuer. The most widely known insurers are the Municipal Bond Insurance Agency (MBIA), the American Municipal Bond Assurance Corporation (Ambac), and the Federal Guaranty Insurance Corporation (FGIC).

mutual fund   the commonly used name for an open-end management company that establishes a diversified portfolio of investments and then continually issues new shares and redeems already outstanding shares representing ownership in the portfolio.

mutual fund supermarket   the name given to the department of a financial services firm that offers a select group of mutual funds from many different sponsors. The largest supermarkets—Charles Schwab's OneSource and Fidelity's Funds Network—contain hundreds of different funds each. A nominal transaction fee is usually charged when investors buy or sell shares of any fund in the supermarket. Initially, most of the funds were no-load funds; however, today's supermarkets include load funds. Among the conveniences that a mutual fund supermarket offers investors are a consolidated statement (which includes all transactions in the various funds) and consolidated tax information at year-end (including the cost basis of the investor's holdings as well as all capital gains and dividend distributions).

NASD   abbreviation for the National Association of Securities Dealers, the self-regulatory body of the over-the-counter market, established in 1938 under the Maloney Act amendments to the Securities Exchange Act of 1934.

NASDAQ   acronym for National Association of Securities Dealers Automated Quotation System, a totally computerized trading market that provides brokers, traders, and market makers with current bid and asked quotes and trade execution for securities listed on NASDAQ. The full name of this stock exchange is NASDAQ-OMX.

NASDAQ Composite index the broadest measure of over-the-counter trading, this market capitalization-weighted index that includes a little over 3,000 domestic and international common stocks that trade on the NASDAQ system.

NASDAQ 100 Index A modified market capitalization-weighted index of the 100 largest domestic and international non-financial companies listed on the NASDAQ Stock Market. The companies included are in the following business sectors: technology, computers, software, biotechnology, telecommunications, retail, etc.

negotiable security a security that can be bought or sold, usually without restriction, and whose title can be easily transferred when it is traded. (*Compare* redeemable security.)

net asset value (NAV) the market value of each share of a mutual fund, which is computed by subtracting the fund's liabilities from its total assets and then dividing the remainder by the total number of outstanding shares. A mutual fund calculates its NAV at the end of each trading day.

net investment income the total amount of dividend and interest income earned by a mutual fund minus all of the associated expenses such as brokerage fees. A mutual fund typically distributes at least 97 percent of its net investment income to shareholders in order to avoid being taxed by the IRS. (*See* conduit tax treatment.)

net worth the difference between the total value of a person's assets and possessions (e.g., home, land, savings accounts, investments, etc.) and the person's total indebtedness (e.g., mortgage, credit cards, school loans, etc.).

new issue Any security being offered and sold to the public in the primary market. The issuance of the security may be an initial public offering (IPO) or the reissuing of treasury stock, called a secondary offering. (*See* treasury stock.)

no-load fund a mutual fund (i.e., open-end management company) that has no front-end sales charge and no back-end load. A no-load fund can, however, have 12b-1 fees. Under current legislation, a mutual fund with 12b-1 fees can call itself "no-load" if these fees do not exceed 0.25 percent. (*See* pure no-load fund.)

nondiversified fund a mutual fund whose concentration of investments does not meet the definition of a diversified fund. Typically this means that more than 5 percent of its net assets are invested in the securities of a single company. (*Compare* diversified fund.)

non-tax-qualified plan a pension or retirement plan in which the contributions are not deductible against the contributor's taxable income. In effect, the contribution is made with after-tax dollars. All earnings on the contributions are still tax-deferred; however, when distributions begin, only the tax-deferred earnings build-up is taxed. (*Compare* tax-qualified plan.)

note   a short-term debt security with a maturity greater than one year. The term is commonly used to refer to U.S. government securities with a maturity of 2 to 10 years.

NYSE Composite index   a weighted index that includes all of the common issues that trade on the NYSE-Euronext.

offer price   synonym for asked price. The price at which an investor's order to buy a securities is executed. (*Compare* bid price and net asset value.)

offshore fund   a managed mutual fund that is domiciled outside the United States. It may have a management company located within the United States, but the fund itself is available only to non-residents calling from outside the country. Offshore mutual fund transactions cannot occur while a customer is on U.S. soil. It must be verified that a customer is calling from outside the United States before discussing offshore funds or taking an order on the telephone.

open-end fund   *See* mutual fund.

open-end management company   legal name for a mutual fund under the Investment Company Act of 1940. (*See* mutual fund.)

option   a contract that gives the holder the right to buy or sell securities at a specified price (the strike or exercise price) for a specified period of time. The writer of the option contract is obligated to sell or buy when the holder exercises the contract. The two types of options are call options and put options. There are option contracts on stocks, debt securities, foreign currencies, commodities, and stock indexes.

OTC   common abbreviation for the over-the-counter market.

over-the-counter (OTC) market   a decentralized, negotiated market in which many dealers in diverse locations execute trades for customers over an electronic trading system or telephone lines. In many cases the dealer is buying securities into and selling them out of its own inventory.

overbought market   usually interpreted as an indicator of a future price decline, a technical term used to describe a stock (or the overall market) whose value has risen quickly and unexpectedly, far above its actual worth. (*Compare* oversold market.)

oversold market   usually interpreted as an indication of an impending price rise, a technical term to describe a stock (or the overall market) whose value has fallen quickly and sharply, far below its actual worth. (*Compare* overbought market.)

P/E ratio   *See* price-earnings ratio.

par   *See* par value.

par value   (1) for common stock, an arbitrary (and essentially meaningless) value assigned the shares at the time it is issued; (2) for preferred stock, a share's fixed value ($100, $50, or $25) upon which dividend payments are based; (3) for a bond, the fixed value (usually $1,000) upon which interest payments are based. Par value, face value, and principal are synonyms when applied to bonds.

participating UIT   a unit investment trust that usually invests in the shares of mutual funds, although it can also buy shares of publicly traded companies. The return from a participating UIT varies with the performance of the securities held in trust.

passively managed fund   a mutual fund that does not have a portfolio manager. An index fund is an example of this type of fund. The securities in the fund's portfolio only change when the components of the index—e. g., the S&P 500—change. There is, therefore, little or no trading in the fund portfolio. Such a fund typically has very low costs and expenses. (*Compare* actively managed fund.)

pass-through certificate   a debt security whose periodic payments consist of both interest and the repayment of principal. GNMA, FNMA, and FHLMC all issue forms of pass-through certificates that as a group are called mortgage backed securities. Additionally, many investment banks and other financial institutions create "private label" MBS.

payable date   (1) the date on which a cash or stock dividend will be paid on common stock; (2) the preset dates on which a mutual fund pay its investment income (dividends and interest and its capital gains to shareholders).

paying agent   also called a disbursing agent, usually a commercial bank or trust company that receives funds from the issuer of a security and is then responsible for distributing dividends, interest payments, and capital gains to mutual fund shareholders.

payroll deduction savings plan   more commonly called a 401(k) plan, a pension plan to which an employee contributes a percentage of his or her salary via payroll deduction These contributions are made with before-tax dollars. In some cases, the employer will match each employee's contribution to the plan up to a certain percentage. A 401(k) plan with this feature is sometimes called a matching plan.

penny stock   any non-exchange-listed stock with a value of less than $5. These are usually low-priced, extremely speculative OTC stock issued by a small, start-up company with no earnings history. These securities are very risky and specific customer authorization is required for the broker to be able to purchase them.

Pink Sheets   Originally named for the color of the paper on which the stock price information was printed and distributed daily, the Pink Sheets is now an electronic price display system run by the Pink OTC Markets. Each market maker displays a two-sided price quote—i.e., a bid price and an offer price—at which to buy or sell an amount of the stock. The quotes are now widely referred to as the Pink Quotes. The companies whose stocks prices are quoted in this market are thinly traded, closely held, or bankrupt. Many are low-priced stocks and foreign issues.

plan completion insurance   normally refers to the waiver of premium provision, it states if a customer is unable to make the payments to a variable annuity contract due to disability (or death in a few cases), then the company providing the insurance will waive the premium during the disability period or complete the contractual agreement.

point   1) for common and preferred stock, the price movement on an individual stock equal to one dollar. 2) for bonds, the price movement equal to ten dollars.

POP   *See* public offering price.

portfolio   a group of stocks, bonds, or other securities that are being held for investment.

portfolio manager   the individual or team of people responsible for researching and selecting the securities to buy into and sell out of a mutual fund portfolio. For providing this service, a portfolio manager earns an annual management fee that is a fixed percentage of the fund's assets. A portfolio manager is also called an investment advisor, money manager, and investment manager. (*See* management fee.)

portfolio transaction fees   *See* turnover costs.

preferred stock   a security that is senior to common stock. It pays a fixed dividend and usually has no voting or preemptive rights. It has preference over common shares both in dividend distributions and in claims on a company's assets in a liquidation.

premium   (1) for closed-end funds, the percentage by which the market value of a fund's shares are trading above the shares net asset value; (2) the amount by which the market value of a bond or preferred stock exceeds its par value; (3) the market price of a call option or a put option.

prepayment risk   Associated with mortgage-backed securities (FNMA, GNMA, FHLMC), this is the risk that the agency that issued the debt security will repay the principal earlier than expected—in effect, retiring the debt before its maturity. This would occur if the mortgage holder sells the property or refinances an outstanding loan at lower interest rate.

price   in technical terms, this is the point at which supply (sellers) and demand (buyers) converge and a trade occurs. In reality, most securities have two prices: the bid price and the offer price. An investor's purchase order is executed at a security's offer price and a customer's sell order is executed at a security's bid price.

price-earnings (P/E) ratio   a ratio in which a stock's current market price is divided by its annual earnings per share. It measures the number of times that a stock's price exceeds its earnings—in short, how expensive the stock is relative to its earnings.

price-to-book value (P/B) ratio   used to compare the market value of a company to the value of its net assets at the worth they are assigned on the company's balance sheet.

primary issue   another name for an IPO or a new issue security.

primary offering   the issuance of new securities by a company to the public.

principal   (1) par value or face value on a bond ($1,000) or perferred stock ($25, $50 or $100); (2) a synonym for a market maker or dealer (i.e., a brokerage firm that buys securities into and sells securities out of its own inventory). A firm acting as a principal in a transaction is permitted to make either a markup or a markdown, but not a commission. (*See* par value.)

profit-sharing pension plan   a pension plan to which an employer makes contributions for each employee only when the company has profits. If the company is not profitable, then there are no mandatory contributions.

proprietary fund   a management company's or brokerage firm's own mutual funds that it creates and markets itself.

prospectus   legally known as Form N-1A, a printed summary of the SEC-filed registration statement that discloses the details of a particular offering of securities, including the mutual fund's or company's business history and that of its management, its past and expected future performance, and audited financial statements. The prospectus must contain enough material information for the investor to judge the merits of investing in the fund or company. Since 1998, mutual funds will be written in more easy-to-read, user-friendly language. And since 2009, all prospectuses must contain a summary prospectus at the beginning of the full statutory prospectus. (*See* registration statement, statutory prospectus and summary prospectus.)

proxy   a form on which an investor votes in absentia or transfers his or her voting authority to another party. Today, shareholders can vote via the internet or phone.

Prudent Man rule   a standard by which fiduciaries are expected to handle accounts over which they have control. Specifically, the law states that the fiduciary is expected to handle the account and make investment decisions the way any prudent, intelligent person would, with emphasis on preservation of capital, reasonable rate of return, and low risk.

public offering price (POP)   (1) for mutual funds, the price at which an investor purchases a mutual fund share, which may include a front-end sales charge; (2) for stocks and bonds, the price at which new shares are sold to the public by their issuers or underwriters. Bonds and preferred stock are usually issued at par value.

publicly traded fund   *See* closed-end management company.

purchasing power risk   *See* inflationary risk.

pure no-load fund   under current legislation, a mutual fund with no front-end load, no back-end load, and no 12-b-1 fees. (*Compare* no-load fund.)

R-squared   measures how well a fund's price movement corresponds to its benchmark index—i.e., how accurate the beta is. R-squared is expressed as a percentage from 0 to 100. An R-squared of 100 means the fund's price changes are explained completely by price changes in its benchmark index. A high R-squared value would indicate that the beta was very reliable. A low R-squared value means the fund behaves quite differently from its benchmark index. The beta would, therefore, be meaningful. Sector funds tend to have lower R-squared values when compared to a diversified index such as the S&P 500. Bond funds could even have an R-squared of 0 when compared to the same index. (*See* Beta.)

rating services   independent companies that rate the risk of default and the quality of the cash flow or assets backing fixed income issues—bonds, preferred stocks, and commercial paper. The three rating agencies include Moody's Investors Service, Standard & Poor's, and Fitch.

real estate investment trust (REIT)   a corporation or trust with a structure similar to a closed-end fund that, instead of investing in securities, invests directly in real estate (called an equity REIT) or in mortgages (called a mortgage REIT). A REIT issues shares to the public backed by the portfolio of real estate and/or mortgages and those shares trade on an exchange like any common stock. The rents on the real estate and interest earned on the mortgages are paid through the REIT as untaxed dividends to shareholders who must include the income on their IRS filings. (*See* closed-end fund.)

realized gain   the cash profit resulting from the liquidation of a security position.

record date   (1) for mutual funds, the deadline date set by a mutual fund's board of directors on which an investor must be recorded as an owner of the shares in order to be eligible to receive a dividend and/or annual capital gain distributions; (2) for publicly traded companies, the deadline date set by a company's board of directors on which an investor must be recorded as an owner of the stock in order to be eligible to receive a dividend payment or stock distribution.

redeemable security a security that can only be bought from and sold back to the issuer. Mutual funds, unit investment trusts, as well as Series EE, Series HH, and Series I saving bonds are redeemable securities. (*Compare* tradable security.)

redemption (1) the sale of a mutual fund share back to the fund or one of its authorized agents; (2) the repayment of the principal or face value of a debt security or preferred stock by the issuer to the holder of the security. Redemption occurs on a security's maturity date or when a security is called.

redemption fee a flat fee that some mutual funds charge investors at any time they redeem part or all of an investor's shares. (*Compare* contingent deferred sales charge.)

regional fund a mutual fund or closed-end fund that invests in the negotiable securities of companies located in a specific geographical area.

registered representative *See* account executive.

registered securities (1) securities that are registered and held in a customer's name at a brokerage firm; (2) securities that are registered with the SEC.

registrar usually a commercial bank or trust company that is responsible for maintaining an accurate list of the names and addresses of a mutual fund's or company's shareholders. The registrar is also responsible for insuring that the transfer agent does not issue too many or too few shares as changes of ownership occur.

registration statement the disclosure document that all companies planning to offer securities to the public in the U.S. are required to file with the SEC under the Securities Act of 1933. The registration statement must be filed before the securities can be issued and it must contain full and fair disclosure of the company's business history, financial status, management, business risks, and planned use for the proceeds from the sale of the new securities. (*See* prospectus.)

Regular Way settlement defined as three business days after the trade date, this is the day on which the brokerage firm or mutual fund company must receive payment for securities that it has bought for a customer, or must pay the customer for securities that have been sold.

regulated mutual fund under subchapter M of the IRS code, a mutual fund that distributes 90 percent or more of its net investment income. By complying with this regulation, a mutual fund does not pay taxes on the net investment income that it distributes to shareholders. The distribution of dividends and capital gains flows from the fund to each shareholder untaxed. The mutual fund then pays taxes only on the remaining net investment income. If a fund distributed less than 90 percent, then the fund would have to pay taxes on all of its net investment income, not just the remainder. (*See* conduit tax treatment.)

Regulation T   the Federal Reserve's regulation that gives it the power to set the initial margin requirement on most non-exempt corporate securities, and thereby govern the amount of credit that brokerage firms can extend to their customers. Currently Reg T is 50 percent.

reinvestment risk   the risk that the dividends, interest, and capital gains received from investments can only be reinvested at a lower rate of return than that earned from the previous investments. (*See* inflationary risk.)

REIT   *See* real estate investment trust.

right of accumulation   a reduction in a mutual fund's front-end sales charge on all subsequent purchases when the value of an investor's shares or the amount of the money invested in a fund reaches a specified dollar amount in the fund's breakpoint schedule. (*See* breakpoint.)

risk-adjusted total return   *See* total return.

risk premium   the extra percentage of return that a fund earns for the risk it assumes. A mutual fund's performance is expressed as the total return in excess of a risk-free investment (usually T-bills). If a fund earned 10 percent during the same period that T-bills earned 3 percent, then 7 percent of the fund's returns (10 − 3 percent) would be attributable to the risk of the fund. This 7 percent is referred to as the risk premium.

Roth IRA   Named after Senator William Roth who sponsored the legislation, an Individual Retirement Account (IRA) in which the contributions to the account are not deductable from earned income. In short the contributions are made with after-tax dollars, not pre-tax dollars as in a traditional IRA. Unlike a traditional IRA, one can continue to contribute to a Roth IRA beyond age $70\frac{1}{2}$ and, upon retirement, withdrawals are usually (but not always) subject to no taxation. (*Compare* Individual Retirement Account.)

sales charge   the percentage of the public offering price that many mutual funds charge when an investor buys their shares. While this percentage is usually deducted up front (a front-end sales charge), it can be deducted when an investor redeems the shares of a mutual fund (a back-end sales charge). By law, the maximum sales charge on a mutual fund is 8.5 percent of the public offering price, no matter how it is charged. Mutual funds with sales charges are known as load funds. Those without these charges are called no-load funds. (*See* low-load fund, no-load fund, pure no-load fund.)

sales load   *See* sales charge.

sales proceeds   for purposes of computing a capital gain, the price at which a security is sold minus any commission or markdown charged. (*Compare* cost basis.)

SEC   abbreviation for the Securities and Exchange Commission, the primary regulatory authority of the U.S. securities industry (created in 1934), responsible for interpreting, supervising, and enforcing compliance with the provisions of the various securities acts.

SEC Yield   the total return of a mutual fund calculated using an SEC-mandated, standardized formula.

secondary market   also called the aftermarket market, a collective term for the markets—exchange and OTC—in which stocks trade after they are issued to the public. Proceeds from transactions in this market go to the investor. There is no secondary trading market for mutual fund shares. All fund shares are bought from and then sold back (redeemed) to the sponsor or its agents. (*Compare* primary market.)

sector fund   a mutual fund that invests in one industry or segment of an industry. Because this type of fund is often not diversified, it has higher levels of unsystematic risk. (*See* systematic risk, unsystematic risk.)

Securities and Exchange Commission   *See* SEC

Securities Investor Protections Corporation   *See* SIPC.

select fund   *See* focused funds.

selling group   a group of companies registered as brokers/dealers, which is responsible for offering and selling mutual fund shares to the public. This is part of a mutual fund distribution system. Selling groups act as agents in the sale of mutual fund shares.

selling short   a strategy used by investors to profit from an anticipated price decline. An investor instructs the brokerage firm to borrow the securities on his or her behalf and then sell them in the market. The customer eventually will have to buy back the securities (and replace them to the lender). If the price has gone down, the customer profits. If the price has risen above the short sale price, then the customer has lost. Selling short is a highly speculative strategy subject to unlimited loss. Many mutual fund managers are prohibited from selling short securities in the fund's portfolio.

sentiment indicators   statistics used to measure the bullish or bearish mood of the market and its investors. These are usually considered to be contrary indicators.

SEP-IRA   *See* Simplified Employee Pension plan.

SEP   *See* Simplified Employee Pension plan.

separate account   the account in which variable annuity investors' monies are invested in a portfolio of securities. It is called a separate account because its assets are kept separate from the insurance company's other investments and assets.

service fee   ongoing compensation for the broker or financial professional who advises customer to invest in a mutual fund. The maximum annual service fee that a mutual fund can charge is 0.25 percent of the fund's total net asset value. The service fee, which is one of the two types of 12b-1 fees is an ongoing charge. (*See* 12b-1 fee.)

settlement date   the date on which the orderly exchange of monies and securities occurs following a purchase or sale. (*See* Regular Way settlement.)

Sharpe ratio   measures a fund's performance relative to the risk associated with the fund.

short sale   *See* selling short.

Simplified Employee Pension (SEP) plan   designed especially for small businesses, a pension plan in which the employer opens an IRA for each employee (including the owner of the business) and makes contributions on his or her behalf. The contribution limits are higher than those for a regular IRA. If the employer contributes less than the maximum allowed under a regular IRA, then the employee can make up the difference. A SEP requires less administration and filing requirements than a regular corporate pension plan.

SIPC   acronym for Securities Investor Protection Corporation, a non-profit, membership corporation created in 1970 that provides limited insurance protection for the customers of broker-dealers that go bankrupt. Each customer's account is covered for up to $500,000 of securities, of which no more than $250,000 can be cash. All registered broker-dealers must be members of SIPC and the member firms are assessed fees that fund SIPC. (*See* ex-SIPC insurance.)

small cap   a company whose total market capitalization is between $500 million and $1 billion. Lipper Inc. defines small cap as a company whose capitalization is between $300 million and $1.5 billion. (*See* market capitalization.)

socially responsible fund   a mutual fund that invests in companies that adhere to humane, health-conscious, environmentally sensitive policies or business practices. This fund avoids companies that do business in countries whose governments are repressive and violate human rights. (*See* green fund.).

soft dollars   a term that describes the practice in the securities industry whereby a brokerage firm that executes trades for institution (e.g., mutual fund, pension fund) charges that institution a commission that is slightly higher than usual. The fee includes the cost of providing research as well as other information and services to the institution.

sovereign debt   long-term bonds and notes issued by a foreign government.

special situation fund   a mutual fund that invests in companies that are candidates for takeover or those that are emerging from bankruptcy.

sponsor   the corporation or trust that creates a mutual fund or a family of mutual funds. Fidelity, for example, is one of the largest mutual fund sponsor in the United States.

sponsored ADR   an American Depositary Receipt in which the foreign company is directly involved—i.e., sponsors—in depositing its shares with a bank that acts as trustee, registering the securities with the SEC, and issuing its receipts to investors in the United States. Each receipt represents an undividend interest in the shares held in trust. Increasingly, sponsored ADRs are called American Depositary Shares (ADS).

Standard & Poor's Corporation   *See* rating agencies.

Standard & Poor's 500 index (S&P 500)   a capitalization-weighted index that includes 500 common stocks that trade on the NYSE-Euronext and NASDAQ OMX. It is a benchmark for mutual fund performance as well as the strength or weakness of the U.S. economy.

statement   a summary of all transactions in an investor's account, as well as the current value of all long and short positions being held in the account. Statements are sent monthly for active accounts; quarterly for inactive accounts.

Statement of Additional Information (SAI)   an addendum to a mutual fund's prospectus that includes more detailed information such as the fund's audited financial statements, the calculation methods used for computing the fund's results, the investment advisor's contract and fees, the fund's investment approach, etc. The SAI is available to investors upon request for free.

statutory prospectus   this is the legal name for the full prospectus that all mutual funds must file with the SEC and make available to customers. When buying a mutual fund, a customer can receive a summary prospectus instead of the statutory prospectus. (*See* summary prospectus.)

stock   a negotiable security representing ownership of a company and entitling its owner to the right to receive dividends. (*See* equity security.)

stock dividend   the issuance of additional shares of stock, instead of cash, as a dividend to shareholders. A stock dividend increases the number of shares outstanding and therefore dilutes a company's earnings per share. (*See* dividend.)

stock exchange   a trading market in which exchange participants execute buy and sell orders for individual and institutional customers in a central location or through an SEC-registered computerized trading platform.

stock-specific risk   commonly referred to as "putting too many eggs in one basket," the risk associated with investing too much money in a single security. Diversification protects against this type of risk. (*Compare* systematic risk.)

street name   industry phrase describing securities owned by an investor, but registered in the name of the brokerage firm. In the records of the depository where the securities are safeguarded, the brokerage firm is listed as the "owner of record." However in the brokerage firm records, the customer is listed as the "beneficial owner" of the securities. It is standard industry practice for all securities left at a brokerage firm to be held in the street name at a registered depository facility. (*See* beneficial owner.)

STRIPS   commonly used acronym for Separate Trading of Registered Interest and Principal of Securities, the U.S government's version of a zero-coupon bond. (*See* zero-coupon bond.)

suitability   the appropriateness of a particular investment for a customer given his or her investment profile, investment objectives, financial means, and other information disclosed on the new account form.

summary prospectus   a section at the front of each statutory prospectus in which the important information about the specific fund is presented in plain English in a standardized format, so that individuals can more easily assess and compare the information. This must be in paper form and can be used to meet the industry's prospectus delivery requirement, as long as the statutory prospectus and other key disclosure items like the Statement of Additional Information (SAI) are available on the Internet or, upon request, in printed form. (*See* statutory prospectus.)

systematic investment plan   a service that permits shareholders to have money automatically debited from their bank accounts and invested in mutual fund shares. Automatic debits may be made quarterly or monthly. Minimum debit amount will vary from fund to fund.

systematic risk   also called market risk, the risk that a decline in the overall market will adversely affect the total market value of a portfolio of securities. Diversification does not protect against this type of risk. (*Compare* stock-specific risk.)

T-Bill   *See* Treasury Bill.

target bond fund   a bond fund that invests solely in zero-coupon bonds. In managing the portfolio, the investment advisor: (1) buys and hold bonds that have been bought at a very low price and therefore have an above market yield, or (2) trades large amounts of zeros as their market prices fluctuate in response to interest rate changes, and thereby realizes the capital gains.

target-date fund originally called a life-cycle fund, an asset allocation fund that adjusts the mix of securities in the portfolio, becoming more conservative and emphasizing preservation of capital, as the fund moves toward a specified year that is usually part of the name of the fund. These funds are designed as a one-size-fits-all retirement planning fund for people who don't want to take the time to personally manage their retirement investment portfolios. They have become a widely offered choice in 401(k) plans.

taxable bond fund a bond mutual fund whose interest income is subject to federal taxes. Bond funds included under this general category are corporate bond funds, government bond funds, and international or world bond funds. (*Compare* tax-exempt bond fund.)

tax-deferred the tax-free build up of interest, dividends, and capital gains in a retirement account. These earnings are subject to taxation only when distributed or withdrawn from the account at some later (deferred) date.

tax-deferred annuity usually called a 403(b) plan, a pension plan specifically for certain tax-exempt, non-profit organizations—e.g., schools, municipalities, hospitals, etc.—to which an employee contributes to a tax-deferred annuity via payroll deduction. The amount is contributed is always made with pre-tax dollars and is therefore a salary reduction for the employee.

tax-efficient mutual fund a mutual fund that, as a part of its investment strategy, tries to minimize the amount of capital gains it generates so that its shareholders do not have to pay taxes on the gains. Most funds try to achieve tax efficiency by keeping portfolio turnover low; hence, index funds are among the most tax efficient. A fund that is not tax efficient generates and pays to shareholders huge capital gains. The taxes that investors must pay on these gains reduce the fund's total return.

tax-exempt bond fund a bond mutual fund whose interest income is not subject to federal taxes. The interest income may, however, be subject to state or local taxes. The term is synonymous with a municipal bond fund. (*Compare* taxable bond fund.)

tax-exempt security a term frequently used to describe a municipal bond whose interest payments are exempt from federal taxes.

tax-managed mutual fund *See* tax-efficient mutual fund.

tax-qualified plan a pension or retirement plan in which the contributions are deductible against the contributor's taxable income. In effect, the contributions are made with pre-tax dollars. All earnings on the contributions are tax-deferred, and when they begin, all distributions from the account are fully taxable. (*Compare* non-tax qualified plan.)

tax shelter   the commonly used name for a limited partnership. (*See* limited partnership.)

technical analysis   (1) research that seeks to predict the future price movement of a stock or the overall market by using price and volume as indicators of changes in the supply and demand; (2) using charts of a stock's past price and volume movements to predict its future price movements. (*Compare* fundamental analysis.)

thin market   also called an illiquid market, a market in which there are few buyers or sellers for a security and which is characterized by increased price volatility.

timing   attempting to buy or sell a security at the optimum moment in its price movement.

TIPS   *See* Treasury Index Protection Securities.

top-down security selection strategy   beginning with a broad (macro) look at factors within the overall economy (e.g., inflation, interest rates, expansion), the portfolio manager then tries to identify which industries will benefit from the anticipated economic environment. Once the industries have been selected, the manager then looks for specific companies within each that will benefit the most. (*Compare* bottom-up security selection strategy.)

total market index fund   an index fund that seeks to match the performance of the broadest measures of the market, the Wilshire 5000 index. This index consists of stocks that trade on the NYSE-Euronext (which now owns the AMEX) and NASDAQ OMX and the number of common stock in the index changes from time to time, with no preset minimum or maximum number.

total return   the percentage return that includes dividends, interest, realized capital gains, and unrealized capital gains earned on money invested in a mutual fund, stock, bond, or other type of security. The total return calculation assumes that all distributions from the fund (dividends, interest, and realized capital gains) were reinvested in the fund. (*Compare* inflation-adjusted total return, load-adjusted total return, risk-adjusted total return.)

tracker fund   a synonym for an index fund. This term is widely used throughout Europe, especially the United Kingdom.

tradable security.   A security that can be bought and sold on a registered stock exchange or in the over-the-counter markets. (*Compare* redeemable security.)

transfer agent   usually a commercial bank or trust company appointed by a mutual fund company to keep track of the daily purchase and sale of fund shares. Also responsible for mailing dividends and other important information and documents to the shareholders.

Treasuries   the commonly used name for U.S. government securities.

Treasury bill   a short-term security issued by the U.S. government with one year or less to maturity. The security is issued at a discount and matures at face value. The difference between the discounted price and the face value is the interest income paid to the holder. The Federal Reserve Board (FRB) holds weekly auctions for four-week, three-month, and six-month T-bills, and monthly auctions for one-year T-bills. T-bills are issued in minimum denominations of $100 face value to the public.

Treasury bond   a negotiable, long-term U.S. government security with 10 to 30 years to maturity. Minimum denomination is $1,000. T-bonds are issued at par value with a coupon rate of interest that is paid semiannually.

Treasury Index Protection Securities (TIPS)   a U.S. government Treasury bond whose principal amount ($1,000) is adjusted every six months by a percentage equal to the change in the Consumer Price Index (CPI). The interest payment, a fixed percentage of the bond's principal, changes as the principal is adjusted upward (in an inflationary economy) or downward (in a deflationary economy). At maturity, the bondholder receives the greater of the inflation-adjusted principal or the bond's par value.

Treasury note   a negotiable, intermediate-term U.S. government security with more than 1 year to a maximum of 10 years to maturity. Minimum denomination is $1,000. Like T-Bonds, T-Notes are issued at par value with a coupon rate of interest that is paid semiannually.

treasury stock   common stock that has been issued and bought back by the issuing corporation. Treasury stock has no voting rights and receives no dividends.

trend   in technical terms, the up, down, or sideways movement of the overall market (as reflected in an average or index) or a stock's price over a period of time, usually longer than six months.

triple tax-exempt security   a term used to describe a municipal bond whose interest payments are exempt from federal, state, and local taxes.

trust   a fiduciary account in which a person or entity, called the trustee, holds title to securities or property for the benefit of another person, usually called the beneficiary.

trustee   traditionally a commercial bank or trust that holds the title to or manages securities or property in a fiduciary account for the benefit of another person. A trustee can also be an individual or a brokerage firm.

turnover costs   the fees incurred when the manager trades securities into and out of the mutual fund's portfolio. These costs consist of commission, markups, and markdowns. High turnover costs can be a drain on a mutual fund's return.

turnover rate   also called turnover, the number of times a manager replaces all of the stocks in a mutual fund's portfolio. Turnover is stated as a percentage. A turnover rate of 100 percent means the portfolio changes completely once a year. 200 percent indicates twice a year. 400 percent indicates four times per year. Each time a portfolio turns over, the manager must pay commissions, markups, or markdowns on the transactions. These changes reduce a mutual fund's total return.

12b-1 fee   named after the 1980 SEC rule, a fee charged by a mutual fund that permits it, under strictly defined circumstances, to charge existing shareholders for the advertising expenses and costs associated with attracting new investors to the fund. They are also referred to as distribution costs. There are two types of 12b-1 fees: (1) asset-based 12b-1 fees, that cannot exceed .75 percent of a fund's net assets; and (2) service-based 12b-1 fees, that cannot exceed .25 percent of a funds net assets. Therefore the maximum 12b-1 fee is 1.00 percent of the fund's total net assets. These fees are ongoing and are not part of a fund's sales charge. (*Compare* sales charge.)

underwriter   (1) in mutual funds, the financial institution, usually a brokerage firm, responsible for the distribution of the mutual fund shares to the public; (2) in stocks and bonds, the investment banking firm that helps companies raise capital by issuing securities to the public.

unit investment trust (UIT)   one of the three types of investment companies defined in the Investment Company Act of 1940. A UIT is organized not as a corporation but as a trust, which issues units (called shares of beneficial interest) represented by an undivided interest in a portfolio of securities. In a fixed UIT, the trust establishes a portfolio that never changes. The portfolio eventually self-liquidates. In a participating UIT, a holding company manages the portfolio of securities. Investors buy units of the holding company. (*See* fixed UIT, participating UIT)

unlisted securities   virtually synonymous with over-the-counter stocks and bonds, a term used to describe any stock or other security that does not trade— i.e., is not listed—on an exchange. Today this term is mostly used to describe stocks whose price information is displayed on the Pink OTC Markets (more commonly called The Pink Sheets or the Pink Quotes), which has no listing requirements.

unmanaged fund   a mutual fund that has no manager to select the securities that make up the investment portfolio. The term has become synonymous with index funds, which produce the return of a selected stock market average or index. Because there is no portfolio manager, the fees associated with this type of fund tend to be very low. (*See* index fund.)

unrealized gain the profit resulting from an increase in the value of a long security position or a decrease in the value of a short security position that is still being held.

unsecured bond a bond backed by the full faith and credit of the issuer. There are no specific assets or property backing the bond.

unsponsored ADR an American Depositary Receipt in which the corporation that issued the stock in the foreign country is not involved in the issuance of the ADRs in the United States. Usually a bank or broker/dealer in the foreign country uses its own funds to acquire the shares that will back the ADR program and handles all the details of the issuance of the ADR. (*Compare* sponsored ADR.)

unsystematic risk *See* stock-specific risk.

uptrend the upward movement of a stock's price or of the market as measured by an average or index over a period of time.

value investing investing in a company's common stock whose market value appears to be a bargain (i.e., the price is below the company's real worth or earnings power, or below the value of comparable companies in the same business sector). The managers use fundamental measures such as price-earnings (P/E) ratio and price-to-book value ratio to find such bargains. As soon as the stock becomes fully valued based on the same measures, the manger will typically sell it out of the portfolio. This is basically a buy-and-hold strategy that focuses on the long-term price movement of a security.

Value Line index a geometrically weighted index consisting of over 1,600 issues that are on the NYSE-Euronext, AMEX, NASDAQ OMX, and Toronto Stock Exchange.

variable annuity an annuity in which the return on the money invested and the amount of the periodic payments to the investor (called the annuitant) will vary with the value of the underlying portfolio. (*See* annuity.)

vesting a period of time over which an employer's contributions to a pension plan becomes the property of the employee. Under ERISA, most pension plans vest over five years, at a rate of 20 percent per year; however, the period can be shorter.

volatility the frequency with which the price of a security moves up and down. The larger and more frequent the movement, the more volatile the security. (*See* beta.)

volume the total amount of a security traded in a given period of time.

warrant usually attached to a new bond or preferred stock issue, a warrant gives the holder the right to buy a stated amount of common stock at a specified price. This specified price (called the exercise price) is usually higher than the current market price of the underlying common stock at the time the bond or preferred stock is issued. Most warrants have a limited life—usually 5 to 10 years; however, some companies have issued "perpetual" warrants that have no expiration date. Warrants are often described as "sweeteners" designed to increase the marketability of the security to which it is attached.

weighting   a method for determining the worth of each company's stock relative to the value of the overall index.

Wilshire 5000 index   considered the broadest measure of the activity and movement of the overall stock market, this index consists of more than 4,000 issues that trade on the NYSE-Euronext, AMEX (now owned by the NYSE-Euronext), and NASDAQ-OMX. While the name suggests that there are 5,000 stocks in the index, in reality there is no minimum or maximum number set. The number can vary substantially from year to year.

wrap account   a brokerage account in which the cost of research, asset allocation, trading, and other services are all included (i.e., wrapped) in one annual fee that is usually a small percentage (e.g., 0.5 percent) of the funds in the account.

Yankee bond   a bond, denominated in dollars, that is issued in the United States by a foreign corporation or government. This bond would be registered with the SEC. Yankee bonds are a type of foreign bond.

yield   the percentage or rate of return that an investor makes on capital invested in a security or in a portfolio of securities.

yield curve   a graph, with a vertical axis depicting the yield and a horizontal axis representing years to maturity, that depicts the yields of bonds with similar quality but different maturities. The shape of the yield curve can be ascending (a.k.a. a normal yield curve), descending (a.k.a. an inverted yield curve), flat, or humped. The shape is dependent on investor expectations for future interest rate levels, actions of the Federal Reserve to tighten or loosen credit, and the supply and demand for debt issues in each maturity segment of the curve.

yield to maturity   the rate of return that a bond would provide if the investor held it to its maturity date. This calculation takes into account the compounding of semi-annual interest payments as well as the discount or premium price of the bond at the time it was purchased.

zero-coupon bond   a bond that makes no semi-annual interest payments over its life. Instead, the security is issued at a discount and matures at face value. The difference between the discounted purchase price and the face value at maturity is the interest income on the bond.

zeros   the commonly used name for zero-coupon bonds.

Index

Actively-managed mutual fund, 24
Adjustable Rate Mortgage
    Government Bond Fund, 66
Administrative services fees, 86
Advisory fees. *See* Management fees
Agency securities, 45
Agent, 21
Aggressive growth funds, 50–52
Annual report, 25
Asset allocation, 25
Asset allocation fund, 69–71
Asset allocation models, 155,
    166–168
Asset classes of funds, 41
Asset protection, 26
Asset-management firms, 24
Automatic investing, 113, 152–153,
    164–165
Automatic investment plan, 113
Averaging down, 166

Back-end load, 93–95
Balance sheet, 136
Balanced fund, 71
Banking funds, 56
Barron's, 149
Basis point, 97
Bear market, 25
Benchmark indexes, 127, 128
Benefits of mutual fund investing,
    3–5
Best Fit Index, 128
Best ideas fund, 59, 60
Blue chip stock, 48

Board of directors, 21–23
Bond funds, 31, 60–68, 142–143
    Adjustable Rate Mortgage
        Government Bond Fund, 66
    bond ratings, 62
    corporate bond funds, 62–63
    criteria for, 61–62
    expenses, 85
    general corporate bond fund, 63
    General Government Bond Fund,
        65
    government bond funds, 63–66
    high-quality corporate bond fund,
        63
    high-yield corporate bond fund,
        63
    international bond funds, 65
    Mortgage-Backed Securities
        Government Bond Fund, 65
    multi-sector bond funds, 67
    National Tax-Exempt Bond
        Fund, 67
    Single-State Tax Exempt Bond
        Fund, 67
    taxable, 62–67
    tax-exempt, 67
    types of, 61–62
    U.S. Treasury Government Bond
        Fund, 65
    world bond funds, 67
Bond quality, 142–143
Bonds:
    bond funds (*see* Bond funds)
    defined, 18

Bonds: (*continued*)
Eurobonds, 63, 67
Federal Home Loan Mortgage
Corporation (FHLMC), 65
Federal Intermediate Credit Bank
(FICB), 66
Federal Land Bank, 66
Federal National Mortgage
Association (FNMA), 65
foreign bonds, 67
Government National Mortgage
Association (GNMA), 65
muncipal, 31
ratings, 62
Treasure STRIPS, 64
Treasury Bonds (T-Bonds), 64
Treasury Inflation Protection
Securities (TIPS), 64–65
Treasury notes (T-Notes), 64
Breakpoints, 91–93, 111–112
BRIC funds, 54–55
Brokerage fees, 86–87
Bull market, 16

Capital appreciation, 39
Capital appreciation funds, 52
Capital gains:
automatic reinvestment of, 116
defined, 28
distribution of, 123–124
embedded capital gain, 147, 148
taxes and, 146–148
Capitalization, 49–50
Cash account, 46
Cash dividends, 123
Cash equivalents, 69, 70
Charles Schwab, 27
Check writing, 153
Classes of shares, 99–103
chart of classes and their fee
structures, 100
chart of comparison of
returns, 102

Closed-end funds, 29–33
defined, 31
vs. mutual funds, 33–34
Wall Street Journal listing of, 32–33
Closed-end management company,
16. *See also* Closed-end funds
Commissions, 9, 90
Common stock, 48
Communications funds, 56
Conduit tax treatment, 125, 146
Confirmation, 28
Contingent deferred sales charge
(CDSC), 93–95
Convenience of mutal funds, 4–5
Convertible securities fund, 72
Country risk, 141–142
Coupon rate, 65
Currency risk, 141
Custodian bank, 26–27
Custodian fees, 87–88

Debentures, 45, 63
Defensive stock, 49
Defined benefit plan, 10
Defined contribution plan, 10
Directors' fees, 88
Distribution, retail/wholesale, 28, 29
Distribution fees, 96–98
Distributor/underwriter, 27–29, 30
Diversification, 3–4, 15
and asset allocation, 166–168
diversified fund, defined, 59
vs. protection, 37–38
Diversified fund, 59
Dividend reinvestment, 8, 116, 153
Dividend reinvestment plan, 91
Dividends, 122–123
automatic reinvesting of, 116
defined, 27
taxes and, 146–147
Dollar-cost averaging, 8, 113–116
Dow Jones Industrial Average
(DJIA), 55

Embedded capital gain, 147, 148
Emerging markets index fund, 73–74
Emerging-growth stock, 49
Enhanced index fund, 74
Equipment trust certificates
  (ETCs), 63
Equity funds, 47–60, 134–143
  aggressive growth funds, 52
  banking funds, 56
  BRIC funds, 54–55
  capital appreciation funds, 52
  chart of types, 51
  communications funds, 56
  core investing, 138
  defined, 47
  equity income funds, 52–53
  financial services funds, 56
  foreign and global equity funds,
    140–142
  growth and income funds, 53
  growth funds, 53
  growth investing, 136–138
  health care funds, 56
  international/foreign funds, 39,
    53–54
  investment style matrices, 140
  natural resource funds, 57
  objectives, 50–58
  precious metals funds, 57
  real estate funds, 57
  sector/specialty funds, 42, 55–56
  small company funds, 57–58
  socially responsible investing, 139
  stock types, 48–50
  technology funds, 57
  utilities funds, 57
  value investing, 135–136
  world/global funds, 58
Equity income funds, 52–53
Established-growth stock, 48
Eurobonds, 63, 67
Exchange privileges, 153–154

Exchange-traded funds (ETFs), 12
Exchanging fund shares, 118–119
Ex-dividend date, 123
Expense ratio, 80, 103–106
Ex-SIPC insurance, 43

Face value, 42
Federal Home Loan Mortgage
    Corporation (FHLMC), 65
Federal Intermediate Credit Bank
    (FICB), 66
Federal Land Bank, 66
Federal National Mortgage
    Association (FNMA), 65
Federal Reserve Board (FRB), 60
Fees and expenses:
  12b-1 fees (distribution/marketing
    fees), 96–98
  administrative service fees, 86
  back-end load, 93–95
  board member fees, 22
  charges and loads, 89–98
  Contingent deferred sales charge
    (CDSC), 93–95
  expense ratio, 103–106
  front-end load, 90–93
  fund expense summary table
    example, 83
  management fees, 26, 80–85
  minimizing, 161–163
  no-load and pure no-load funds,
    98
  operating expenses, 80–89
  other expenses, 85–89
  overview, 79–80
  redemption fees, 95
  transaction costs, 6
  transfer agent fees, 87–88
Fidelity Daily Income Trust, 9
Financial adviser, 101
Financial crisis of 2008, 12–13
Financial profile, 36

Financial services funds, 56
Financial statements, 85
First in, first out (FIFO), 120
Fixed asset allocation fund, 70
Fixed income funds. *See* Bond funds
Flexible asset allocation fund, 71
Focused fund, 59
Foreign bonds, 67
Foreign funds, 53–54, 140–142
Forward pricing, 108–109
Front-end load, 90–93, 110
Fund assets, protection of, 26
Fund classification, 41
Fund evaluation sheet example,
    131, 133
Fund families, 20–21, 22
Fund manager, 23–26, 163–164
Fund of best or top fund managers,
    76–77
Fund of funds, 76–77
Fund performance. *See* Performance
Fund pricing, 34
Fund size, 34
Fund structure. *See* Structure of
    mutual funds
Fund survey sheet example, 132
Fund types, 41, 43–44, 51

GARP (growth at a reasonable price),
    137
General corporate bond fund, 63
General Government Bond Fund, 65
Global funds, 140
Goals, 36. *See also* Investment
    objectives
Gold funds. *See* Precious metals funds
Government bond funds, 64–65
Government National Mortgage
    Association (GNMA), 65–66
Government Securities Money
    Market Fund, 44–45
Growth and income funds, 53

Growth funds, 53
Growth measures, 124–133
Growth stocks, 40

Health care funds, 56
Highflyers, 51
High-quality corporate
    bond fund, 63
High-yield corporate bond fund, 63
Historical timelines, 6, 8, 10, 11
History of mutual funds:
    1924–1970, 6–8
    1970–1980, 9
    1980–Today, 9–13
    timelines, 6, 8, 10, 11
Hub and spoke arrangement, 46
Hybrid funds, 69–72

Income return, 129–130
Income stock, 48–49
Income stocks, 40
Index funds, 12, 72–76, 148
    emerging markets index fund, 74
    enhanced index fund, 74
    large capitalization index fund, 75
    long-term bond index fund, 75
    small capitalization index fund, 75
    total market index fund,
        75–76
    Willshire 5000 index fund, 76
Individual Retirement Accounts
    (IRAs), 10
Initial investment amounts, 155
Initial public offerings (IPOs), 50
Insider, 138
Insider trading, 139
Interest fees, 88
Interest rate risk, 143
International Bond Funds, 65
International funds, 39, 53–54, 141
Investing rules of thumb (7),
    161–169

Investment advice, 155
Investment advisor/manager, 23–26
Investment advisory service, 81
Investment company, 16
Investment Company Act of
    1940, 6, 16
Investment costs, 34
Investment dollars, 37
Investment grade, 42
Investment grade bond, 64
Investment income, 122
Investment objectives:
    defined, 16
    of fund, 39–42
    of investor, 35–39
Investment pools, 16
Investment style, 134–140
    core investing, 138
    growth investing, 136–138
    insider trading, 139
    matrices, 140, 143
    socially responsible investing,
        138, 139
    value investing, 135–136
IPOs (Initial public offerings), 50

Junk bond, 60, 61

Large capitalization index fund,
    74–75
Large-cap company, 49
Lead managers, 24
Legal and audit fees, 88
Lehman Brothers, 42
Letter of intent (LOI), 112
Life-cycle fund, 70
Liquidity, 30
Load fund, 80
Load-adjusted total return, 126
Long-term bond index fund, 75
Low-load funds, 93
Lump-sum purchase, 92

Management company, 20–21
    defined, 16
    types of, 17
Management fees, 26, 80–85
Mark to market, 108–109
Market capitalization, 49–50
Market timing, 168–169
Marketing fees, 96–98
Massachusetts Investment Trust, 16
Measures of investment growth, 124
Micro-cap company, 50
Mid-cap company, 50
Money market mutual funds, 42–47
    costs of, 46
    defined, 41
    taxable funds, 44–45
    tax-exempt funds, 44, 45
    types of, 43–44
Money market securities, 39
Monitoring fund performance,
    165–166
Monthly Investment Plan (MIP), 7–8
Morningstar fund evaluation sheet,
    133
Morningstar Reports, 131, 149
Mortgage bonds, 63
Mortgage-Backed Securities
    Government Bond Fund, 65
Mortgage-backed security (MBS), 65
Multi-class fund, 99
Multi-Sector Bond Funds, 67
Municipal bonds, 31, 33
Mutual fund, defined, 15
Mutual fund supermarkets, 18, 20,
    28
Mutual funds vs. closed-end funds,
    33–34

NASDAQ, 75
National Tax-Exempt Bond Fund, 67
National tax-exempt money market
    fund, 45

Natural resource funds, 57
Negotiable commissions, 9
Net asset value (NAV), 89–90, 108, 124
No-load funds, 98
Non-independent board members, 22

Offer price, 90
Online information, 154–155
Open-end management company, 16, 17–18
Operating expenses, 80–89
  administrative service fees, 86
  brokerage fees, 86–87
  custodian and transfer agent fees, 87–88
  directors' fees, 88
  interest fees, 88
  legal and audit fees, 88
  management fees, 80–85
  miscellaneous expenses, 89
  shareholder service fees, 88–89
Options, 52

Pass-through certificate, 67
Payroll deduction, 8
Performance, 121–150
  bond funds, 142–143
  capital gains distributions, 123–124
  comparisons to make in evaluating, 148–149
  dividends, 122–123
  equity funds, 134–143
  growth measures, 124–133
  information sources for evaluating, 149–150
  investment style and risk, 134–143
  monitoring, 165–166
  net asset value (NAV) increase, 124
  portfolio composition, 143–144
  risk profile and, 129
  short-term vs. long-term, 163

  and taxes, 146–148
  total return, 124–129
  turnover, 145–146
Performance evaluation, 26
Portfolio composition, 143–144
Portfolio drift, 12
Portfolio manager, 23–26
Precious metals funds, 57
Preferred stock, 48
Price-earnings (P/E) ratio, 135
Price-to-book value (P/B) ratio, 135
Pricing of funds, 34
Professional management, 4
Proprietary funds, 27, 30
Prospectuses, 20, 24
  defined, 21
  and index funds, 55–56
  and performance analysis, 149
Proxy, 22
Public offering price (POP), 90, 110
Publicly traded funds. *See* Closed-end funds
Purchasing fund shares, 109–116
Pure no-load funds, 98
Purpose of investment, 36

Real estate funds, 57
Realized/unrealized gains, 123–124
Record keeping, 157
Redeeming fund shares, 117–118, 119–120
Redemption, 19
Redemption fees, 95
Registrar, 27
Reinstatement privilege, 156
Reinvestment of dividends/capital gains, 116
Reserve Primary Money Market Fund, 42
Retail distribution, 28
Retirement accounts, 10
Right of accumulation, 92, 93

Risk, 134–143
  bond funds, 142–143
  and core investing, 138
  country risk, 141–142
  currency risk, 141
  equity funds, 134–142
  and growth investing, 136–138
  interest rate risk, 143
  and value investing, 135–136
Risk tolerance, 37–39
Rules of thumb (7) for mutual fund
     investing, 161–169

Sales charge, 81
Secondary market, 20
Sector funds, 42, 55–56
Securities Investor Protection
     Corporation (SIPC), 43
Select fund, 59
Selling groups, 28, 31
Selling short, 51
Shareholder reports, 156
Shareholder retention, 39–40
Shareholder service fees,
     88–89
Shareholder services, 151–159
  automatic investing, 152–153
  check writing, 153
  dividend reinvestment, 153
  exchange privileges, 153–154
  investment advice and asset
     allocation models, 155
  low initial investment amounts,
     155
  online information, 154–155
  reinstatement privileges, 156
  shareholder reports and other
     documents, 156
  simplified record keeping, 157
  systematic withdrawal, 157–158
  tax-deferred retirement
     accounts, 158

web sites, 158–159
  wire transfers, 159
Single-state, double tax-exempt
     money market fund, 45
Single-state, tax exempt bond fund,
     67
SIPC insurance, 43
Size of funds, 34
Small capitalization index fund, 75
Small company funds, 57
Small-cap company, 50
Sovereign debt, 67
Special situation funds, 58
Specialty funds. *See* Sector funds
Splicing, 40
Sponsor, 18, 20
Standard and Poor's 500 Index (S&P
     500), 56
Standard and Poor's Mutual Fund
     Reports, 150
Statement, 29
Statement of additional information
     (SAI), 86, 87, 149, 156
Statement of operations, 84
Stock funds. *See* Equity funds
Stock types, 48–50
Stocks, defined, 18
Structure of mutual funds, 18–29
  advisors/managers, 23–26
  board of directors, 21–23
  custodian bank, 26–27
  diagram, 19
  distributor/underwriter, 27–29
  management company, 20–21
  sponsor, 20
Subadvisors, 24
Systematic risk, 134
Systematic withdrawal, 157–158

Target bond fund, 68
Target-date fund, 70–71
Taxable bond fund, 63

Taxable money market funds, 44–45
Tax-deferred account, 47, 158
Taxes:
  and dividend/capital gains
    reinvestment, 116
  and fund exchanges, 119
  and fund performance, 146–148
Tax-exempt bond fund, 64
Tax-exempt money market funds,
    44, 45
Tax-exempt securities, 44
Team leaders, 24
Technical analysis, 168
Technology funds, 57
Time horizon for investment, 36–38
Timelines, 6, 8, 10, 11
Timing, market, 166–168
Total market index fund, 75
Total return, 124–129
Tradable funds, 12. *See also*
    Exchange-traded funds (ETFs)
Transaction costs, 4, 15
Transfer agent, 27
Transfer agent fees, 87–88
Treasury bills, 9
Treasury Bonds (T-Bonds), 64
Treasury inflation protection
    securities, 64–65, 66
Treasury Notes (T-Notes), 64
Treasury STRIPS, 64
Triple tax exempt, 67
Truth in Advertising rule, 12
Turnover:
  defined, 86
  performance and, 144–146
  12b-1 fees, 96–98

Types of investment companies, 7
Types of mutual funds, 41

Underwriter, 30. *See also* Distributor/
    underwriter
U.S. Treasury Government Bond
    Fund, 65
U.S. Treasury Money Market Fund,
    45
Utilities funds, 57

Value Line Fund Survey Reports,
    132, 149
Vanguard Group, 72–73
Volatility:
  defined, 38
  and growth funds, 53
  and income investing, 130

Wall Street Journal, 149
  closed-end fund listing, 32–33
Warehousing, 28
Web sites of funds, 158–159
Weighting, 75
Wholesale distribution, 29
Willshire 5000 index fund, 76
Wire transfers, 159
World Bond Funds, 67
World/global funds, 58

Yankee bond, 61, 63
Yield, 46

Zero coupon bond, 66